1 7 7 6

Come into the Kitchen Cook Book

A collector's treasury of America's great recipes

Mary and Vincent Price's Come into the Kitchen Cook Book

Heritage Recipes
Helen Duprey Bullock

Modern Recipes
Eileen Gaden

Decorative Color Illustrations
Charles M. Wysocki

Wine In America
Robert Jay Misch

Wine Making In The Home
Clem Stein, Jr.

Line Illustrations
Nicholas Amorosi

Stravon Educational Press • New York

Standard Book Number 87396-020-3
Library of Congress Catalog Card Number: 70-91414

Editorial Staff

Coordinating Editor	Robert H. Doherty
Associate Editor	Elvin Abeles
Assistant Editor	Robert Segal
Research	Celia G. Green
Copy	Betty W. Brinkerhoff
Home Economists	Hazel S. Detwiler
	Eileen Gaden Associates
	Nancy Garvey
Cover Design	Doris Gamble
	Pasquale Del Vecchio
	Donald Havrda
Book Design	Morton Garchik

Every recipe in this book has been tested. Occasionally, a particularly interesting old form of a recipe is also included; to distinguish it from the modernized version, the old recipe is given in italic print.

The Heritage Recipes in this book originally appeared in *A National Treasury of Cookery* by Mary and Vincent Price, copyright 1967 by Heirloom Publishing Company.

A description of each full-color picture and its source is given in the list of "Illustrations" appearing on page 11. The food illustrations on pages 17 and 53 are through the courtesy of *Ladies' Home Journal,* photo by Mike Cuesta.

Manufactured in the United States of America by Rand McNally & Company

Preface

IN THE DAYS OF the early American settlers, the kitchen was the center of family living. Usually the kitchen *was* the room for living —for the fire on the hearth supplied all the light and warmth both for the work of the household and for its leisure activities.

Here the fisherman mended his nets. The farmer carved yokes for his oxen. Here the children played. And the housewife spun and wove. And cooked the meals.

And what meals they were! Foods fresh from the orchard, the garden, the fields. Fish from the river or the sea. Game and fowl in abundance.

From Massachusetts to the Golden West, from Kansas to New Orleans, America was blessed with food so bountiful and so varied that no other country has known its equal.

In the days when our forebears could cook only those foods they grew, or caught, or raised themselves, the recipes of one region were truly "foreign" to the people of another. Today the foods and recipes of *every* region may be enjoyed by all of us.

Here, then, are recipes that span a continent—and cover four centuries. Recipes that celebrate our American heritage in their very names: Indian Slapjack. Lone Star Chicken. Jackson Cake. Mrs. Madison's Whim. And recipes that mirror modern America: Hero. Corned Beef Cheeseburger.

Here, too, is a complete section on wines. The story of wine making is delightful, but you will return again and again to the helpful information that will make wines seem like familiar friends: How to shop for domestic or imported wines. Which wines to serve with various foods. Hobbyists—or culinary artists—will find a fine dissertation on how to produce a home variety of this nectar of the Greek and Roman gods. But lest you run afoul of the "revenuer," read carefully the requirements to qualify legally as a home vintner.

A word, also, about the color illustrations, for which we are indebted to Charles M. Wysocki. We hope the charm with which they decorate these pages will not obscure their value as history. For each illustration is authentic in every detail. Each is a true gem of Americana.

Today, as more and more of us turn back to the quiet pleasures of good cooking and good company, we invite you to try these treasured American recipes. Our wish for you is a warm and welcoming kitchen —now, as in the days gone by, the heart of a happy home.

MARY AND VINCENT PRICE

Publisher's Note

VINCENT PRICE is the distinguished American actor known to millions of theatergoers for his many successful roles on both stage and screen. Less well known but probably more cherished by him is the career he originally embarked upon—that of art historian. A graduate of Yale University in art history, he actively pursues this first love as art collector, consultant, and lecturer. He is a member of the Art Department faculty at the University of Southern California, and he has published a highly regarded book on art history and appreciation, *I Like What I Know*. His hobby (which now amounts to a third career) is collecting interesting and unusual recipes from all over the world, gleaned from his extensive travels. With his wife Mary, a noted costume designer and an authority on Americana, he constantly tests in their own beautiful kitchen the recipes he comes upon in his travels. The hobby has already resulted in two books of outstanding culinary merit. The first, *A Treasury of Great Recipes*, presented unique recipes from the world's greatest restaurants. This was followed by *A National Treasury of Cookery*, consisting of American recipes from pre-Colonial days to the end of the 19th century. The present book, *Come Into the Kitchen Cook Book*, based on *A National Treasury of Cookery*, brings American cookery right up to the minute—practically into the 1970's.

HELEN DUPREY BULLOCK works at doing what she likes best—saving sites and homes of historic and patriotic value from the real estate developer's bulldozer. She is an officer of the National Trust for Historic Preservation, an organization chartered by the U.S. Congress for the purpose of preserving and restoring homes, lands, or buildings of historic significance that are about to be sold and razed. She travels extensively in the United States, lecturing and showing local patriotic groups how to go about salvaging such sites for their own communities. It was almost inevitable that she would, during her travels, come upon another prize of Americana—its recipes. Her reputation as a collector of American recipes (she is a graduate in American history) resulted in her being invited by the Williamsburg Historical Society to compile and publish a book of American recipes. This she did, and her famous *Williamsburg Art of Cookery* is a treasured reference guide in many an American kitchen.

EILEEN GADEN is the coauthor of four cook books on contemporary cooking and was for ten years an associate editor of a leading food magazine. She now has her own food consulting and publicity firm, creating and testing food for television and magazines. Among her clients are the leading food processors and distributors in America.

ROBERT JAY MISCH describes himself as a traveler by addiction and a wine man by decision. As a traveler he has covered a good part of this country and Europe, which he has described in books, lectures, and a syndicated newspaper column. As a wine man he is the author of *Quick Guide to Wine*, *Robert J. Misch's Foreign Dining Directory*, and *Quick Guide to the World's Most Famous Recipes*, published by Doubleday & Company. He is a member of the Chevaliers du Tastevin and of the Wine Committee for the U.S. State Department, he holds the French "Medaille Agricole des Vins de France," and he is a Commander in the Bontemps de Barsac-Sauternes.

CLEM STEIN, JR. is, by vocation, an executive of a large corporation. In private life, however, he is an enthusiastic home vintner with a missionary's zeal for converting the rest of America to the delights of his avocation. Although he has been making wine since boyhood (he actually helped his father create the family wine cellar back in his native Ohio), he decided for the occasion of this book to produce a new supply just to check out his instructions. With the help of a friend and fellow home vintner, Dr. Nicholas Srankovelgia, the test was proved out. The resultant nectar? In his own word, "*Magnifique*."

CHARLES M. WYSOCKI is a painter and illustrator with a national reputation in both art forms. He has won more than fifty awards in national and local art shows, and his paintings are in the permanent collections of many museums and are prized by prominent private collectors. He studied art in his native Detroit and later at the Art Center School of Los Angeles. Of his art he writes, "My paintings are like my family and me, gentle and peaceful. I feel the greatness and beauty of America, and this country becomes for me an endless source of inspiration."

NICHOLAS AMOROSI is a scientific illustrator for the American Museum of Natural History. He has produced thousands of drawings ranging from archaeological reconstructions of ancient pottery to decorative illustrations for children's books, and he is an authority on Eskimo and American Indian artifacts and folklore material. He received his art education at Pratt Institute, the Art Students' League of New York, and the National Academy School of Fine Arts, all in New York City. For relaxation he paints, and his canvases are on display at the Galerie Internationale in New York City.

Contents

Illustrations

xi

Introduction

THIS OFFERING OF HERITAGE recipes is neither a primer nor an encyclopedia of American cookery; it is rather a sampler of treasures from the past. Time-tested and handed down for generations before they ever became embalmed between the pages of a printed book and reduced to chemical formulas, these recipes are traditional in certain areas and periods, and with groups of different foreign origin. Omissions are conspicuous but deliberate. With such a wide variety of recipes to try which evoke an era or an ethnic tradition, preference has been given to foods which can be prepared and enjoyed today in the modern home, and to ingredients which are easily available.

We have come a long way since the early days of America. Now an Indian pudding may be bought in one-pound cans, and instead of pickling, smoking, and curing bacon by the flitch, in today's urban America it may be acquired more simply in a neat cellophane package. For gelatin we are not purists enough to propose the calf's-foot method, nor the use of isinglass (concocted from the swimming bladders of fishes). Our shortenings are the basic butter, lard, and oils consistently used before the era of modern substitutes. We specify cake yeast. We yield on use of canned or frozen vegetables and foods which would be unavailable otherwise in certain areas and seasons.

Tastes in spirituous beverages, also, have changed substantially since 1738, when Tavern Keeper Henry Wetherburn's "biggest Bowl of Arrack Punch" bought 200 acres of land in Goochland, Virginia, for Thomas Jefferson's father, Peter; or when rum was a staple in the trade of Yankee sailing ships.

But in food, tradition is more persistent. Boston is still the land of the bean and the cod (with many tasty additions); Old New Yorkers can wax emotional over tomatoes in the chowder; and throughout the South there are two mortal sins, trampling on the Confederate flag and putting sugar in the corn bread.

When Jefferson purchased the first Louisiana territory from which thirteen states were later carved, American cuisine gained two of its richest treasures, Creole and Cajun cookery.

Game, seafood, and wild fowl were so abundant that they were common fare in the pioneer cabin, the great houses of Southern plantations, and the elegant hostelry of the large cities. They were also served on the luxurious floating palaces, the steamboats, that plied the Mississippi and connected with the expanding rivers of the West.

Food was the chief element of political rallies held throughout the nation on the Fourth of July. Whether it was Kentucky Burgoo, Southern Brunswick Stew, Philadelphia Snapping Turtle, or Yankee Clambake, table barbeques and torrents of political oratory were the order of the day and the best cooks vied in providing cakes and pies.

As the population moved westward, sourdough went in every prospector's pack and in every covered wagon. The seekers for El Dorado brought with them the traditions of cookery as varied as their origins, adapting them to native provender. There were railroad workers and railroad magnates, cowhands and cattle barons. In Bishop Hill, Illinois, descendants of the Swedish Colony still eat Lutfisk at Christmas and delight in Janson's Temptation. The Cornish miners brought a taste for their famous pasties with them to Michigan from a tradition that was old three centuries before, when it was commonly said the Devil himself would fear to appear in Cornwall lest he be baked in a pasty. The real melting pot of America was the cooking pot.

While Victoria ruled in England, Americans saw the period of the Gilded Age, The Four Hundred, when the chefs of the villas of Newport had chefs, and dinners might include as many as 27 courses with appropriate wines. The recipes give a clue to this era of elegance, and include such solid bourgeois favorites as Brownstone Front Cake, which bears a remarkable resemblance to its architectural prototype then in high fashion.

Each recipe in this book has been kitchen tested with modern quantities, but faithfully chosen ingredients. Detailed instructions are provided. Today's cooks do not have to begin by washing the salt from the butter, cutting sugar from the loaf and pounding it fine and sifting it, nor are most of them able to follow directions that assume the cook knows what to do when told, "add Milk [not saying how much] and put them in the Oven until *enough* [meaning done]." Of course, if they are not *enough*, "do not take them from the Oven or they will be undone and unwholesome."

HELEN DUPREY BULLOCK

THE 20TH CENTURY HAS made its own contributions to the panorama of American cookery. Many of the favorite dishes of today are pure modern Americana—as witness Texas Spareribs and Country Casserole. Others are borrowed and adapted from the great cookery of foreign lands—such as Cold Senegalese, Chicken Trianon, Sauerbraten, and Sukiyaki. All are designed, however, to bring to the kitchen of the 1970's the same qualities of variety and hearty goodness that marked American cookery of the earlier days.

EILEEN GADEN

Recipes of Early America

To all men at all times a journey to a new country has been an adventure. To the early settlers of this country the spirit of adventure was backed by necessity in some cases and desire on the part of all not only to escape the tired old world but to create a brighter new one.

And new and strange it was indeed. But those men and women from every country in Europe sought it out as eagerly as children seek to find their individuality in the tyrannical world of grownups. They came to make their mark, leaving the world they knew behind but bringing with them its anciently great life force. The mark of each is still upon our land and is still its driving force.

It was a wilderness, but from pre-Jamestown reports by Captain Arthur Barlowe and Thomas Hariot there were "large forests overrun with deer, rabbits, hares, and woodfowl in great abundance" and "the soil is deep, sweet, healthy and the most fruitful in the world." Certainly the earliest to arrive had hard times and hungry ones. The comparatively rich and varied tastes that they had left behind had to be changed drastically, but the women were industrious and inventive and learned to use what their rich but tough land had to offer.

SALT-GLAZED STONEWARE "BELLARMINE" JUG

This chapter is a bit of history of what those people ate and how their taste for food was developed and was appreciated while they subdued the wilderness and made useful the soil from which a new republic would grow. Generations passed. By the time these recipes were recorded there were already two million settlers in a hundred-mile-wide strip between the mountains and the sea. But they were no

15

longer English, Dutch, and Germans, they were citizens of America. It was British America to be sure, but even that would change, and soon.

From the indigenous Indians they took a native grain, maize or corn as we call it, and learned a hundred new lessons in good eating. Englishmen were hardest to convince of the merits of what the Indians called *pagstowr* and they called it variously "Guinea wheat or Turkey wheat." But their wives accepted it gladly and learned to make many breads from it and from those breads delicious stuffings for the abundant fowl. Memories of porridge and oatmeal must have inspired the corn mush, then known as Indian pudding, that was immortalized by Joel Barlow under the name of Hasty Pudding. It would not tempt a connoisseur, in the 17th or 20th century, but it did win the approval of the 19th-century kitchen pundit Priscilla Homespun: ". . . there are few better articles, either for economy or health, than this neglected old English country food . . ."

Of course, Hasty Pudding was not "old English," but more American than blueberry pie. So are many of the other dishes recorded here. Yet it must be confessed that they are merely reconstructions, after the manner of those delightful communities built by 20th-century builders with 20th-century materials to simulate the "look" of the colonial era.

TIN BISCUIT OVEN

Still I can not feel cynical in reaching Sturbridge Village via the Massachusetts Turnpike or in accepting motel accommodations at Colonial Williamsburg. Nor should anyone apologize for using a blender rather than a mortar and pestle to prepare forcemeat. How the settlers would have welcomed that miraculous machine! You may recognize that the Olykoek ("oily cake") is now a doughnut; it was considered a "yankee cake" by the Virginia Housewife in her 1824 cook book, but originally it had a very different accent . . . Dutch.

The first formal cook books used in those years were either printed in Europe or copied from those that had been printed here. (The first such reprint in America was done in Williamsburg in 1742 by William Parks of E. Smith's *Compleat Housewife*.) The recipes were handed down in the immemorial manner, mother to daughter or daughter-in-law, mistress to servant and vice versa. Some manuscript recipes survive; most, however, were copied from printed books; but they do enshrine an ancient tradition of colonial cookery. Hopping John is indubitably venerable, and Benjamin Franklin gave us a "receipt" for mincemeat that was less novel and far less useful than the lightning rod. The ancient recipes are not restorable; the facsimiles, however, are reasonable.

Shoulder of Venison, page 30
Steamed Stuffed Onions, page 138
Spinach Soufflé with Glazed Carrots, page 139

**Kitchen, Kenmore
Fredericksburg, Virginia**

**Kitchen, George Wythe House
Williamsburg, Virginia**

THE SNOW CAME LAST NIGHT
AND THE DOOR IS FROZEN TIGHT
THE SOUP IS IN THE POT
THE FIRE IS COZY AND HOT
A PLACE IS AT THE TABLE
COME IN IF YOU ARE ABLE

TURNIP SOUP

Stew down a knuckle of veal; strain, and let the broth stand still next day; take off the fat and sediment, and warm it, adding turnips cut in small dice; stew till they are tender; put a bit of pounded mace, white pepper, and salt. Before you serve, rub down half a spoonful of flour, with half a pint of cream, and boil with the soup; pour it on a roll in the tureen; but it should have soaked a little first in the soup, which should be as thick as middling cream.

BRASS CLOCK JACK

1 veal knuckle (about 1½ pounds)	¼ teaspoon pepper
Water	½ teaspoon ground mace
10 to 12 small white turnips, peeled and shredded	1 cup light cream
	1 tablespoon flour
1 teaspoon salt	2 slices toast, cut in quarters

Cook the veal in water to cover for 1 hour. Strain the broth; cool it and remove fat. Return the broth to the kettle, adding enough water, if necessary, to make 3 cups of liquid. Add the turnips, salt, pepper, and mace. Cover and cook over medium heat until the turnips are tender, about 10 minutes. Stir the cream into the flour, blending well. Pour a little of the hot liquid from the turnips into the cream mixture. Then stir the flour mixture into the turnips, cooking and stirring until smooth and bubbling. Adjust seasonings, if necessary. Put the toast into a tureen and pour the soup over it. Makes 6 to 8 servings.

HOTCH POTCH

Ham or beef soup bone
1 cup dried green split peas
2 medium onions, cut up
½ medium head lettuce, cut up
1 teaspoon salt

1½ quarts water
4 lamb steaks, shoulder or leg
  chops, ¾ inch thick
Salt and pepper

In a Dutch oven or stew pot, place the soup bone, split peas, onion, lettuce, salt, and water. Cover and simmer over low heat for 2 hours. Meanwhile season the lamb steaks with salt and pepper and brown well in a skillet. When the peas are tender, remove the soup bone and add the lamb to the vegetables; cook about 30 minutes longer. Place the meat and vegetables in a tureen, pour the "gravy" over all. Makes 4 to 6 servings.

CHOWDER

4 slices salt pork, partially
  broiled
1 medium onion, cut up
1 large fillet of haddock or
  other firm fish
Pepper as desired

12 saltine crackers
½ cup milk
1 cup white wine
Water
1 tablespoon all-purpose flour
2 tablespoons snipped parsley

In a large saucepan, arrange the slices of pork, cover with the onion. Sprinkle the fish with pepper, then cut it in strips and place on the onion. Soak the crackers in the milk until soft, then beat lightly and spoon over the fish. Add the wine and 1 cup of water; cover and simmer over low heat about 45 minutes. Remove and discard the salt pork, spoon the fish mixture into a deep serving dish. If desired, thicken the "gravy" with the flour blended with 2 tablespoons of cold water, add with the parsley to the gravy and stir over low heat for a few minutes, until of desired consistency. Pour over the fish mixture and serve hot. Makes about 4 servings.

BEEF SOUP

2 pieces beef hind shank bone
  with meat
½ teaspoon black pepper
2 teaspoons salt
3 medium onions, cut up
2 small turnips or 1 parsnip,
  diced
6 carrots, cut up

3 quarts water
Parsley sprigs
Celery leaves
½ teaspoon dried thyme leaves
1 cup sliced celery
2 tablespoons brown sugar
Croutons

In a large kettle, place the bones with meat, sprinkle with pepper and salt. Add the onions, turnips, carrots, and water to cover. Simmer covered about 4 hours, skimming when needed. Tie the parsley and celery leaves together with thread. Add to the soup with the thyme and sliced celery. Continue cooking about 1 hour longer. Just before serving, remove the "bouquet" of parsley. Remove the bones and cut off the meat. Place the meat in a tureen. In a small skillet, melt the brown sugar in a ladleful of the soup; stir into the kettle. Adjust the seasoning. Pour the soup with vegetables over the meat in the tureen. Top each serving with croutons. Makes about 6 (main-dish) servings.

CAROLINA CORN SHRIMP PIE

2 pounds shrimp (raw, shelled and deveined, or thawed frozen)
3 whole eggs
3 cups milk
¼ cup chopped green bell peppers
¼ cup chopped small green onions
½ cup chopped celery hearts
2 cups corn scraped from the cob, or 2 cups canned creamed style corn

Dash of Tabasco sauce, or Bermuda pepper sauce
1 teaspoon Worcestershire sauce
1 teaspoon prepared mustard
¼ cup butter
Salt
Pepper
Unsalted crackers
Cracker crumbs

Line a well-buttered shallow casserole with crackers. Beat the eggs with the milk and add the shrimp and vegetables. Add seasoning and rectify to taste. Pour into the casserole and sprinkle with cracker crumbs. Dot with butter. Bake 1 hour at 350° F. Serves 10 to 12.

BAKED CRABMEAT

2 cups cooked crabmeat (2 6-ounce packages frozen)
3 tablespoons melted butter
¼ teaspoon grated nutmeg
¾ teaspoon salt

¼ teaspoon pepper
2 teaspoons cider vinegar
⅔ cup fine toast crumbs
2 slices buttered toast, cut in quarters

Flake the crab well. In a bowl combine the crab, 2 tablespoons of the melted butter, nutmeg, salt, pepper, vinegar, and crumbs. Toss lightly with a fork to mix well. Heat the oven to 400° F. Turn the crab mixture into a buttered 1-quart baking dish. Drizzle with the remaining butter. Bake for 15 to 20 minutes or until lightly browned on top. Serve on toast points. Makes 3 to 4 servings.

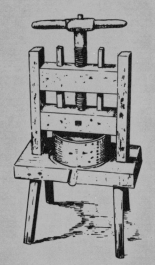

CHEESE PRESS

FLOUR SIFTER

BUTTER PADDLE

SCALES

WATER BUCKET

STOVE PLATE

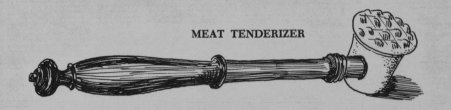

MEAT TENDERIZER

CLAM FRITTERS

3 dozen cherrystone clams
  Salt and pepper
1¼ cups milk
2 eggs, separated

½ teaspoon salt
1¼ cups all-purpose flour
Fat for frying

Wash the clams and arrange them in a large kettle. Add water to cover and simmer until the shells open. Drain, and run cold water over the clams. Remove them from the shells and chop coarsely. (Makes about 1½ cups chopped clams.) Sprinkle the clams with salt and pepper. Beat egg yolks; blend in milk, the ½ teaspoon salt, and flour. Beat egg whites stiff. Fold them into flour mixture. Stir in clams. Using a tablespoon, drop batter into hot fat. Fry, turning to brown both sides. Drain on paper towels. Makes 6 generous servings.

FRIED CLAMS

3 dozen steamer clams
½ teaspoon salt
⅛ teaspoon cayenne pepper
3 egg yolks

2 tablespoons light cream
1 cup fine cracker crumbs
Butter

Wash clams and steam them in boiling water until the shells open. Remove them from the shell, rinse, drain well on paper towels. Sprinkle the clams with salt and cayenne pepper. Beat together the egg yolks and cream. Dip clams in the egg mixture, then roll in cracker crumbs, coating well. Heat butter in a skillet. Fry the clams until lightly browned on both sides, adding more butter from time to time as needed. Serve hot. Makes 6 servings.

OYSTER AND SWEETBREAD

2 dozen large oysters	¼ teaspoon ground mace
1 pair sweetbreads (about	¼ cup butter
1½ pounds)	¼ cup flour
3 lemon slices	½ teaspoon salt
½ teaspoon salt	1 cup light cream
¼ teaspoon pepper	

Drain the oysters, reserving ¾ cup liquor. Wash the sweetbreads in cold water. Let stand in cold water 20 minutes. Drain. Combine the sweetbreads and lemon slices in a saucepan. Cook, covered, in boiling salted water for 30 minutes. Drain and cover the sweetbreads with cold water. When cool enough to handle remove any connecting membrane and cut them into 1-inch pieces. Combine the oysters and sweetbreads. Sprinkle with the salt, pepper, and mace. Melt the butter in a small saucepan. Blend the flour and ½ teaspoon salt. Slowly stir in the cream and reserved oyster liquor. Cook, stirring, over medium heat until the sauce is smooth and thickened. Stir in the sweetbreads and oysters. Pour into a 1½-quart casserole. Bake at 375° F. for 25 minutes or until bubbling and hot. Makes 5 to 6 servings.

PICKLED OYSTERS

4 dozen large oysters	3 tablespoons white wine
8 peppercorns	¼ cup cider vinegar
¾ teaspoon salt	2 tablespoons peppered sherry
¼ teaspoon ground mace	

Simmer the oysters in their liquor until they begin to curl around the edges. Strain off and reserve the liquor. To it add the peppercorns, salt, mace, wine, vinegar, and sherry. Simmer the liquid for 10 minutes. Cool. Put the drained oysters into a quart container with a cover. Pour the liquid over them. Store, covered, in the refrigerator at least 1 day before serving. Makes about 3 cups.

To make peppered sherry, add 6 drops of Tabasco for each 2 tablespoons of sherry and use for seasoning.

OYSTER FRITTERS

3 large eggs	1¾ cups all-purpose flour
1 cup milk	4 dozen large oysters
¾ teaspoon salt	Fat for frying

Beat eggs thoroughly. Gradually blend in the milk, salt, then flour. Beat smooth. Let the batter stand at room temperature for 1 hour. Drain the oysters on paper towels. Dip them, one at a time in the batter, coating well. Fry in hot fat, turning once to brown both sides well. Drain on paper towels. Makes 8 generous servings.

PICKLED MACKEREL

Clean and divide, then cut each side in three; or, leaving them undivided, cut each fish in five or six pieces. To six large mackerel, take near an ounce of pepper, two nutmegs, a little mace, four cloves, and a handful of salt, all in finest powder; mix, and making holes in each bit of fish, thrust the seasoning into them; rub each piece with some of it; then fry them brown in oil; let them stand till cold, then put them into a stone jar, and cover with vinegar: if to keep long, pour oil on the top. This done, they may be preserved for months.

3 medium mackerel
¾ teaspoon black pepper
1½ teaspoons ground nutmeg
3 teaspoons ground mace
¼ teaspoon ground cloves
3 tablespoons salt
Cooking oil
About 2 cups vinegar

Clean the fish and slice each into about 6 pieces. In a shallow bowl, combine the pepper, nutmeg, mace, cloves, and salt. Dip the cut pieces of fish in the spice mixture, coating well and piercing the skin to season the fish well. In hot oil, brown the fish on all sides. Let cool. Place in 2 1-quart jars and pour in vinegar to cover fish; then pour a layer of oil on top. Refrigerate for a week before serving. Makes about 8 servings for appetizer course.

BAKED ROCKFISH

1 3- to 4-pound whole fish
   (rockfish, striped bass,
   red snapper)
Salt and pepper
4 cups coarse dry bread
   crumbs
⅔ cup finely diced onion
1 teaspoon salt
2 egg yolks, beaten
¼ cup melted butter
¼ teaspoon ground cloves
3 tablespoons port wine
3 tablespoons catsup
2 tablespoons water
2 tablespoons lemon juice
¼ cup buttered bread crumbs
Lemon slices

Wash the fish and dry it well with paper towels. Remove the head and tail if desired. Sprinkle the cavity with salt and pepper. In a large bowl combine crumbs, onion, salt, egg yolks, melted butter, and cloves. Blend lightly. Use to stuff the cavity; close the cavity with the small skewers laced with twine. Arrange the fish in a large shallow baking dish. Heat the oven to 375° F. Combine the wine, catsup, water, and lemon juice. Pour half of the wine mixture over the fish. Bake for 12 minutes per pound, or until it begins to flake when tested with a fork. Sprinkle with buttered crumbs and drizzle with the remaining wine mixture. Continue to bake until the crumbs are lightly browned and the fish is very tender, about 10 minutes longer. Serve garnished with lemon slices. Makes 6 to 8 servings.

SUGAR SIFTER

BAKED SHAD

3½–pound shad, split and boned
1 cup forcemeat mixture
  (recipe on page 31)
½ cup water
½ cup red wine
2 tablespoons vinegar

Few whole cloves
Clove garlic
Salt and pepper as desired
2 tablespoons melted butter or
  margarine

Preheat the oven to 400° F. Grease a shallow baking pan and lay the fish in it. Stuff the fish with forcemeat and skewer. Add the water, wine, vinegar, cloves, and garlic. Sprinkle the fish with salt and pepper, brush with the melted butter. Bake for 45 minutes, basting occasionally. Remove the fish to a serving platter; if desired thicken the gravy with flour. Makes about 6 servings.

STEWED COD

2 pounds sliced fresh cod or
  2 12-ounce packages
  frozen cod fillets,
  defrosted
1½ teaspoons salt
½ teaspoon ground nutmeg
¼ teaspoon pepper
1 teaspoon dried parsley flakes
¼ teaspoon powdered thyme

½ teaspoon dried basil
1 cup dry white wine
½ cup water
3 tablespoons melted butter
¼ cup flour
3 tablespoons lemon juice
1 dozen small oysters
¼ cup liquor drained from
  oysters

In a large, heavy saucepan combine the cod, salt, nutmeg, pepper, parsley, thyme, and basil. Add the wine and water. Cover and simmer 6 to 8 minutes or until fish flakes when tested with a fork. Remove the fish to a heated platter. Blend together the butter, flour, lemon juice, oysters, and oyster liquor. Stir the mixture into liquid in the saucepan. Cook, stirring, until the sauce is smooth and bubbling. Strain and serve over the cod. Makes 4 servings.

ROAST DUCK WITH
VIRGINIA CORNBREAD STUFFING

1 duck	Salt
Virginia cornbread	Pepper
½ cup onion, finely chopped	Giblets
1 cup celery, coarsely chopped	2 eggs
Butter	Flour
½ cup parsley, coarsely chopped	Stock (from the giblets)

Break up Virginia cornbread to make 4 cups. Sauté the onion and the celery, including tender top leaves, in butter until tender. Add the parsley to the cornbread, salt and pepper to taste. Add the giblets which have been parboiled and chopped. Moisten with the eggs, lightly beaten, and fill the duck loosely. Rub the outside of the duck with salt, pepper, and flour. Place on the rack of a roasting pan. Start in a hot oven at 500° F. for about ½ hour. Reduce heat to 300° F. and complete the cooking for about 1½ hours, basting with the juices in the bottom of the pan. To make gravy, pour off most of the fat, leaving about 2 tablespoons. Add 2 tablespoons of flour and blend. Add a cup of the hot seasoned stock in which the giblets were parboiled, blend and serve.

Virginia cornbread is made with white stoneground meal, according to any one of several recipes to be found on the packages of this meal, widely sold wherever people have developed a taste for "ole Southern cooking." There is only one inviolable rule about Virginia cornbread: under no circumstances should sugar be added. Having observed this rule, this favorite dressing may easily be made and used in both wild and domestic duck.

CHICKEN FRICASSEE

1 3-pound chicken, cut up	1 cup chopped parsley
2 tablespoons melted butter	3 cups light cream
12 small onions, thinly sliced in rings	Salt
	Pepper

Heat the oven to 400° F. Wash the chicken pieces and blot them dry in paper towels. Brush them with melted butter on all sides and sprinkle with salt and pepper. Spread the chicken pieces on a baking sheet and bake 30 minutes. Remove the chicken from the oven and place in a skillet on a layer of onions, then sprinkle with parsley. Add another layer of onions, chicken, and parsley. Pour ½ cup of cream into the baking sheet and stir in any butter and juices from the chicken. Pour over the chicken and add the remaining cream. Cover and cook 20 minutes or until the onions are tender. Makes 6 servings.

ROAST STUFFED TURKEY

About 12-pound hen turkey
1 quart soft bread crumbs
Grated rind of 1 lemon
¼ teaspoon pepper
1 teaspoon salt
1 teaspoon nutmeg
Butter or margarine, melted

Turkey liver, gizzard, and
   heart
All-purpose flour
1 egg, hard-cooked, discard
   white
2 cups hot water

KETTLE TILTER

Rinse inside of the turkey well, drain. Combine the bread crumbs, lemon rind, pepper, salt, and nutmeg with ½ cup of melted butter. Fill the cavity with the bread mixture. Brush the turkey with melted butter. Roast at 325° F. for about 4 hours, basting occasionally with more butter and pan drippings. Meanwhile cook the liver, gizzard, and heart in small saucepan in boiling water. Remove the liver when cooked, about 5 minutes; continue cooking the gizzard and heart until tender, about 45 minutes. Rub the liver with 2 tablespoons of flour to make a smooth paste. Chop the gizzard and heart fine and add to "liver paste." Add the egg yolk, and salt and pepper to taste. Skim fat from the drippings and add the liver mixture to the remaining drippings. Blend in the hot water. Turn into a small saucepan, simmer for 10 minutes, stirring frequently. Serve with the turkey. Makes about 20 servings.

CHICKEN PILAU

Boil a pair of fowls; when done, take them out and put your rice in the same water, first taking out some of the liquor. When the rice is done, butter it well; cover the bottom of your dish with half of it; then put the fowls on it, and add the remainder of the liquor; cover the fowls with the other half of the rice, make it smooth, and spread over it the yolks of two eggs, well beaten. Bake in a moderate oven.

1 6-pound roasting chicken	1 teaspoon salt
2 quarts water	1 tablespoon butter or
1 teaspoon salt	margarine
1 cup regular rice	2 egg yolks, beaten

Simmer the chicken in water and salt until tender (about 2 hours). Drain off the broth; reserve. Remove the chicken from the bones; cut into bite-size chunks (about 6 cups). Cook the rice as the label directs, using 2 cups of the reserved broth with salt and butter. Place half of the cooked rice in a buttered 2-quart casserole, then put the chicken on rice. Pour the remaining broth over the chicken and rice. Cover the chicken with the remaining rice. Spoon beaten yolks over the rice. Bake in 350° F. oven 1 hour, or until golden and bubbly. Makes 8 servings.

CHICKEN PUDDING

2 3-pound frying chickens disjointed (split breasts, separate drumsticks and thighs)	1 teaspoon oregano
	2 teaspoons salt
	1 teaspoon coarsely ground black pepper
1 chicken breast, split	½ cup chopped parsley
3 stalks celery, including tops	Butter
1 large mild onion	Flour
6 sprigs parsley	

Make a stock by using the giblets, necks, and backbones and simmering with celery, onion, sprigs of parsley, oregano, salt, and pepper for about 40 minutes. Strain and reserve the broth. Chop the giblets.

Combine flour, salt, and pepper in a bag; shake pieces of chicken a few at a time until coated. Sauté in butter until well browned. Place the chicken in a large round chicken pudding dish or large shallow casserole. Thicken the drippings with flour and make a gravy, using two cups of the strained chicken broth. Add the chopped parsley. Pour over the chicken. Add a Yorkshire Pudding topping and spread evenly (a recipe for such a batter is described on page 32). Start in a hot oven (450° F.) for 15 minutes. Reduce to 350° F. and continue baking for 20 to 25 minutes. Make a gravy with 2 tablespoons of butter, two of flour, and the remaining broth. Add the chopped giblets and serve in a separate sauce boat.

SHOULDER OF VENISON

CAST-IRON KETTLE

Let the meat hang until you judge proper to dress it, then take out the bone: beat the meat with a rolling pin. Lay some slices of mutton fat that has lain a few hours in a little port wine, among it: sprinkle a little black and Jamaica pepper over it, in finest powder: roll it up tight, and fillet it. Set it in a stewpan that will only just hold it, with some mutton or beef gravy, not strong, half a pint of port, and some pepper and pimento. Simmer, close covered, and as slow as you can, for three or four hours. When quite tender, take off the tape, and set the meat on a dish, and strain the gravy over. Serve with currantjelly sauce.

¼ pound mutton or lamb fat, pounded flat
1 cup port wine
5 to 6 pounds boned shoulder of venison (or beef)
½ teaspoon salt
½ teaspoon pepper
¼ teaspoon allspice
1 tablespoon butter or margarine
1 tablespoon flour
1 cup water
Currant jelly

Soak the fat in the wine about 1 hour. Wrap the fat around the meat; tie with butcher's string. Place the meat in a close-fitting Dutch oven. Sprinkle the meat with the salt, pepper, and allspice; pour on the wine the fat soaked in. Start to cook over low heat. As soon as the wine begins to simmer, stir in the butter kneaded with the flour. Cook covered for 3 or 4 hours or until the meat is fork tender. From time to time check the liquid and add water as needed. Remove the meat to a platter; skim any fat from the gravy. Serve with currant jelly. Makes 10 servings.

VEAL BIRDS
WITH FORCEMEAT

Cut long thin collops: beat them well, and lay on them a bit of thin bacon the same size; and spread forcemeat on that, seasoned high, with the addition of a little garlik, and Cayenne. Roll them up tight, about the size of two fingers, but not more than two or three inches long. Put a very small skewer to fasten each firm. Rub egg over them, and fry of a fine brown, and pour over them a rich brown gravy.

DUTCH OVEN

3 ounces beef suet, ground
3 ounces veal, ground
2 strips bacon, finely chopped
2 cups soft fine bread crumbs
1 teaspoon grated lemon peel
2 tablespoons finely snipped
    parsley
½ teaspoon salt
    Few grains pepper

½ teaspoon mace
1 clove garlic, minced
6 slices veal (about 1½
    pounds) pounded very
    thin
6 strips bacon
1 egg, beaten
    Shortening

To prepare the forcemeat, combine the beef suet, ground veal, chopped bacon, bread crumbs, lemon peel, parsley, salt, pepper, mace, and garlic. Place each veal slice on a bacon strip. Place a tablespoon of the forcemeat mixture on the veal slices. Roll up the veal and bacon to rolls about 1½ inches thick and about 3 inches long and skewer firmly. Brush the veal rolls with the egg. In a large skillet, brown the rolls well on all sides in hot shortening. Serve with brown gravy. Makes 6 servings.

STUFFED BAKED HAM

1¼ cups dry bread crumbs
¼ teaspoon pepper
½ teaspoon ground allspice
½ teaspoon ground cloves
½ teaspoon ground mace
¼ cup brown sugar
2 tablespoons melted butter or
    margarine

4 tablespoons water
    About 10 pounds boiled
    ham, bone in, skin
    removed
1 egg, beaten
3 tablespoons granulated
    sugar

Preheat the oven to 325° F. Combine 1 cup of bread crumbs, the pepper, allspice, cloves, mace, brown sugar, and butter. Blend in the water gradually. With a knife cut out 1-inch deep plugs in diagonal lines over surface of ham and fill with the spice-crumb mixture. Brush the ham with the egg; sprinkle with ¼ cup bread crumbs, then with the granulated sugar. Bake for 2½ hours. To serve, slice as usual. Makes about 25 servings.

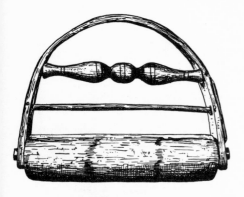

ROLLING PIN

ROAST BEEF
WITH YORKSHIRE PUDDING

5-pound top sirloin of beef	1 piece bacon
Salt	1 small onion, sliced
Pepper	1 carrot, split
Flour	¼ cup beef bouillon

Sprinkle the meat with salt and pepper; dredge with flour. Place the bacon, onion, carrot, and bouillon in a roasting pan; set meat on this. Bake in a 350° F. oven 1 hour and 15 minutes (allow 15 minutes per pound). Baste with drippings. When the meat is done remove from the oven. Increase temperature to 450° F. Drain off all but 2 or 3 tablespoons of drippings.

YORKSHIRE PUDDING

¾ cup flour	1 cup milk
1 teaspoon salt	3 eggs, well beaten

To flour and salt in a bowl, stir in just enough of the milk to form a smooth batter. Combine the rest of the milk with the eggs and pour into the roasting pan. Bake 20 to 30 minutes or till Yorkshire pudding is puffed and golden. Cut in 8 to 10 squares. Arrange around the roast; spoon on pan drippings and juices from the meat. Makes 8 to 10 servings.

BOSTON BAKED BEANS

2 cups pea or navy beans
   Water, salted
¼ pound strip or slab bacon
   or pork
¼ cup molasses
1 teaspoon salt

¼ teaspoon soda
1 onion, peeled (optional)
1 tablespoon mustard
   (optional)
¼ teaspoon black pepper
   (optional)

Soak the beans overnight in 2 quarts of water. Cook the beans plus another quart of water and salt for about 1 hour or until the skins start to crackle or pop. Drain, reserving the liquid. Cut the meat into pieces and score the rind; place in a 2- or 3-quart bean pot. Put the cooked beans in the pot. Add the molasses, salt, soda, and any or all of the optional ingredients. Pour on enough of the bean liquid to cover the beans. Cover the pot and bake in 350° F. oven 5 to 6 hours, adding bean liquid or more water so that beans do not dry out. Makes 6 to 8 servings.

HOPPING JOHN

2 cups dried black-eyed peas
1½ quarts cold water
1 pound bacon
5 cups boiling water

2 cups long-grain rice
1 tablespoon salt
½ teaspoon pepper

Combine the peas and cold water in a large, heavy kettle with a tight-fitting cover. Bring to a boil. Cover and cook over medium heat for 1 hour. Remove the cover. Turn heat to high and cook until the peas are almost dry. Cut the bacon into 1½-inch lengths. Add the bacon, boiling water, rice, salt, and pepper. Stir; bring to a boil; cover and simmer for 25 minutes or until moisture is absorbed and the rice tender. Serve topped with some of the bacon pieces. Makes 8 to 10 generous servings.

SALAD WITH DRESSING

2 hard-cooked eggs, sliced
1 tablespoon cold water
2 tablespoons salad or olive oil
1 teaspoon salt
1 teaspoon sugar
1 teaspoon prepared mustard
2 tablespoons cider vinegar

2 tablespoons tarragon vinegar
1 small head lettuce
1 small head romaine
½ head chicory
1 bunch watercress
2 bunches young scallions

In a small bowl, carefully remove the yolks from the egg slices, reserving the egg-white rings. Mash the yolks, blend smooth with the water; then blend in the oil, salt, sugar, mustard, and vinegars. Refrigerate. Just before serving place the chilled, crisped, cut-up salad greens in a salad bowl; pour the dressing over the greens, garnish with the scallions and rings of egg white. Toss at the table. Makes about 10 servings.

JOHNNYCAKE

1 cup cornmeal
2 cups water
½ teaspoon salt

1 tablespoon butter or
    margarine

Put the cornmeal in a saucepan. Stir in the water, salt, and butter. Cook, stirring constantly, until mixture thickens. Cool. Shape into 2 cakes about 6 by 3 inches. Place on a hot, greased baking pan and bake in a 400° F. oven for 30 minutes. Makes 4 servings.

BATH BUNS

2 packages active dry yeast
½ cup warm water
½ pound butter (1 cup)
4 cups sifted all-purpose flour
4 eggs, well beaten
2 cups confectioners' sugar

½ teaspoon nutmeg
1 teaspoon caraway seeds
    (optional)
Preserved fruits (citron,
    lemon, or orange peel)

Sprinkle the yeast over the warm water; let stand a few minutes to dissolve. With a pastry blender, or 2 knives used scissors fashion, blend the butter into the flour until all fat particles are coated. Stir in the eggs. Cover the bowl with cloth. Set the dough to rise until double in bulk, then stir in the sugar, nutmeg, and caraway seeds. Drop by heaping spoonfuls onto a greased cookie sheet. (Be sure to leave room—they spread.) Sprinkle preserved fruits on each. Bake in a 375° F. oven 25 minutes or till golden. Remove from pan. Makes 24 buns.

INDIAN SLAPJACKS

One quart of milk, 1 pint of indian meal, 4 eggs, 4 spoons of flour, little salt, beat together, baked on griddles, or fry in a dry pan, or baked in a pan which has been rub'd with suet, lard or butter.

1 egg, well beaten
1 cup milk
½ cup yellow cornmeal

½ cup flour
½ teaspoon salt
Shortening

Combine the egg and milk; stir into combined cornmeal, flour, and salt. Drop batter by tablespoonfuls onto a hot, greased griddle. Cook till the edges are done. Turn; cook on the other side. Makes 18 4-inch slapjacks.

Kitchen, Webb House
Wethersfield, Connecticut

Kitchen, Millbach House
Lebanon County, Pennsylvania

**Kitchen, Governor's Palace
Williamsburg, Virginia**

**Kitchen, Hempstead House
New London, Connecticut**

SALLY LUNN

1 package active dry yeast
¼ cup warm water
2 tablespoons butter or
   margarine

1 cup milk, warmed
3 cups sifted all-purpose flour
2 eggs, well beaten
½ teaspoon salt

Sprinkle the yeast over the warm water; let stand to soften. Warm the butter in the milk. Put the flour in large bowl and make a well in it. Add the eggs, salt, milk mixture, and softened yeast. Mix well; pour into well-buttered 9-inch square pan. Cover; let stand in a warm place 1 to 1½ hours, or until doubled in bulk. Bake in a 375° F. oven about 30 minutes, or until golden. Serve hot, cut in squares. Makes 9 servings.

NAPLES BISCUIT

½ cup flour
½ cup confectioners' sugar
2 eggs

Sift together the flour and the sugar. Beat the eggs until very thick (about 4 minutes). Beat in the flour mixture in 4 parts. Mixture will be thin. Bake in Naples biscuit tins or lady-finger pans, or in a well-greased 9-inch square pan. Bake at 375° F. for 15 minutes. Cool on a wire rack; cut into 12 cakes. Makes ¼ pound.

CRULLERS

4 cups sifted all-purpose flour
1½ cups confectioners' sugar
½ teaspoon cinnamon
¼ teaspoon nutmeg

¼ pound butter
3 eggs, well beaten
Shortening
Confectioners' sugar

In a large bowl combine flour, sugar, cinnamon, and nutmeg. With a pastry blender, or 2 knives used scissors fashion, blend the butter into the flour mixture until all the fat particles are coated. Stir in the eggs to form a dough, adding a little water if necessary. Knead the dough well on a floured board. Divide the dough into 4 pieces and knead these separately, then form back into a single piece of dough and knead again. Roll the dough into squares ½-inch thick. Cut into narrow ½-inch strips. Twist the strips into various shapes. Fry in a deep fat fryer set at 400° F. until golden, turning them once. Cool on paper toweling. Sprinkle with confectioners' sugar. Makes about 2 dozen.

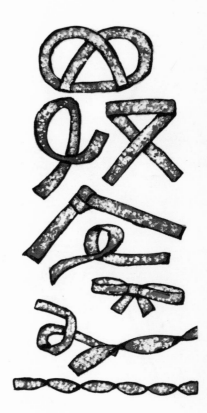

OLYKOEK

To one pint of raised bread dough, add one cup of sugar, and half a cup of butter, with spice to your taste. Work these last well into the dough and set it to rise. When it becomes light, and while the lard for frying them in, is heating, roll out part of the dough, cut it into squares an inch and a half in size, lay two or three raisins in each, and close the dough over them to prevent any opening. Before frying, try the heat of the lard first with a small bit of dough; if it rises immediately to the surface, the lard is sufficiently hot; then drop in your balls.

1 cup milk	2 eggs, well beaten
1 package active dry yeast	1 cup softened butter or
¼ cup lukewarm water	margarine
6 cups sifted all-purpose flour	Raisins (optional)
1 teaspoon salt	Fat
1 teaspoon cinnamon	Confectioners' sugar, or
½ teaspoon nutmeg	granulated sugar and
1 cup brown sugar	cinnamon

WAFER IRON

Scald the milk; cool to lukewarm. Soften the yeast in warm water. Combine the flour, salt, cinnamon, nutmeg, and brown sugar. Combine the milk, yeast and flour mixture (dough will be thick). Stir in the eggs. Cover and set in a warm place to rise until doubled in bulk. Punch down. Work in the butter till smooth and blended. Roll dough ½-inch thick on lightly floured board, cut with a doughnut cutter; sprinkle with raisins. Let them rise again then fry in fat that is hot enough to brown a 1-inch cube of bread in 60 seconds. Fry till golden on both sides; drain on paper. Sprinkle with sugar, or sugar and cinnamon. Makes about 40.

MAIDS OF HONOR

Pastry for 2-crust pie	1 tablespoon lemon juice
2 eggs	2 tablespoons flour
½ cup granulated sugar	Strawberry or raspberry
½ cup almond paste	jam
1 to 2 tablespoons dry sherry	
2 tablespoons melted butter	
or margarine	

Roll out the pastry; cut circle ½ inch larger all around than diameter of the tart shells. Line 8 to 10 tart shells 3½ inches in diameter with the pastry and place them on a cookie sheet. Beat the eggs until very light and fluffy; gradually beat in the sugar. Soften the almond paste with sherry, butter, and lemon juice. Add to the batter. Stir in the flour. Drop a teaspoonful of jam in each shell; pour on batter. Bake in a 350° F. oven for about 45 minutes or until puffed, golden, and firm. Makes 8 to 10 servings.

ALMOND CAKE

5 eggs
2 cups sifted confectioners' sugar
½ cup finely ground blanched almonds

1 tablespoon rose water
1 cup sifted cake flour

ICING

1 egg
1½ cups confectioners' sugar
½ teaspoon lemon or almond extract

Preheat the oven to 400° F. Separate the eggs, putting the yolks in a large mixing bowl and the whites in a medium bowl. First beat the whites until stiff but not dry. Beat the yolks until light and lemon-colored. Gradually beat in the sugar, then the almonds, then the rose water. Fold half of the whites into the egg-yolk mixture, then sift half the flour over the batter and fold in to blend well. Fold in the remaining egg white, then the flour, and gently blend well. Turn into a greased 9- x 9- x 1¾-inch baking pan. Bake about 25 minutes or until the top springs back when lightly touched. Cool in the pan on a rack.

Make the icing in a small bowl: blend the egg white with the sugar, beat until smooth, add the extract. Spread on the cake and decorate as desired while the icing is wet. Mark into squares as desired; cut through when the icing is set. Makes 12 to 24 pieces.

CHEERS FOR THE GINGERBREAD BOYS!
LITTLE MOUTHS SMACKING WITH JOYS
MAMA BAKES THEM BROWN AND HOT!
GINGERBREAD BOYS EAT A LOT.

SOFT GINGERBREAD

¼ pound whipped butter, softened (1½ sticks)
1 cup brown sugar
2 tablespoons ginger
1 teaspoon each cinnamon and ground cloves

2 cups molasses
6 cups sifted all-purpose flour
6 eggs, well beaten
2 cups sour milk or buttermilk
1 teaspoon baking soda

In a large bowl mix the butter and brown sugar till smooth; add the ginger, cinnamon, and cloves. Stir in, one after the other, until just blended the molasses, flour, eggs, and sour milk combined with soda; beat well. Pour into a greased and floured 14- x 9- x 2-inch baking pan. Bake in a 350° F. oven for 1 hour, or until a cake tester inserted in center comes out dry. Cool on a wire rack 10 minutes, then remove from pan. Makes 12 to 15 servings.

SAVOY OR SPONGE CAKES

6 egg yolks	6 egg whites
1¼ cups granulated sugar	½ teaspoon salt
1 tablespoon lemon juice	1½ cups sifted cake flour
1 teaspoon grated lemon peel	

In a large mixing bowl, beat the egg yolks until thick and lemon-colored. Gradually beat in 1 cup of the sugar, the lemon juice, and the peel. In a medium bowl, beat the egg whites with the salt, until soft peaks form, then gradually beat in the remaining ¼ cup sugar, beating until stiff. Turn onto the egg-yolk mixture, sift the flour over the egg whites and fold in until thoroughly blended. Fill about 24 lined cupcake cups two-thirds full with the fluffy batter. For a sponge cake, turn into an ungreased 10-inch tube pan. Bake the cup cakes at 350° F. for 15 to 20 minutes until golden and the cake shrinks away from sides. Cool on racks. Bake the tube cake at 325° F. for about 1 hour or until done. Invert pan to cool the cake. Makes about 24 large or 30 medium cup cakes, or 1 10-inch tube cake.

POUND CAKE

1 pound butter	1 pound sifted all-purpose
2 cups sugar	flour (4½ cups)
1 pound eggs (10 eggs, separated)	1 teaspoon baking powder
	1 teaspoon mace
1 tablespoon lemon juice	2 teaspoons almond flavoring
	¼ cup brandy

Cream the butter with 1 cup of the sugar. Beat the egg yolks until light and lemon colored, and gradually beat in the remaining cup of sugar. Add the lemon juice and beat into the butter mixture. Mix in the dry ingredients and add the flavoring and brandy. Beat the egg whites until they form peaks, but are not dry. Fold into the batter. Bake in greased and floured Turk's head mold or 10-inch tube pan at 325° F. for about 1 hour. May also be baked in 2 loaf pans 8 x 8 x 3 inches.

PUMPKIN PIE

1 9-inch unbaked pie shell	¾ cup granulated sugar
1½ cups canned or mashed cooked pumpkin	½ teaspoon salt
	1 teaspoon mace
3 eggs, well beaten	½ teaspoon ground nutmeg
1½ cups heavy cream	½ teaspoon ground ginger

Make the pie shell with a high scalloped edge, refrigerate several hours. Preheat the oven to 425° F. In a large bowl (with a pouring lip if you have one) combine the pumpkin with the eggs, then the cream, sugar, salt, and spices. Blend well, then pour into the chilled pie shell. Bake for 15 minutes, then reduce the heat to 350° F. before serving. Makes about 8 servings.

SAFFRON CAKE

1 cup milk
1 cup granulated sugar
½ teaspoon salt
½ pound butter or
  margarine
1 teaspoon saffron
2 tablespoons boiling water
4 cups all-purpose flour

½ teaspoon ground cloves
1 teaspoon each mace and
  cinnamon
½ cup warm water
2 packages active dry yeast
3 eggs, beaten
1 tablespoon rose water
1 teaspoon caraway seeds

In a medium saucepan, scald the milk; stir in the sugar, salt, and butter, cool to lukewarm. Combine the saffron and boiling water, let stand. Sift together the flour, cloves, mace, and cinnamon. Into a large mixing bowl, pour warm water; sprinkle the yeast over the water and stir to dissolve. Add the milk mixture, eggs, rose water, saffron liquid, caraway seeds, and half the flour mixture. Beat at medium speed until smooth. Beat in the remaining flour. Pour the batter into a greased 13- x 9- x 2-inch baking pan. Let rise in a warm place until double in bulk, about 1 hour. Preheat oven to 325° F. Bake the cake for about 1 hour or until it tests done. Cool in the pan on a rack. Cut as desired. Makes about 18 squares.

BUTTER MOLD

HASTY PUDDING

1 cup cornmeal
1 cup cold water
3 cups boiling water

½ teaspoon salt
Sugar

Combine the cornmeal and cold water. In a very heavy pot, bring 3 cups of water with ½ teaspoon of salt to a boil. Carefully stir in the corn meal mixture, making sure that it does not lump. Cook over low heat, stirring occasionally, for 1 hour or until the mixture is very thick. Serve with sugar. Makes 3 or 4 servings.

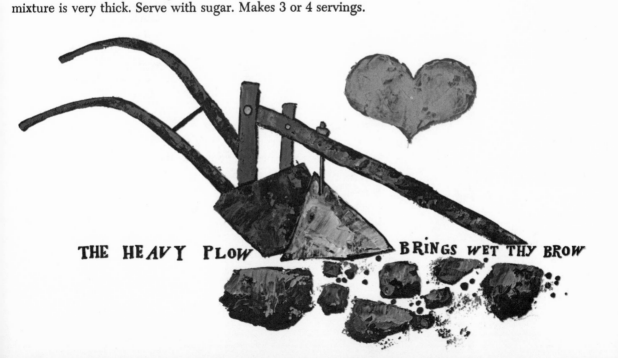

THE HEAVY PLOW   BRINGS WET THY BROW

PLUM PUDDING

1 pound ground beef suet	1 teaspoon allspice
4 cups all-purpose flour	4 eggs, beaten
1 (11-ounce) package currants	1 cup brandy
1 (15-ounce) package raisins	½ teaspoon salt
Rind of 1 lemon	½ cup milk

In a very large bowl or container, combine the ingredients and blend well. Turn the mixture into 3 tall (1-pound) coffee cans or any suitable metal container or pottery mold, filling ⅔ full. Cover the tops with foil, tie on with string. Set the molds in a steamer or large kettle with a rack on the bottom. Add enough water to the kettle so that the molds are half immersed in water, adding more water as needed. Cover and steam for about 9 hours. Cool. Store in the refrigerator until needed.

Before serving: Heat the puddings by steaming over hot water as directed above, for about 1 hour. Unmold the puddings, sprinkle with confectioners' sugar. To flame, heat ½ cup brandy in a small saucepan, set it aflame and pour over the puddings.

BLANC MANGE

1 envelope unflavored gelatin	½ teaspoon mace
2 cups heavy cream	1 teaspoon almond extract
1 cup confectioners' sugar	

Sprinkle the gelatin over the cream in a skillet; let stand a few minutes. Add sugar, mace, and extract. Cook, stirring until mixture comes to a boil. Pour into individual custard or soufflé cups. Makes 6 servings.

TRIFLE

8 ounces sliced sponge cake, split lady fingers or macaroons	½ teaspoon almond extract
	½ cup seedless raspberry jam or marmalade
1 cup white wine	½ cup heavy cream
2 cups custard sauce or "baked" custard from 1 package egg custard mix	2 teaspoons granulated sugar
	1 tablespoon white wine
	Red currant jelly for garnish

PEWTER SPOON AND MOLD

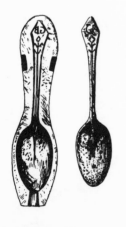

In a 2- to 3-quart glass serving bowl, place sponge cake (or split lady fingers or macaroons) along the bottom and sides. Pour 1 cup of wine evenly over the cake. Make the custard as the package label directs. Pour into the bowl, over soaked cake. Let stand in the refrigerator. Just before serving, spoon a layer of jam or marmalade over the custard. Whip the cream, gradually adding the sugar and 1 tablespoon wine, beating until stiff. Spoon the cream over the jam. Garnish with bits of jelly. Makes 6 to 8 servings.

CUSTARD

¼ teaspoon cinnamon
1 tablespoon granulated sugar
1¾ cups milk
   Small piece bay leaf
1 teaspoon grated lemon rind
3 tablespoons granulated sugar

1 tablespoon flour
2 egg yolks, beaten
¼ cup cold milk
¼ teaspoon almond extract
1 teaspoon brandy

In a saucepan combine the cinnamon and 1 tablespoon sugar, then add 1¾ cups milk, bay leaf, and rind; bring to boil. Meanwhile in a bowl combine the remaining sugar, flour, yolks, then milk. Ladle some of the hot milk into the yolk mixture, beating constantly. Stir the yolk mixture back into the hot milk mixture in the saucepan. Cook over medium heat, stirring, until the mixture just comes to a boil; reduce the heat and continue to cook and stir for 5 minutes; remove from the heat. Stir in the extract and brandy. Strain into individual dessert dishes; chill. Makes 4 servings.

BRANDIED PEACHES

4 pounds firm peaches
   Boiling water
4 cups granulated sugar

2 cups water
2 cups brandy

Wash and prick the peaches with a fork through the flesh to the stone. Place the peaches in a large kettle and pour boiling water over them to cover. Peel or pare skins, blanching in boiling water again if necessary to loosen skin. In a medium saucepan, dissolve the sugar in 2 cups of water, bring to boil; place a few peaches in the boiling syrup, cooking a few at a time (turning them occasionally) for about 10 minutes until the peaches are barely tender. Remove the peaches and gently pack in wide-neck quart jars. Cool the syrup; then stir in the brandy and pour over the peaches in jars, dividing the syrup equally and covering peaches completely. Add more brandy to fill jars to top if needed. Seal tightly. Makes 3 (1-quart) jars of peaches.

LONDON SYLLABUB

2 cups port or white wine
½ cup granulated sugar

½ teaspoon ground nutmeg
2 quarts cold milk

In a serving bowl, blend the wine with the sugar and nutmeg. Place the milk in a blender, 2 cups at a time, and beat until frothy (or shake the milk in a jar); pour into the serving bowl. Stir, and serve in glass punch cups. Makes about 20 (4-ounce) servings. Note: To make Devonshire style, top each serving with whipped cinnamon cream made as follows: whip 1 cup heavy cream, then gradually beat in 1 tablespoon granulated sugar and 1 teaspoon ground cinnamon.

Recipes of the Young Republic

THE YEARS COVERED in this chapter span the birth and adolescence of the young American republic. By 1820 there were almost ten million Americans to enjoy the independence won after two wars. America was extrovert, yet not too confident. Adolescence had set in.

Literature and the arts reflected the lack of confidence. Peale and Stuart depicted patriotic themes but went to school abroad. Benjamin West expatriated himself to England, where he presided over the Royal Academy. The writers of the era were little noted nor long remembered, except for Washington Irving, who recalled: "My native country was full of youthful promise. Europe was rich in the accumulated treasures of age."

Among these treasures were kitchen lore. English cook books continued to pour from American presses. *The Compleat Housewife,* after its debut in Williamsburg in 1742, was published from New York in 1764. Susannah Carter's *The Frugal Housewife* appeared in 1772 both in London and in Boston; the latter edition was graced by Paul Revere's plates. Came the war; but in 1792 (and for another decade) the Carter anthology continued to help ex-colonials with their kitchen problems. *The Art of Cookery* by Hannah Glasse, the British edition of which had appeared when Washington was a teen-ager, reached the American scene in 1805. Maria Eliza Rundell's *A New System of Domestic Cookery* went through 67 London editions and almost as many in America from 1806 to 1844.

A true American entry slipped demurely on stage in 1796. Covered

COFFEE MILL

in paper, its 48 pages included one detailing errors committed because "the author . . . not having an education sufficient to prepare the work for the press, the person that was employed by her . . . did omit several articles very essential in some of the receipts, and placed others in their stead . . ." Nevertheless, the book had charm, and it *was* a pioneer. Significantly entitled *American Cookery,* and said to be "Adapted to this country, and all grades of life," it was signed by Amelia Simmons, an American orphan. It was reprinted, with added material, until 1822 and made a belated curtain bow (with the author's name) at Woodstock, Vt., in 1831. In 1963 it was recast in the role of a genuine American antique.

Simmons affirmed the American setting. "This treatise is calculated for the improvement of the rising generation of Females in America," the Orphan prefaced. She observed that "the cultivation of Rabbits would be profitable in America, if the best methods were pursued. . . ." Concerning apple culture, she inserted an exhortation to "preserve the orchard from the intrusion of boys, &c. which is not too common in America." And now, at last, melons and "cranberries" and apple pie and three kinds of Indian pudding, to say nothing of an epic on dressing a turtle, appear for the delectation of "American Ladies." The latter continued to favor the English competition, of course, but the offerings in the present volume adopt only those recipes known to be accepted in America in the era of the Young Republic.

As for refrigeration: in 1820 Frederic Tudor of Boston learned how sawdust would insulate ice from the weather, and he shipped the frozen harvest of New England ponds to the West Indies and Southern ports. But for most Americans, ice was where you chopped it. The advice of Amelia Simmons remained relevant: "To have sweet butter in dog days, and thro' the vegetable seasons, send stone pots to honest, neat, and trusty dairy people, and procure it pack'd down in May, and let them be brought in in the night, or cool rainy morning, and partake of no heat from the horse, and set the pots in the coldest part of your celler, or in the ice house."

At long last in the case of the great American drama, the American diet was given a leading role, and while we would never be without foreign supporting players—and why should we, since they play their part so well—pride in our native cookery could at least show top billing.

SHAKER STOVE

LOAF SUGAR GRATER

GUMBO SOUP

2 pounds round steak
½ cup flour
4 to 5 tablespoons butter or margarine
1 large onion, chopped
1 quart fresh tomatoes, quartered, or 2 1-pound cans whole tomatoes
2 quarts water
1½ tablespoons salt
¼ teaspoon freshly ground pepper
1 large green pepper, seeded and cut in strips
½ pound fresh whole okra or 1 (10-ounce) package frozen
1 teaspoon tarragon
1 teaspoon thyme
1 bay leaf

Cut the meat in strips 2 inches long, ½ inch wide, and ½ inch thick. Flour the meat and cook in the butter in a Dutch oven until brown. Add the onion and cook until lightly colored. Put in the tomatoes, water, salt, and pepper. Cover and simmer for 1 hour. Add the green pepper, okra, tarragon, thyme, and bay leaf. Cook another hour. Serve in a soup tureen. Makes 10 to 12 servings.

CHICKEN AND OKRA SOUP

4 slices bacon
1 tablespoon shortening
1 3-pound chicken, cut in pieces
2 10-ounce packages frozen okra
2 teaspoons salt
4 fresh tomatoes, cut up
1 green pepper, chopped
1 quart boiling water

In a large heavy soup pot or Dutch oven cook the bacon and remove; reserve. Add the shortening to the pot and brown chicken pieces. Add the okra, salt, tomatoes, green pepper, and water. Simmer covered 1 to 1½ hours or till chicken is tender. Correct seasonings. Makes 6 to 8 servings.

CLEAR TOMATO SOUP

7 medium size whole tomatoes (or 1 1-pound 12-ounce can)
2 pounds beef shin, cut up
1 beef knuckle, split
1 carrot, pared
1 onion, peeled
1 stalk celery
2 sprigs parsley
2 quarts water
1 teaspoon Worcestershire sauce
½ teaspoon brown sugar
½ teaspoon salt
⅛ teaspoon pepper
Croutons

In a large kettle combine the tomatoes, shin, bone, carrot, onion, celery, parsley, and water. Bring to a boil; continue to cook, stirring and skimming occasionally. Strain; add the Worcestershire, brown sugar, salt, and pepper. Bring to a boil; correct the seasonings. Serve garnished with the croutons. Makes 1 quart, or 4 to 6 servings.

GASPACHO

2 slices toast
4 red-ripe tomatoes, peeled
    and sliced
2 medium-size cucumbers,
    peeled and thinly sliced
¼ cup chopped onion
¼ cup tomato juice
½ teaspoon salt
¼ teaspoon pepper
1 teaspoon prepared mustard
⅓ cup olive oil

Prepare the toast and cut it into small cubes. Prepare the vegetables. Blend together the tomato juice, salt, pepper, mustard, and oil. In 6 soup bowls, arrange a layer of toast cubes, tomato, and cucumber slices. Sprinkle with chopped onion. (Use one fourth of total ingredients allowing for 4 layers.) Drizzle with about one fourth of dressing. Repeat until all ingredients are used. Chill. Makes 6 to 8 generous servings.

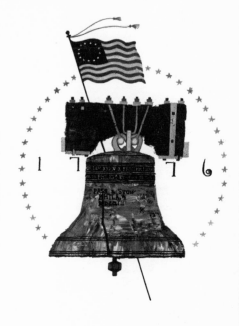

PEA SOUP

2 pounds split peas (1 quart)
1½ pounds lean beef, cut up
½ pound slab bacon, cut up
2 teaspoons powdered mint or
    6 fresh leaves
1 to 2 tablespoons salt
2½ quarts water
2 cups cut-up celery
1 tablespoon celery seed
Croutons

Cover the peas with water and soak overnight. Drain off the water. Place peas in a large soup pot with the beef, bacon, mint, salt, and water. Cook for 3 hours over very low heat. Skim and stir occasionally. Add the celery and celery seed; cook 1 hour longer or until the peas are entirely dissolved and the celery is quite soft. This is a very thick soup. You may prefer to add more water to thin it. Strain soup; correct seasonings. Serve with croutons. Makes 10 to 12 servings.

BRUNSWICK STEW

4 to 5 pounds pullet,
    quartered
1½ quarts water
2 slices bacon, cut up
1 medium onion, sliced
1 (1-pound 12-ounce) can
    peeled solid pack
    tomatoes
1 (10-ounce) package frozen
kernel corn or 3 ears
    fresh corn, kernels cut
3 medium potatoes, sliced
1 (10-ounce) package frozen
    lima beans
Dash cayenne pepper
Salt
½ cup soft bread crumbs

In a Dutch oven or a 6-quart heavy saucepan, cook the chicken in the water with the bacon and onion about 1 hour or until the meat is almost tender. Remove the bones from the chicken and cut into bite-size pieces; return the meat to the Dutch oven. Add the tomatoes, corn, potatoes, beans, and cayenne. Cook until the vegetables and meat are tender. Salt to taste. Just before serving, stir in the bread crumbs. Makes about 6 servings.

PAN

SCALLOPED OYSTERS

24 oysters in shell
1½ cups fine bread crumbs
Butter or margarine

Scrub the oyster shells and open (or have your fish man do this). Arrange the oysters on the half shell in a baking pan. Sprinkle 1 tablespoon of the crumbs on each oyster and dot with butter. Bake in a 375° F. oven about 10 minutes or until the oysters are done and the crumbs tinged with brown. Allow 4 per serving. Makes 6 servings.

CAROLINA DEVILED CLAMS

½ cup chopped celery
½ cup chopped onions
1 chopped green pepper
½ to ¾ teaspoons curry powder
3 tablespoons butter
2 dozen medium clams
  chopped

¾ cup cracker crumbs
2 tablespoons mayonnaise
2 teaspoons Worcestershire
  sauce
3 drops Tabasco sauce
2 eggs, well beaten
1 tablespoon lemon juice

Sauté celery, onions, green peppers, and curry in 2 tablespoons of butter until tender. Put the vegetables into a bowl and add clams, ½ cup of the cracker crumbs, mayonnaise, Worcestershire, Tabasco, eggs, and lemon juice. Toss with a fork. Fill 6 ramekins and sprinkle remaining crumbs on the top of each. Dot with remaining butter. Bake in 350° F. oven for 15 minutes until lightly browned. Serves 6.

BAKED SHRIMP AND TOMATO

Beaten Biscuits or crisp,
  hard crackers
3 tablespoons butter or
  margarine
1½ pounds shrimp: shelled,
  deveined, cooked, cut up
  or split

Pepper
½ teaspoon mace
1 (1-pound) can stewed
  tomatoes
Salt

Preheat the oven to 450° F. In a greased 1½-quart baking dish, lay half the biscuits or crackers on the bottom; dot with butter, then put a layer of shrimp, sprinkle with pepper and ¼ teaspoon mace; half of the tomatoes and juice, dot with butter, sprinkle with salt. Repeat layering with shrimp, pepper, mace, butter, the rest of the tomatoes, and sprinkle with salt. Top with the remaining biscuits or crackers, dot with butter. Bake for about 20 minutes or until top is brown. Makes 4 to 6 servings.

BEATEN BISCUITS

3 cups sifted all-purpose flour	½ cup butter or margarine
½ teaspoon salt	½ cup milk
1 tablespoon granulated sugar	

In a large mixing bowl, sift flour, salt, and sugar together. Cut in butter until mixture resembles coarse cornmeal. Stir in milk and knead to a smooth dough. Place the dough on a floured board and pound dough with a rolling pin (about 25 minutes). As the dough flattens, bring edges to center, folding the dough in layers. Preheat oven to 350° F. Roll the dough about ¼ inch thick. Cut out with 1½-inch round biscuit cutter, placed on ungreased baking sheet. With a fork, prick the tops of the biscuits. Bake for 30 minutes or until light golden. Makes about 7 dozen.

FRIED SMELT

1 dozen cleaned large smelt (about 1½ to 2 pounds)	2 tablespoons cold water
¼ cup all-purpose flour	⅓ cup fine dry bread crumbs
2 egg yolks, well beaten	1 teaspoon salt
	Fat for frying

Wash the fish, if necessary. Blot dry on paper towels. Dip them in flour, then in combined egg yolks and cold water. Coat well and roll in crumbs. Sprinkle with salt. Heat fat in a large heavy skillet and fry the smelt, turning to brown lightly on both sides. Makes 4 servings.

BOILED DUCK WITH ONION SAUCE

Duckling, about 4½ pounds	Parsley sprigs
Salt	6 medium onions, peeled
All-purpose flour	¼ cup butter or margarine
Few celery leaves	2 tablespoons heavy cream

Rinse the duckling cavity well, drain and pat dry. Sprinkle with salt, dredge the duckling in flour and set in a large saucepan or a Dutch oven, with the celery leaves and parsley sprigs. Add water to cover the duck, bring to a boil, skim the foam from the surface, and simmer about 1½ hours or until tender. Meanwhile, cook the onions in boiling salted water until tender. Drain well, chop the onions and return to the saucepan; add the butter and cream. Serve over the duckling. Makes about 4 servings.

SPICED BEEF ROUND

5- to 6-pound bottom round of beef	1 tablespoon allspice
1 teaspoon saltpeter	½ cup brown sugar
½ cup coarse salt	¼ pound beef suet
1 tablespoon pepper	1 cup water
	Pie dough

Rub the beef with saltpeter; refrigerate for 5 or 6 hours, then season with salt, pepper, allspice, and brown sugar. Refrigerate the meat for 10 days, turning occasionally.

Wash the meat. In a large covered baking dish place the suet with the meat on top of it. Pour on the water. Seal the casserole with a strip of dough. Bake in 350° F. oven 3 hours. Pour off the juices; cool. Makes 8 to 10 servings.

CORNED BEEF AND CABBAGE

5 pounds corned beef	2 carrots, scraped and sliced
3 to 5 quarts water	1 onion, sliced
2 or 3 turnips, peeled and sliced	2 small heads of cabbage, quartered
6 to 8 medium-size potatoes, peeled and quartered	1 tablespoon flour

Place the corned beef in a large pot; cover with water; cook about 6 hours or until the meat is tender, adding water as needed. Remove the cooked meat to a platter. Add the turnips, potatoes, carrots, and onion to the meat broth. Cook 20 to 30 minutes until the vegetables are tender. Set the cabbage on top 10 minutes before you think the vegetables will be done. Remove the vegetables from the pot; keep warm. Mix flour into a smooth paste with a little water; stir into the broth and cook, stirring a few minutes; season to taste. Serve the broth as a soup. Slice the beef and surround with vegetables. Makes 8 to 10 servings.

BEEF À LA MODE

¼ pound fat bacon or salt pork
1 cup vinegar
2 teaspoons salt
½ teaspoon freshly ground
  black pepper
¼ teaspoon ground cloves
1 teaspoon each thyme,
  savory, marjoram
2 teaspoons finely chopped
  parsley

4 to 5 pounds bottom round of
  beef
1 cup chopped onions
2 tablespoons fat
2 carrots, cut in chunks
1 cup turnips, cut in chunks
2 stalks celery, cut in chunks
1 cup water
1 cup port wine

Cut the bacon (or the pork) into slices 1 inch thick; dip them in the vinegar and then into a seasoning mixture of the salt, pepper, cloves, thyme, savory, marjoram, and parsley. With a sharp knife make enough holes in the beef deep enough and wide enough so that you can insert the slices of bacon. Rub the beef with the rest of the seasoning mixture.

In a Dutch oven brown the onions in fat; drain off the fat. Place the meat in the Dutch oven with the carrots, turnips, celery, and water; cover and simmer gently. From time to time turn the meat and gradually add the vinegar. Cook 4 hours or until fork-tender. Remove the meat and the vegetables to a platter. Spoon off fat from the gravy. Add the wine and reheat. Makes 10 to 12 servings.

BEEF HEART STEWED

1 beef heart (about 3 pounds)
  Butter or margarine
2 slices bread
  Pepper
  Salt

1 medium onion, finely
  minced, or ½ teaspoon
  dried thyme (optional)
  Hot water
  All-purpose flour

Cut the fibrous parts out of the top and inside of the heart; wash well and drain. Butter the bread, place in a shallow dish, and sprinkle with pepper, salt, and the onion or thyme, as desired. Add about 3 tablespoons of hot water to moisten the bread. Stuff the heart with the seasoned bread mixture; close the opening with skewers. Place the heart in a heavy saucepan, add 1½ quarts water to cover; cook until tender, about 2 hours. Drain and measure the broth, returning only 1 cup to the saucepan with the meat. Soften ¼-cup butter, dredge in 2 tablespoons flour, stir into the broth in the saucepan. Add ½ teaspoon pepper and 1 teaspoon salt; cover and braise over moderate heat, turning frequently to brown the meat on all sides.

Remove the meat to a serving platter, remove the skewers. Stir 1 cup of hot water into the drippings, bring to boil and pour over the heart. Slice meat to serve. Makes about 6 servings.

BEEF RAGOUT

4 to 4½ pounds rump of beef, cut in 1-inch cubes
¾ cup flour
2 to 3 tablespoons salad oil
1 cup hot water
7 ounces beer (about 1 cup)
1 teaspoon salt
¼ teaspoon pepper
½ teaspoon each parsley flakes and rosemary leaves
¼ teaspoon each savory, marjoram, and basil
1 cup carrots
1 cup celery
1 strip of lemon peel 3 inches by 1 inch
1 onion, peeled
8 to 10 whole cloves
2 tablespoons catsup

Coat the beef cubes in flour; brown in hot oil in a Dutch oven. Pour in the water, beer, seasonings, carrots, celery, lemon, and the onion studded with the cloves. Cover and cook gently 1½ hours, stirring occasionally, or until the meat is tender. Remove the onion and stir in catsup. Correct the seasonings. You may add sliced mushrooms, artichoke bottoms boiled and quartered, or hard-cooked egg yolks. Makes 6 servings.

PLAW

2½ pounds veal cutlet, in one piece
1 quart water
1 teaspoon salt
½ teaspoon pepper
½ to 1 teaspoon curry powder
½ teaspoon parsley flakes
2 tablespoons butter or margarine
1 cup raw regular rice

Place the meat in a soup pot or Dutch oven; cover with water; add salt and pepper. Simmer, covered, 1 hour or until the meat is fork tender. Remove the meat from the broth and cut into ½-inch-thick strips 3 or 4 inches long. Measure the liquid and add water if necessary to make 3 cups. To the liquid in the pot add the curry, parsley, butter, and rice. Bring the liquid to a boil, then lower the heat and cook 10 minutes. Add the cut-up meat and cook 5 to 10 minutes longer. The rice should be tender and very little liquid left. Makes 4 servings.

SILVER COFFEE POT
BY PAUL REVERE

**Alabama Rice Bread, page 83
Clear Tomato Soup, page 46
Pumpkin Pie, page 40**

ASPARAGUS BUNCHER

Kitchen, Mount Vernon
Mount Vernon, Virginia

Kitchen, Tryon Palace
New Bern, North Carolina

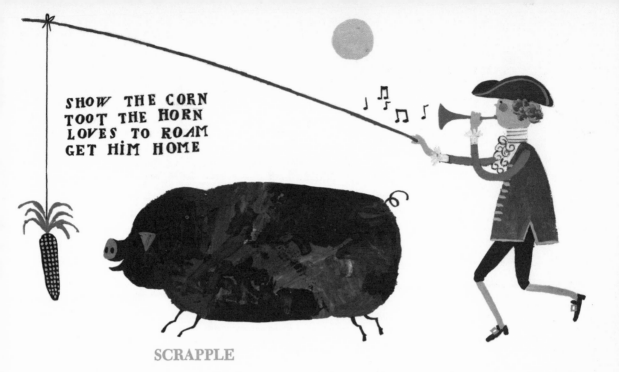

SHOW THE CORN
TOOT THE HORN
LOVES TO ROAM
GET HIM HOME

SCRAPPLE

1½ pounds boneless pork
   Water
2 teaspoons salt
½ teaspoon pepper

1 teaspoon ground sage
1 cup yellow cornmeal
   Bacon fat

In a 3-quart saucepan, place the meat with water to cover and salt; cook about 2 hours, until the meat is very tender. Remove the meat, measure the broth and add water if necessary to make 3 cups of liquid. Mince the meat very fine, and return with the broth to the saucepan. Add the pepper and sage. Mix the cornmeal with 1 cup of cold water, then stir into the meat and broth. Cook over low heat until thickened, stirring frequently. Then cover and continue cooking over low heat for 10 minutes longer. Rinse a 9- x 5- x 3-inch loaf pan with cold water. Turn the cornmeal mixture into the pan. Chill well. Unmold and cut into ½- to ¾-inch slices; flour them and brown slowly in hot bacon fat. Makes about 6 to 8 servings.

POTATOES IN CREAM

1 tablespoon butter or
   margarine
1 tablespoon flour
½ teaspoon salt
⅛ teaspoon pepper

1 tablespoon minced onion
1 cup heavy cream
1 quart sliced potatoes,
   cooked
1 teaspoon chopped parsley

In a large saucepan melt the butter then mix in the flour, salt, and pepper to make a smooth paste. Stir in the onion and cream. Cook stirring until the mixture is smooth and thickened. Add the potatoes and continue to cook until the potatoes are heated through; sprinkle on the parsley. Makes 6 servings.

SUCCOTASH

½ pound dried lima beans
   (about 1¼ cups)
¼ pound salt pork, sliced
   ½-inch thick

½ teaspoon cayenne pepper
½ teaspoon salt
Water
1 can (12-ounce) kernel corn

Soak the beans overnight, then drain. Place the salt pork on the bottom of a Dutch oven or heavy saucepan. Add the beans, pepper, salt, and water to cover. Simmer for 1½ hours or until beans are tender, stirring occasionally and adding more water if needed. Just before serving stir in the corn; serve hot with salt pork. Makes 1 quart or 8 servings.

CORN CASSEROLE

6 ears of corn
4 eggs
1 tablespoon cream

¾ teaspoon salt
⅛ teaspoon pepper
1 teaspoon sugar

Cook the corn in boiling salted water till tender; drain. Cut the corn from the cob (about 3 cups). Separate the eggs. Combine the yolks, cream, salt, pepper, sugar, and corn. Beat the whites until they form stiff peaks. Fold whites into the corn mixture. Pour into a well-greased 1½ quart casserole. Bake in 425° F. oven 20 minutes or until puffy and golden. Makes 6 servings.

EGGS AND TOMATOES

3 tablespoons butter
1 tablespoon finely chopped
   onion
3 large red-ripe tomatoes,
   skinned and coarsely diced

¾ teaspoon salt
¼ teaspoon pepper
3 eggs, well beaten

Melt the butter in a large, heavy skillet. Add the onion and cook for 2 minutes or until the onion is transparent. Add the tomatoes, salt, and pepper. Cook, stirring frequently, for 5 to 6 minutes or until the tomato pulp can be easily mashed. Mash slightly. Stir in the beaten eggs and continue to cook, stirring occasionally, for 2 minutes, or until the eggs are set. Makes 4 to 5 servings.

MRS. MADISON'S WHIM

6 eggs, separated
1 pound butter or margarine,
    softened
2 cups granulated sugar
¼ cup brandy
1 teaspoon nutmeg

4 cups sifted cake flour
½ teaspoon baking soda
1 tablespoon hot water
1 (11-ounce) package raisins,
    floured (with ¼ cup flour)

Preheat oven to 300° F. In a medium bowl, whip the egg whites until stiff. In a large mixing bowl, cream the butter; gradually add the sugar, then the egg yolks.

Beat well, add the brandy and nutmeg. Blend in the flour. Dissolve the soda in hot water, stir into the batter; add the raisins, mix well. Gently fold in the egg whites. Turn into 2 (1½-quart) loaf baking dishes (8- x 5- x 2-inches) or 1 (3-quart) tube pan. Bake in a slow oven for 1½ to 2 hours, or until a cake tester inserted in the center of the cake comes out clean. Makes 1 large tube cake or 2 small loaf cakes.

BUCKWHEAT GRIDDLE CAKES

1 envelope granular yeast
3 cups lukewarm water
1½ teaspoons salt

¼ teaspoon baking soda
2 cups buckwheat flour
½ cup white cornmeal

Sprinkle the yeast over the warm water in a bowl. Blend together the salt, soda, buckwheat flour, and cornmeal. Stir about half of the flour mixture into the water with yeast. Beat until smooth. Add the remaining flour and beat again until mixture is smooth and blended. Let stand for about ½ hour in a warm place (about 85° F.) free from drafts, or until the surface of the batter is bubbly. Beat again. Heat griddle; grease lightly and fry the cakes, using about 3 tablespoons batter for each. Turn to brown both sides. If batter thickens, add a little milk if necessary. Cakes should be about the thickness of a silver dollar. Serve with butter and maple syrup. Makes about 20 to 24 2½-inch cakes or enough to serve 6.

HARD GINGERBREAD

1½ cups molasses
1 egg, beaten
½ cup brown sugar
1 teaspoon ground ginger
½ teaspoon each ground cloves,
    mace, allspice, nutmeg
½ teaspoon each coriander
    seeds and caraway seeds
    (optional)

1 pound butter or margarine,
    melted
About 2 pounds (8 cups)
    all-purpose flour

In a large bowl, combine the molasses with egg, then add the brown sugar and spices. Add the melted butter. Add the flour gradually, then knead into a stiff dough. Wrap in waxed paper. Chill. Preheat the oven to 375° F. Roll out ¼ of the dough at a time on a floured board and cut out gingerbread men or other shapes as desired. Bake on ungreased baking sheets for about 10 minutes, depending on thickness of the dough. Makes about 7 dozen (5-inch) gingerbread men.

MORAVIAN SUGAR CAKE

¼ pound butter or margarine
    (½ cup)
2 cups warm milk
1 package active dry yeast
¼ cup warm water
6 cups sifted all-purpose flour
1 teaspoon salt

1 egg, well beaten
1 teaspoon oil of cinnamon or
    powdered cinnamon
¼ cup soft butter or margarine
1 cup brown sugar
2 teaspoons cinnamon
2 teaspoons granulated sugar

JARS, JUGS, BOTTLES AND CROCKS ★ ★ ★ ★ ★
SQUARE-HEAD NAILS AND GRANDFATHER CLOCKS
CHICKENS, COWS, HORSES AND PIGS.★ ★ ★ ★
PLUMS, PUMPKINS, APPLES AND FIGS ★ ★ ★
JOYS FROM THE FARM WE LOVE ALL YEAR ★
THIS IS OUR HOME, SMALL AND DEAR.★ ★ ★ ★

Dissolve ¼ pound butter in the warm milk. Sprinkle the yeast over the warm water; let stand a few minutes to dissolve. Place 4 cups of the flour and the salt in a large bowl; make a well in the center. Pour the milk mixture and yeast into the well; stir to mix well. Cover the bowl and set in a warm place to rise about 2 hours. When the dough has risen and is bubbly stir in the egg, remaining flour, and oil of cinnamon. Put the dough in a well-greased 9- x 9- x 3-inch square pan; set to rise again. When the batter has doubled in bulk combine the remaining butter, brown sugar, and cinnamon into a smooth paste. With a knife make gashes all over the top of the cake. With a spoon fill each gash with some of the brown sugar mixture and pinch or push dough over the sugar mixture to be sure it won't run out. Sprinkle the top of the cake with granulated sugar. Bake in 375° F. oven about 40 minutes or until the top is golden brown; cool 10 minutes; remove from the pan onto a wire rack. Cut the cooled cake into 9 to 12 servings.

COCONUT MACAROONS

3 egg whites
2 cups sifted confectioners' sugar
3 to 4 cups fine grated coconut

Beat the egg whites till very frothy, then beat in the sugar and continue beating until the mixture is very stiff. Snip or chop the coconut very fine. Stir the coconut into the egg-white mixture to form a very stiff paste. With floured hands very gently roll a tablespoonful at a time into small balls. Place a few inches apart on a greased cookie sheet. Bake in 425° F. oven 8 to 10 minutes. Remove from the pan at once. Makes about 4½ dozen.

JUMBLES

¼ pound butter or margarine
   (½ cup)
2 cups sifted all-purpose flour
2 eggs, well beaten

½ cup finely grated coconut
½ teaspoon rose water
   (optional)
Granulated sugar

With a pastry blender or 2 knives scissors-fashion blend the butter into the flour. Blend in the eggs, coconut, and rose water to form a stiff dough. Pinch off a lump about a tablespoonful at a time. Roll lumps of dough between the palms of your hands to form a rope about 4 inches long and ½ inch wide. Form into a ring; sprinkle with sugar. Bake on a well-greased cookie sheet in 450° F. oven 10 minutes or until tinged with brown. Remove at once to a wire rack. Makes 2½ dozen.

APPLE PANDOWDY

10 large apples
½ cup sugar
½ teaspoon cinnamon
¼ teaspoon nutmeg
   Dash salt

½ cup light molasses
¼ cup water
3 tablespoons melted butter
Pastry for 9-inch pie shell

Make a pie crust as usual and roll out. Brush with melted butter, and cut in half. Fold over, and repeat the operation. This makes a very flaky pastry. Chill while peeling the apples.

Peel, core, and slice apples into thin pieces. Mix the sugar, spice, and salt, and combine with apple slices; place in a baking dish. Combine the molasses, water, and melted butter, and pour over apples. Cover with pastry. Cook in a 400° F. oven for 10 minutes; then turn heat down to 325° F. and cook for 30 minutes, or until pastry begins to brown and the apples are juicy. At this point remove from the oven and "dowdy" the crust by cutting through crust and apples with a sharp knife. Return to the oven for another 10 minutes. Serve warm with cream or ice cream. Six to eight servings.

BOURBON AND BLACK WALNUT CAKE

2 cups white sugar	¼ teaspoon salt
2¼ cups brown sugar, firmly packed	1 teaspoon freshly grated nutmeg
1½ cups butter (3 sticks)	1 pint 100-proof bourbon whiskey
6 eggs	
5½ cups all-purpose flour, sifted	1 pound black walnut meats

Mix the white and brown sugar until free from lumps. Cream the butter in a large mixing bowl and add half the sugar mixture. Cream thoroughly. Then cream some more. This will govern the texture of your cake. In a separate bowl beat the eggs until light and fluffy, and add the remaining sugar. Stir into the butter mixture. Sift the flour, salt, and nutmeg and add to the batter, alternating with the whiskey, beginning and ending with the flour. Add the walnut meats, but do not bother to fold; a little extra beating will tend to bruise the walnuts, releasing the oil and flavor into the cake. Pour into a well-greased and floured 10-inch tube pan or, if you prefer smaller cakes, into 4 small loaf pans. Bake in a 300° F. oven for 1½ to 2 hours for the large cake, or 1¼ hours for the smaller ones, or until the cake shrinks slightly from the sides of the pan. Remove from the oven and allow to stand for 15 minutes, then turn out on a cake rack. When completely cool, wrap in foil and store in the refrigerator. Do not freeze. The crust of this cake will be rather hard and dry, and the inside should have a moist texture.

RHUBARB CHESS PIE

9–inch prebaked pie shell	1 cup fresh rhubarb, cut in ½-inch pieces
1 tablespoon butter	
1 cup sugar	1 cup milk
¼ cup flour	¼ teaspoon salt
2 eggs	¼ teaspoon nutmeg

Cream together the butter and sugar. Add the flour. Separate the eggs. Beat the yolks and add to the remaining ingredients. Beat the whites until stiff but not dry and mix gently with the other ingredients. Pour into the pie shell and bake at 350° F. for 45 minutes. The shell may be baked for 5 minutes before the filling is added—an insurance against sogginess.

SILVER SUGAR BOWL

APPLE PIE

2 tablespoons brown sugar
2 teaspoons grated lemon rind
2 teaspoons ground ginger
1 teaspoon cinnamon
½ teaspoon mace
¼ teaspoon ground cloves

2 tablespoons orange
  marmalade
2 pounds greening or other
  pie apples
Pastry for 9-inch pie shell

Combine the brown sugar, rind, spices, and marmalade, and sprinkle half of it in the bottom of a deep-dish pie plate (9 inches in diameter and 2 inches deep). Pare, quarter, and slice the apples thin (about 6 cups). Put half of the apples in the dish; repeat layering with the rest of the spice combination and the apples. Cover the dish with waxed paper and refrigerate.

Roll the pastry into a circle slightly larger than the pie plate. Fit the pastry onto the top of the pie. In the middle of the pastry make a small hole with the point of a knife; notch the edges. Bake in 425° F. oven for 40 minutes, or until the apples are tender. Makes 6 to 8 servings.

TIPSY CAKE

6-inch sponge cake layer
¼ cup brandy
¼ cup white wine
1 to 2 tablespoons
  confectioners' sugar

Custard based on 2 cups
  milk or cream
Blanched almonds

Put the cake into a 9-inch pie plate or serving dish. Sprinkle the combined brandy and wine over the cake; let it soak up a few minutes. Sprinkle the sugar over the cake; pour on the custard; refrigerate. Garnish with split or chopped almonds. Makes 6 to 8 servings.

This is affording exquisite pleasure   extremely gratifying

TANSEY

6 eggs, separated
1 pint heavy cream
½ cup granulated sugar
½ cup white wine or sherry
¼ pound Naples biscuit (or lady fingers) broken up

¼ teaspoon nutmeg
Few drops green food coloring (optional)
1 pastry-lined 10-inch pie plate

Place the egg yolks in a saucepan and beat slightly. Stir in the cream, sugar, and sherry, and add the biscuits and the nutmeg. Cook stirring until the mixture thickens. Add the green coloring if desired. Beat the egg whites until they form stiff peaks and fold in the hot cream mixture. Pour into the pastry-lined pie plate. Bake at 450° F. for 10 minutes, then reduce the heat to 350° F. and bake for 30 minutes longer. The pie will be puffy and golden. Cool on a wire rack. The pie will sink somewhat as it cools. Makes 8 servings.

PISTACHIO CREAM

½ pound shelled pistachio nuts
1 tablespoon brandy

2 cups light cream
3 egg yolks, well beaten

Reserve a few whole nuts for garnish. Grind the rest, or pulverise them in the blender. In a small saucepan blend together the nuts and brandy. Combine the cream and beaten egg yolks; stir into the nuts. Cook over low heat, stirring constantly, until mixture thickens and bubbles around the edges of the pan. Remove from the heat at once. Pour into a bowl; cover, and chill. Serve topped with bits of the reserved pistachio nuts. Makes 4 servings.

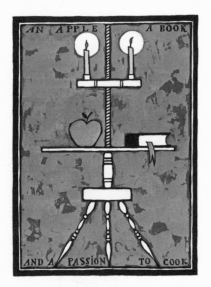

ALBEMARLE PEACH CHUTNEY

1 quart peeled and sliced peaches
½ cup cider vinegar
1½ cups dark brown sugar
2 tablespoons grated onion
1 cup diced, peeled apple
½ cup seedless raisins

1 teaspoon mustard seed
2 teaspoons ginger
½ teaspoon salt
1 teaspoon cumin powder
1 teaspoon grated lemon rind
1 tablespoon lemon juice

In a heavy pot place the peaches and rest of the ingredients. Cook slowly, stirring until the ingredients are well blended. Continue to cook until the mixture is soft and thickened. Pack into sterilized jars while hot and seal. Makes 3 cups.

Recipes of Ante Bellum America

IN THE FORTY YEARS preceding the Civil War, Americans moved "across the wide Missouri" to the western ocean. The northwestern frontier was pushed from Minnesota to Oregon, and the Cumberland Road led, however deviously, to the goldfields of California. The Golden Land, despite its very brief existence as a republic, shrugged off its identity as a sun-drenched Mexican province and flowered into statehood.

In the East, canals laced the woodlands, and New York City took on the nickname Gotham. The Irish came to New England, the Yankees migrated to the Midwest and beyond, and cotton became king in Dixie. The splash of the paddlewheel followed the river traffic up the Mississippi Valley, and "Johnny Appleseed" was followed by McCormick's reaper, producing an endless horizon of wheat and corn. It was the time for the expansive and the new.

DOUGH KNEADER

Cookery changed with the times, but not spectacularly. The fireplace slowly yielded to the black range that could use coal as well as wood. Jars capped with paper and earthenware crocks with lids fixed by various devices continued to preserve most fruits. But the method of making and sealing tins progressed during this period, and at its close some five million cans (mostly tomatoes and meats) were marketed in a year, one can or less per family. Natural ice became more available, and artificial ice was developed. Ice houses, though not taken for granted, were hardly restricted to the owners of mansions. Eliza Leslie, the most prolific purveyor of household information, felt it necessary to describe refrigerators: "large wooden boxes standing on feet and lined with tin or zinc." She urged all to procure one, or two if possible, but they were luxuries.

Progress did not invariably stimulate huzzas. "The old-fashioned fire-place and open chimney were more favorable to health than our modern stoves, grates, and furnaces," observed Mrs. Cornelius, The Young Housekeeper's Friend, at the end of the era. Health concerned at least half the culinary preceptors in those days. A high moral tone sold not only temperance tracts, but also cook books, such as those compiled by Lydia Child (author of the novel *Hobomok* and *An Appeal in Favor of That Class of Americans Called Africans*), Sarah Josepha Hale (editor of *Godey's Lady's Book*), and Catharine Beecher, not the least distinguished Beecher sibling (others being Harriet Beecher Stowe and Henry Ward Beecher). Undeservedly less celebrated was Mrs. Horace Mann, also a crusader for Abolition and Temperance, who hoped her book would aid in "redeeming the race from its present degradation." Mrs. Mann verged on health faddism, her *Christianity in the Kitchen, a Physiological Cook Book* denouncing saleratus and baking soda *(inter alia):* "Our stomachs were not made to digest metals, and when we powder them and eat them we try to cheat nature." However, she cited Justin Liebig, an esteemed pioneer in organic chemistry; it was his work that led to the small revolution set off by baking powder. (My grandfather, an early pioneer in the baking-powder business—"Dr. Price's," he called his formula—made a fortune which, woe is me, he subsequently lost.) We also owe to Mrs. Mann the approving notice that "Dr." Syvester Graham (whose name still hallows a flour) apologized in a newspaper for having been sick. Her logic runs: "Why is not dyspepsia disgraceful, like *delirium tremens?*"

WROUGHT IRON

TOASTER

The actual emergence of an American cuisine was partly confirmed by the healthy development of regional cook books that reflected this phenomenon. (One called *Everybody's Cook and Receipt Book: But More Particularly Designed For Buckeyes, Hoosiers, Wolverines, Corncrackers, Suckers, and All Epicures Who Wish to Live With the Present Times* appeared in Cleveland in 1842.) At the same time such gastronomists as Anthelme Brillat-Savarin and Charles-Elmé Francatelli were reaching customers in America for an introduction to the mysteries of *haute cuisine*. President Van Buren was evidently not the only gourmet in the land. Americans love to eat and to eat well.

RARE ARE THE TAILS OF THIS FABULOUS OX

THE OX WITH THREE TAILS IS LOVED WITH A PASSION
HIS SOUP BRINGS HAILS AND IS QUITE THE FASHION

OXTAIL CREOLE

1 or 2 disjointed oxtails
   (about 2½ pounds)
   Flour
2 or 3 tablespoons bacon fat
1 cup diced cooked ham
1 onion, chopped
2 quarts water
¼ cup pearl barley
1½ teaspoon salt
4 peppercorns
3 allspice berries
1 bay leaf
1 sprig of fresh thyme or ½
   teaspoon dried

½ teaspoon basil
1 small onion
3 whole cloves
½ cup chopped celery
½ cup diced carrot
1 8-ounce can stewed tomatoes
1 tablespoon flour
2 tablespoons butter or
   margarine
1 teaspoon cayenne pepper
1 teaspoon Worcestershire
   sauce
½ cup claret, Madeira, or
   sherry

Dredge the oxtails in flour. In a deep heavy kettle brown the oxtails in hot fat. Add the ham and onion and sauté till both are lightly browned. Add the water, barley, salt, peppercorns, allspice, bay leaf, thyme, and basil; simmer gently 3 or 4 hours or until the meat is tender. Be sure to watch the liquid and add water if necessary. Now add the whole onion studded with cloves, celery, carrot, and tomatoes; continue cooking until the vegetables are tender. Knead 1 tablespoon flour with the butter and cayenne. Stir into the soup with the Worcestershire and wine. Cook and stir till smooth. Makes about 6 servings.

PEWTER LADLE

HARICOT OF LAMB

4 medium turnips or potatoes, pared and cut in large cubes	Salt
	Pepper
6 to 8 medium carrots, sliced	¼ teaspoon dried marjoram
2 tablespoons all-purpose flour	1 tablespoon walnut catsup or Worcestershire
6 shoulder lamb chops	

Cook the turnips or potatoes with the carrots until almost tender; drain, reserving 2 cups liquid. In a heavy skillet or a Dutch oven, stir the flour to brown evenly; remove from the pan and set aside. Sprinkle the chops with salt and pepper, then in the same heavy skillet, brown the chops on both sides; remove and set aside.

Make gravy by blending the browned flour into the pan drippings, add ½ teaspoon salt, marjoram, and catsup or Worcestershire. Stir until smooth. Place the chops and the cooked vegetables into the gravy, cover and simmer 15 minutes. Makes 6 servings.

WALNUT CATSUP

2 (4-ounce) cans shelled walnuts	¼ teaspoon ground mace
	¼ teaspoon nutmeg
3 tablespoons salt	¼ teaspoon ginger
1 quart vinegar	¼ teaspoon ground cloves
6 shallots, finely chopped	¼ teaspoon pepper
2 teaspoons grated horseradish	½ cup port wine

In a half-gallon jar, or earthenware crock, dissolve the salt in the vinegar, stir in the walnuts. Let stand 48 hours, stirring occasionally. Drain the liquid into a kettle; put the walnuts through a food chopper or blender and add to the kettle. Add the shallots, horseradish, mace, nutmeg, ginger, cloves, pepper, and wine. Simmer gently for 45 minutes and cool. Strain the catsup and pour into bottles, seal and store for several weeks.

FIRE CARRIER

BEEFSTEAK POUNDER

SCOTTISH CABBAGE SOUP

2 pounds mutton or lamb, cut
    in bite-size cubes
¼ cup pearl barley
1 onion, chopped
2 teaspoons salt

¼ teaspoon pepper
2 quarts water
2 quarts shredded cabbage (1
    head)

Into a soup pot put the meat, barley, onion, salt, pepper, and water. Cook 1 hour or until the meat is tender, then add the cabbage and cook 30 minutes longer. Makes 2 quarts of very thick soup.

CARROT SOUP

1 stick butter (½ cup)
2 cups shredded carrots, firmly
    packed (about 5 to 6
    medium)
1 cup celery, thinly sliced
1 large onion, grated or thinly
    sliced
3 medium-size red-ripe
    tomatoes, cut in quarters

4 peppercorns
1 slice toast broken into fine
    crumbs
1 cup boiling water
1 13¾-ounce can chicken broth
1 cup tomato juice
1 teaspoon salt

Melt the butter in a heavy saucepan that has a cover or in a Dutch oven. Add the vegetables. Cook, stirring, over a low heat until the vegetables just begin to brown. Add the peppercorns, toast crumbs, and boiling water. Cover and simmer for 30 minutes or until the vegetables are very tender. Remove the cover and, over high heat, stirring frequently, reduce the liquid in the pan until it is almost absorbed. Strain, reserving any broth. Purée the vegetables in a blender, or press through a sieve. Return the pulp to a saucepan. Add the chicken broth, tomato juice, and salt. Heat slowly for 10 minutes or until the mixture is about the consistency of cream. Makes 6 servings.

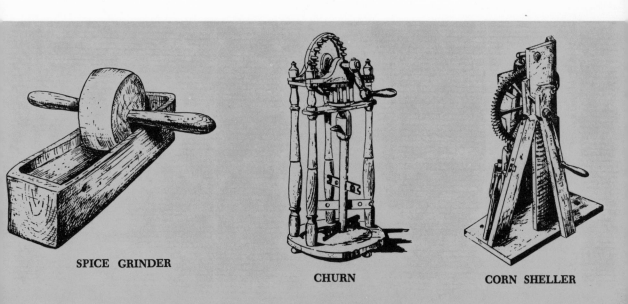

SPICE GRINDER   **CHURN**   **CORN SHELLER**

POTATO SOUP

1 quart peeled and cubed
   potatoes
1 carrot, pared

2 stalks celery
1½ quarts chicken bouillon
1 cup stale bread crumbs

Place the potatoes, carrot, and celery in a soup pot with 1 quart of the bouillon. Cook, covered, for 10 minutes or until the potatoes are soft. Add the bread and cook 10 minutes longer. Put through a food mill or blender. Return the purée to the soup pot; add the remaining bouillon and heat 3 minutes longer. Correct the seasonings. Makes 7 cups or about 6 servings.

CATFISH SOUP

¾ pound salt pork, diced
   Boiling water
½ teaspoon marjoram leaves
¼ teaspoon pepper
   Few sprigs parsley
2 cups minced celery
1½ to 2 pounds of catfish or
   whole flounder, boned
   (have fish man give you
   bones)

1 quart cold water
2 tablespoons butter or
   margarine
2 tablespoons flour
2 cups milk
2 egg yolks, lightly beaten
   Fresh chopped parsley
   Toasted croutons

Pour the boiling water over the diced pork; drain. In a soup pot combine pork, marjoram, pepper, parsley, celery, fish bones, and the quart of water. Bring to a boil, then simmer 30 minutes, skimming. Meanwhile melt the butter in a large saucepan; stir in the flour to form a smooth paste; stir in the milk and cook, stirring until smooth and slightly thickened. Stir some of the hot milk mixture into the egg yolks, then return the egg mixture to the rest of the milk mixture; stir; remove from the heat. Remove the fish bones and parsley. Cut up the fish in 1-inch pieces and add to the hot pork pot and cook 5 minutes longer. Stir in the milk mixture; simmer 1 minute; correct seasonings; sprinkle on some parsley and the toasted croutons. Makes 2 quarts or 8 generous servings.

FRIED TROUT

4 to 6 trout, cleaned
   Flour
1 to 2 egg yolks
   Fine bread crumbs
   Butter or margarine

Salt
Pepper
Worcestershire sauce
Lemon juice

Dredge the fish with flour; dip in yolk and then bread crumbs. Fry in butter. Season with salt and pepper. Sprinkle with Worcestershire and lemon juice. Makes 4 to 6 servings.

SHRIMP PIE

2 slices bread, crusts removed
2 tablespoons melted butter
2 pounds cleaned, cooked
  shrimp or 2 7-ounce
  packages cleaned frozen
  shrimp, cooked

3 tablespoons white wine
½ teaspoon salt
⅛ teaspoon pepper
¼ teaspoon ground nutmeg
¼ teaspoon ground mace

Crumble or grate the bread into fine crumbs. Toss in melted butter, coating the crumbs well. Blend together half of the crumbs and all remaining ingredients. Turn into a 9-inch pie pan. Top with the remaining buttered crumbs. Bake at 350° F. until lightly browned—about 20 minutes. Serve in shells (or bake in shells) if desired. Makes 4 servings.

SHRIMP JAMBALAYA

1½ pounds green shrimp (not
  jumbo)
  Celery tops
1 slice onion

2 tablespoons mild vinegar
1 tablespoon creole seafood
  seasoning
2 teaspoons salt

Put the shrimp in a pot and cover with cold water. Add the tops of a bunch of celery and the other ingredients. Simmer gently until the shrimps turn pink. Remove from the fire. Cool and shell under running water. Place in the refrigerator and cool until the vein can be removed easily.

TO PREPARE GUMBO

1 medium onion, chopped
4 to 6 pieces of celery,
  chopped
4 tablespoons butter
1 medium green pepper,
  chopped
1 No. 2 can of tomatoes
1 small can tomato paste
1 dash Tabasco

1 teaspoon Worcestershire
2 teaspoons salt
¼ teaspoon pepper
1 pinch sugar
1 cup sliced mushrooms
1½ pounds cooked shrimp (as
  prepared above)
1 teaspoon gumbo filé
2 tablespoons chopped parsley

Sauté the onion and celery in the butter until clear. Add the green pepper, tomatoes, and tomato paste and simmer about 30 minutes until the celery is tender. Season with the Tabasco, Worcestershire, sugar, salt, and pepper. Add the mushrooms and shrimp and cook slowly until the shrimp are heated through and the mushrooms are tender. Stir in the gumbo filé just before removing from the heat. Serve over rice. Garnish with the parsley.

TINDER SET

FUNNEL

SCOOP

DEVILED SHRIMP AND RICE

2 pounds shelled, deveined shrimp or 2 7-ounce packages shelled, deveined frozen shrimps
2 tablespoons butter
⅓ cup chopped onion
1 minced clove garlic
1 cup raw long-grain rice
1 1-pound 12-ounce can tomatoes

2 cups chicken broth
1 small bay leaf
3 tablespoons chopped parsley
½ teaspoon dried marjoram leaves
1 to 2 teaspoons chili powder
2 teaspoons salt
⅛ teaspoon pepper
Dash cayenne

Heat the oven to 350° F. If using frozen shrimp, defrost them. Melt the butter in a small skillet. Add the onion and garlic and brown it lightly. Blend together all ingredients in a 2-quart casserole. Cover and bake for 1 hour or until the rice is dry and fluffy and liquid absorbed. Makes 6 servings.

SHRIMP STUFFED IN BELL PEPPERS

1½ pounds shelled, deveined shrimp
3 stalks celery, tops and all, cut in 3-inch lengths
2 teaspoons salt
1 bay leaf
1 small onion
3 whole cloves
6 medium-size green peppers
1½ cups cooked rice
2 beaten eggs

¼ cup milk
3 tablespoons chopped celery
1 tablespoon chopped green pepper
1 tablespoon minced green onion
1 teaspoon salt
1 tablespoon Worcestershire sauce
¼ cup coarse toast crumbs
2 tablespoons butter

Place the shrimp, celery stalks, 2 teaspoons salt, and bay leaf in a large saucepan. Stud the onion with cloves and add to the pan. Cover the ingredients with cold water. Bring to a boil. Reduce the heat and cook 1 to 2 minutes or until the shrimp are pink. Drain. Remove the onion, bay leaf, and celery pieces; discard them. Cut off tops of the peppers. Remove seeds. Cook them in boiling water 3 minutes. Drain and plunge them into cold water. Drain again well. Dice the shrimp, reserving 6 whole shrimps. Mix with the rice, eggs, milk, chopped celery, pepper, and green onion. Stir in the remaining salt and Worcestershire sauce. Stuff the peppers with the rice mixture and press a whole shrimp into the stuffing. Sprinkle with crumbs and dot with butter. Bake at 375° F. for about 30 minutes or until the peppers are very tender and the crumbs browned. Serves 6.

**Kitchen, Pennsylvania Dutch Farmhouse
Hershey, Pennsylvania**

**Kitchen, Nathan Hale Homestead
Coventry, Connecticut**

Kitchen, Van Cortlandt Manor House
Croton-on-Hudson, New York

Kitchen, Ford Mansion
Morristown, New Jersey

PIGEON OR SQUAB PIE

6 pigeons or squabs (about 5
    pounds drawn weight)
6 livers from birds
½ teaspoon salt
¼ teaspoon pepper
2 tablespoons parsley
    Butter or margarine

1 pound sirloin or round steak
    cut paper thin
½ pound mushrooms, chopped
1 cup chopped parsley
4 hard-cooked egg yolks
1¼ cups brown gravy
    Puff pastry

Rinse the birds in cold water, drain and pat dry. Chop the livers and mix with salt, pepper, and parsley. Place some of the liver mixture and a dot of butter in each bird. Truss the birds. Line the bottom of a 14- x 9- x 2-inch baking dish with the beef, then with a layer of mushrooms and parsley. Set the birds on this, separating each from the other with hard-cooked egg yolks. Pour the brown gravy over the birds. Cover the top of the baking dish with puff pastry, being sure to secure edges. Make gashes or a design down the center of the pastry. Bake in a 450° F. oven 8 to 10 minutes, then lower the heat to 350° F. and bake 1 hour and 45 minutes or until the pastry is golden brown, and the birds are cooked. Makes 6 servings.

PUFF PASTRY

1 cup butter
2 cups sifted cake flour
¼ to ½ cup ice water

Allow half of butter to soften. Cut remaining butter into flour with 2 knives scissors-fashion or with pastry blender until all the tiny particles of fat are coated with flour. Add ice water a little at a time, toss with fork, use only enough water to hold ingredients together.

On lightly floured board roll out dough ¼-inch thick and square shaped. Spread two thirds of dough with a quarter of the softened butter; fold unbuttered third over center third and fold remaining buttered third over to cover first third, buttered side down. (You should have 3 layers of dough with butter between each layer.) Roll the dough to about ¼-inch thickness and make it square again. Spread with another quarter of the butter. Fold as before; chill thoroughly (about 1 hour each time). Roll, spread with butter, fold and chill 2 more times. Roll into rectangle large enough to fit top of casserole. Bake in 450° F. oven 8 to 10 minutes, then reduce heat to 350° F. and bake as directed in Pigeon Pie or longer until golden and puffed.

FRIED CHICKENS

2 3-pound frying chickens,
   cut up
  About ¾ cup flour
2 teaspoons salt
  Shortening or vegetable oil
2 tablespoons butter

2 tablespoons finely chopped
   parsley or 2 teaspoons
   parsley flakes
½ teaspoon salt
⅛ teaspoon white pepper
1 cup milk

Wash the chicken pieces and blot them dry on paper towels. Measure the flour and the 2 teaspoons salt into a clean paper bag. Shake the chicken, a few pieces at a time, in flour mixture until well coated. Melt ½ inch of shortening in each of 2 large, heavy skillets. Fry the chicken until golden brown on all sides, adding more shortening as needed. Cover the skillets and cook over low heat for 20 to 30 minutes, turning occasionally.

In a small saucepan melt the butter. Stir in the parsley, remaining salt, and pepper. Blend well. Add the milk. Heat slowly until the sauce begins to bubble around the edges. Thicken if desired. Arrange the chicken on a serving platter and pour on the sauce. Garnish with parsley. Makes 6 servings.

CHICKEN PANCAKES

3–pound young chicken
  Celery tops
1 onion, grated
1 teaspoon thyme

Salt
¼ teaspoon freshly ground
   pepper
½ cup chopped parsley

Simmer chicken until tender, with a few celery tops, onion, thyme, and salt. Remove meat from bones and chop very fine. Do not grind. Season to taste (pepper and parsley are advised) Add just enough of the following sauce to bind, and set aside in the refrigerator until required.

CHICKEN PANCAKE SAUCE

Chicken broth
Milk
Butter, flour

Chicken bouillon cube
  (optional)
Cheddar cheese

Make a rich cream sauce with the chicken broth and enough milk added to make a quart. Chicken fat may be used instead of butter in blending the flour. If salt is needed spice the flavor with a chicken bouillon cube. Set the sauce and cheddar aside and make your pancakes as described below:

2 eggs, well beaten
1 cup flour   1 cup milk

½ teaspoon salt
1 teaspoon cooking oil

Mix ingredients thoroughly and allow to stand for 15 minutes. Cook pancakes in butter, one at a time. This should make 14 pancakes. Use a rounded or heaping tablespoonful of chicken in each pancake, rolling and placing in a rectangular casserole about 1½ inches deep. Cover with the sauce and grate a sharp cheddar over the top. Refrigerate until ready. Heat in a 350° F. oven until the pancakes are hot through and the cheese is bubbly.

RABBITS IN CASSEROLE

2½-pound package frozen,
  ready-to-cook, domestic
  rabbit, cut-up, thawed
All-purpose flour
Shortening
Water

1 cup white wine
½ teaspoon salt
Dash pepper
½ teaspoon sweet basil
½ teaspoon marjoram

Dredge the cut-up rabbit in the flour. In a Dutch oven or heavy saucepan, heat the shortening and brown the meat well on both sides. Add 1 cup water, the wine, salt, pepper, basil, and marjoram. Cover and simmer over a low heat about 1 hour or until the meat is tender. Remove the rabbit to a warm serving platter. If a thicker gravy is desired, dissolve 1 tablespoon flour in ¼ cup water; stir into the hot gravy. Cook while stirring a few minutes until thickened. Pour the gravy over the rabbit on the platter. Makes about 4 servings.

BEEF CAKES

2 cups finely minced cold rare
  roast beef
2 cups grated dry bread
  crumbs
1 tablespoon chopped parsley
1 tablespoon grated onion
1 teaspoon salt

¼ teaspoon pepper
1 egg, beaten
1 tablespoon beef drippings or
  melted butter
2 tablespoons pickle relish
1 cup mashed potatoes
2 tablespoons butter

Heat oven to 400° F. Blend together the beef, crumbs, parsley, onion, salt, pepper, egg, drippings, and pickle relish. Mix well. Form the mixture into flat cakes about 3½ to 4 inches in diameter. Arrange them in a well-greased baking dish or cookie sheet. Spread with potatoes, dot tops with butter and bake in the pre-heated oven until the potatoes are lightly browned, 15 to 20 minutes. Makes 4 to 6 servings.

FORCEMEAT BALLS

1 pound ground beef
2 tablespoons snipped parsley
2 tablespoons onion, finely
  chopped
1 teaspoon salt

Dash pepper
½ teaspoon mace
All-purpose flour
Shortening

FOOD CHOPPER

Combine the meat, parsley, onion, salt, pepper, and mace. With floured hands, roll the meat mixture, a teaspoon at a time, into small balls. Brown the meat balls quickly in the hot shortening. Makes about 48 small meat balls.

SAUSAGE GRINDER

ROAST PIG

1 suckling pig, 10 to 12 pounds
12 cups dried bread crumbs
1 cup butter or margarine
¾ cup minced onion
1 cup chopped celery
2 cups chopped apples
2 tablespoons salt
1 teaspoon pepper
1 tablespoon each dried sage, thyme, and marjoram
Broth or water
1 cup wine
Minced onion, chopped parsley, flour , watercress , cranberries, apple

Wash the pig in several changes of cold water and pat dry. Place the bread crumbs in a large bowl. In a heavy skillet melt the butter or margarine and sauté the onion and celery until soft. Mix in the apples and seasoning. Add to the bread crumbs. Moisten with the hot broth or water. Cool and stuff the pig loosely; skewer and lace opening. Truss the legs to the body. Place a block of wood in the pig's mouth so it will stay open for the apple garnish. Cover the ears with foil or brown paper. Place in a roasting pan with 1 cup wine. Roast in a 350° F. oven. Allow 25 minutes per pound. Cover the pig with foil or brown paper if browning too fast. Baste frequently with the drippings from the pan. While the pig is roasting boil the pig's heart, in water to cover, until it is tender, then add the liver, onions, and parsley; cook until the liver is tender. Chop them fine and mix with the pan drippings and some of their cooking liquid. Skim off the fat and thicken the gravy with flour. Cook for a few minutes; keep hot.

If the pig is too large for your oven, have the butcher cut it through the middle, and roast it in 2 pans. To serve, put together and garnish with a garland of watercress and cranberries. Remove the wood and insert the apple. Surround with parsley.

THE PIG, THE PIG, THE CUTE LITTLE PIG
ATE A LOT AND GREW SO BIG.
HOPPITY, SKIPPITY, JIGGITY JOG
NOW LITTLE PIGGY IS A BIG FAT HOG.

FRICANDELS OF VEAL

1 cup French bread or roll crumbs	1 teaspoon salt
½ cup milk	¼ teaspoon pepper
3 eggs, beaten	1 egg, slightly beaten
3 pounds loin of veal, ground very fine	1 cup fine bread crumbs
	½ cup shortening or oil
	1 cup boiling water

Soften the bread crumbs in milk; combine with the eggs, then with the meat, salt, and pepper. Shape 1 cup of the mixture at a time into an oval. Roll in egg, then bread crumbs. Fry in fat till golden brown. Pour off any fat. Pour on the water; cover; simmer 30 minutes. Serve with pan juices. Makes 6 generous servings.

FRICANDEAU OF VEAL

DOUGH KNEADER

6- to 7-pound leg of veal	2 cups water
6 slices bacon	1 teaspoon salt
1 onion, sliced	¼ teaspoon pepper
6 carrots, peeled	

Have the meat man remove the bone from the meat and saw the bone into several pieces. Spread out the veal and lay strips of bacon on the veal; roll up; tie. In a Dutch oven place the bones, onion, carrots, water; lay meat on top. Sprinkle with salt and pepper. Simmer 2 hours or till the meat is fork-tender. Mash the carrots; slice the meat and arrange on the mashed carrots. Makes 8 servings.

STUFFED EGGPLANT

Parboil them to take off their bitterness. Then slit each one down the side, and extract the seeds. Have ready a stuffing made of grated breadcrumbs, butter, minced sweet herbs, salt, pepper, nutmeg, and beaten yolk of egg. Fill with it the cavity from whence you took the seeds, and bake the egg plants in a Dutch oven. Serve them up with a made gravy poured into the dish.

2 medium-sized eggplants
1½ cups grated dry bread
    crumbs
6 tablespoons melted butter
1 teaspoon oregano
¼ teaspoon powdered thyme
¼ teaspoon grated nutmeg

2 teaspoons finely snipped
    chives (optional)
¾ teaspoon salt
¼ teaspoon freshly ground
    black pepper
2 egg yolks

Cook the unpeeled eggplants in 1 quart of boiling water for 15 minutes or until tender but firm. Cool slightly. Cut them in half lengthwise; scoop out the seeds and pulp. In a bowl combine the chopped pulp and seeds, crumbs, ¼ cup of the melted butter, oregano, thyme, nutmeg, chives, salt, and pepper. Beat the egg yolks slightly and stir them into the crumb mixture, blending well. Stuff the eggplants with the crumb mixture and drizzle with the remaining melted butter.

Heat oven to 375° F. Arrange the eggplants in a shallow baking pan, cover with foil; bake 20 minutes. Remove the foil and continue to bake 10 minutes longer or until the stuffing is lightly browned. Makes 8 servings.

STEWED MUSHROOMS

1 pound fresh mushrooms
¼ teaspoon nutmeg
½ teaspoon salt
   dash pepper

2 tablespoons butter or
   margarine
  All-purpose flour
2 tablespoons cream or milk
1 egg yolk, beaten

Wash the mushrooms and remove the stems. Cook the stems in water to cover for 15 minutes; remove the stems and reserve for other recipes. Add caps to the mushroom liquid remaining in the saucepan. Add the nutmeg, salt and pepper. Roll the butter in flour and add to the mushroom caps. Cover and simmer 15 minutes. Just before serving, stir in cream or milk and the egg yolk. Makes about 4 to 6 servings.

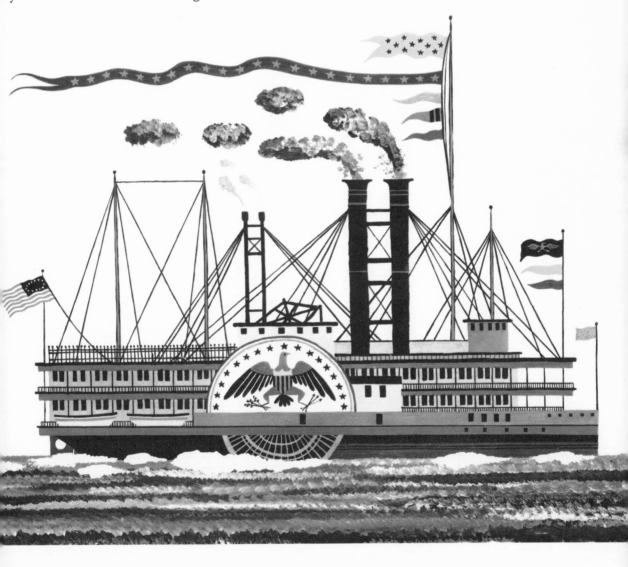

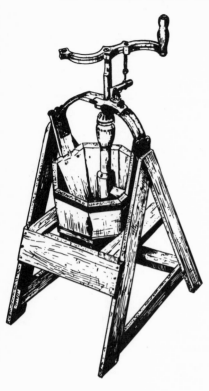

BUTTER WORKER

TOMATOES ESCALLOPED

1½ cups soft bread crumbs
1 (1-pound 12-ounce) can
  peeled tomatoes or 6
  medium size ripe
  tomatoes, peeled
½ cup saltine cracker crumbs

3 tablespoons butter or
  margarine
½ teaspoon salt
Dash pepper
¼ teaspoon nutmeg
2 teaspoons granulated sugar

Preheat an oven to 375° F. In a greased 1½-quart baking dish, sprinkle a layer of the bread crumbs, then half of the tomatoes, the cracker crumbs, dot with half of the butter or margarine; add the remaining tomatoes, salt, pepper, nutmeg, and sugar. Top with the remaining bread crumbs and dot with the remaining butter. Bake in a moderate oven for 30 minutes until the top is golden and bubbly. Makes about 6 servings.

OMELET SOUFFLÉ

4 eggs
1½ cups sifted confectioners'
  sugar

2 tablespoons lemon juice
1 teaspoon butter or margarine
Whipped cream

While you beat the eggs place a 1½-quart casserole in 425° F. oven. Separate the eggs. Beat the whites stiff. Beat the yolks and then slowly beat in the sugar, add the lemon juice. Fold yolks into whites. Melt butter in the hot casserole. Quickly pour in the egg mixture. Bake 15 to 20 minutes or till puffy and golden. Serve with whipped cream. Makes 4 servings.

DUTCH SALAD

1 small head lettuce
1 tablespoon butter
¾ cup diced ready-to-eat ham,
  fat and all

3 tablespoons wine vinegar
2 tablespoons water
¼ teaspoon salt
Dash cayenne

Wash the lettuce. Dry the leaves on paper towels and tear them into large pieces. Melt the butter in a saucepan. Fry the ham in butter, stirring until lightly browned. Pour the vinegar and water into the ham. Put the lettuce into a mixing bowl. Sprinkle it with salt and cayenne. Pour the hot vinegar mixture over and toss lightly. Serve at once. Makes 4 to 5 servings.

HOMINY BREAD

½ cup hominy grits
   Water
½ teaspoon salt
2 tablespoons butter or
   margarine

2 eggs beaten
2 cups milk
1 cup white cornmeal

In a double boiler top, cook the hominy grits with 2½ cups water and the salt. Stir while bringing to a boil; then place over boiling water, cover and cook 45 minutes. Preheat oven to 425° F. Into the hot cooked hominy, stir the butter, eggs and 1 cup milk; then stir in the cornmeal and the remaining milk. Pour into a greased 1½-quart baking dish. Bake in a hot oven for about 45 minutes or until the top is puffy and golden. Serve immediately with a spoon. Texture should be "custardy" as a spoonbread. Makes about 8 servings.

SWEET POTATO PONE

2 eggs
4 tablespoons brown sugar
¼ teaspoon ginger
¼ teaspoon nutmeg
¼ teaspoon salt

1 teaspoon cream
1 tablespoon melted butter or
   margarine
1 quart grated raw sweet
   potato

Beat the eggs till light and fluffy. Beat in the sugar, ginger, nutmeg, salt, cream, and butter. Fold potatoes into the egg mixture. Pour into a well-greased 8- x 9-inch square pan. Bake in a 400° F. oven 20 to 25 minutes or till set. Cool. Cut in circles. Makes 12 servings.

THESE BUNS ARE REALLY QUITE good

MADEIRA BUNS

¼ cup butter
½ cup sugar
1 egg
1½ cups flour
2 teaspoons baking powder

¼ teaspoon freshly ground
 nutmeg
½ teaspoon ginger
½ cup sherry or Madeira
1 teaspoon caraway seeds

Cream together the butter and sugar until light and fluffy. Add the egg and beat until light. Sift together the flour, baking powder, nutmeg, and ginger. Add the dry ingredients to the creamed mixture alternately with the wine, ending with the dry ingredients. Fold in the caraway seeds. Divide into 12 baking cups. Bake in a 350° F. oven for 30 minutes.

BUTTERMILK GRIDDLE CAKES

1 egg
2 cups buttermilk
½ teaspoon salt

½ teaspoon baking soda
2 tablespoons boiling water
2½ cups all-purpose flour

Beat the egg; add to the buttermilk. Stir in the salt and mix well. Dissolve the soda in boiling water; stir into the buttermilk mixture. Gradually add the flour, stirring all the while. Beat the batter until smooth. Bake on a hot greased griddle, turning to brown cakes on both sides. Makes 10 to 12 4-inch cakes.

SHAKER BROWN BREAD

1 cup cornmeal
1 cup rye flour
1 cup graham or whole-wheat
 flour
1 teaspoon salt

¾ teaspoon baking soda
1¾ cups sour milk
¾ cup molasses
2 tablespoons melted butter
1 cup snipped raisins

In bowl combine the cornmeal, flours, salt, and soda. Stir in the milk, molasses, butter, and raisins. Divide between 3 clean, well-greased, 1-pound cans. Cover tops with foil and tie with a string. Set the pans on a rack in a deep kettle. Pour on about 4 inches of boiling water. Cover the pot and steam for 2 hours. Add boiling water as necessary. Remove the cans to a cookie sheet; remove the foil. Bake in 350° F. oven for 30 minutes. Cool on a wire rack about 10 minutes, then remove from the cans. Makes 3 cans of bread.

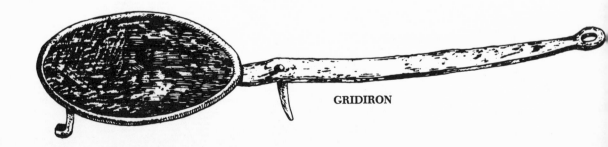

GRIDIRON

ALABAMA RICE BREAD

1 cup hot cooked rice
1 tablespoon butter
1 cup milk
3 eggs, lightly beaten
½ cup cornmeal
1 teaspoon salt

Combine the hot rice and the butter. Add the milk to the lightly beaten eggs; stir in the cornmeal and the salt. Add to the rice mixture. Divide the mixture between 12 muffin cups, being sure to get some rice into each cup. Bake in a 425° F. oven for 25 minutes. Makes 1 dozen muffins.

FEDERAL BREAD

1 pint light cream
¼ cup butter or margarine
1 teaspoon salt
2 packages active dry yeast
½ cup warm water
4½ to 5 cups flour
2 eggs, beaten

Scald the cream; add the butter and salt; cool. Soften the yeast in warm water. Make a well in the center of the flour in a bowl; add the eggs, cream, and yeast. Stir smooth and beat 1 minute. Divide the batter between two 8- x 4½- x 3-inch greased pans. Set the pans, covered, in a warm place to rise till doubled in bulk. Bake at 375° F. about 30 minutes or until the loaves are golden; remove from the pans; cool. Makes 2 loaves.

JACKSON CAKE

½ cup butter or margarine
1¼ cups granulated sugar
2 eggs
1 tablespoon lemon juice
1½ cups sifted all-purpose flour
½ teaspoon double-acting baking powder
½ teaspoon salt
1 cup finely chopped walnuts
1 cup snipped raisins

Cream the butter with sugar. Beat in the eggs one at a time, then the lemon juice. Alternately add flour mixed with baking powder and salt; beat smooth. Stir in nuts and raisins. Bake in a foil-lined 9- x 5- x 3-inch pan in 375° F. oven for 1 hour, or until a cake tester inserted in the center comes out clean. Cool on rack 10 minutes; remove from the pan. Makes 1 loaf cake.

WEBSTER CAKES

½ pound sweet butter
3 cups sifted all-purpose flour
2 cups sifted confectioners' sugar
¼ teaspoon salt
5 eggs, well beaten
1 tablespoon lemon juice
1 tablespoon wine or brandy
1 cup currants

With a pastry blender or 2 knives used scissors-fashion blend the butter into the combined flour, sugar, and salt. Add the eggs and rest of the ingredients. Divide between 2 well-greased and floured 9-inch square pans. Bake in 425° F. oven for 20 minutes or till golden. Serve in squares or diamonds. If desired cakes may be iced; if so, mark the cakes as they are to be cut before the icing dries. Makes 24 servings.

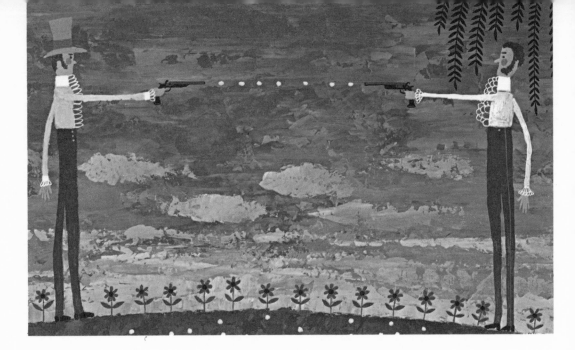

HARRISON CAKE

2 eggs
1¼ cups granulated sugar
1 tablespoon melted butter or
    margarine
½ cup milk

1 cup sifted all-purpose flour
½ teaspoon baking soda
¼ teaspoon nutmeg
¼ teaspoon salt

Beat the eggs till light and fluffy. Gradually beat in the sugar, then the butter and milk. Combine the flour, soda, nutmeg, and salt. Beat into the batter until smooth and bubbly. Pour into a well-greased and floured 9-inch square pan. Bake in 375° F. oven 25 to 30 minutes or till the cake is golden and a cake tester inserted in center comes out clean. Makes 9 squares.

ELECTION CAKE

1 package active dry yeast
¼ cup warm water
1 tablespoon sugar
1 cup flour
¼ cup milk, scalded
½ cup butter or margarine
1 cup granulated sugar

2½ cups flour
½ teaspoon salt
1 teaspoon nutmeg
1 egg, beaten
½ cup raisins
½ cup citron, cut up
½ cup brandy

Soften the yeast in warm water. Stir in 1 tablespoon sugar and 1 cup of flour. Let rise in a warm place. Meanwhile, to the milk add the butter and remaining sugar. Place the flour, salt, and nutmeg in a large bowl. Make a well in the center; add the egg, the cooled milk mixture, fruits, and brandy; beat well. Pour the batter into a well-greased and floured 9- x 5- x 3-inch baking dish. Let rise again. Bake in a 350° F. oven for 45 minutes or until golden and baked through. Makes 1 loaf.

MISSOURI PIE

2 eggs
1 cup granulated sugar
1½ tablespoons flour

¼ cup melted butter or
    margarine
8-inch unbaked pie shell

Beat the eggs till very thick. Combine the sugar and flour and slowly beat into the eggs, then beat in the butter. Quickly turn the mixture into the pie shell. Bake in a 375° F. oven for 40 minutes or until the pie is very puffed and golden brown. Cool (pie will fall). Makes 6 servings.

APPLE FRITTERS

1 pound apples
½ cup water
2 eggs
1 cup milk
2 cups sifted all-purpose flour
¼ teaspoon salt

1 tablespoon lemon juice
1 teaspoon lemon rind
Shortening
Confectioners' sugar
Nutmeg

Pare and core the apples; cut them into chunks. Cook with water 5 minutes just to soften slightly. Beat the eggs till thick and fluffy; slowly add the milk. Stir the egg mixture into the flour and salt. Stir in the apples, lemon juice, and rind. Drop ¼ cup of the batter at a time into fat in a deep fryer heated to 375° F. Fry till golden. Dust with sugar and nutmeg. Makes 12 to 15 fritters.

CHEESE DELIGHTS

½ cup butter
½ pound sharp unprocessed
    cheddar, grated
½ pound (2 cups) all-purpose
    flour

½ teaspoon salt
¼ teaspoon cayenne pepper
Blanched almonds

Cream the butter and cheese and mix in the flour, salt, and pepper. Chill and roll to ¼-inch thickness and cut with a small round cutter. Press a half of blanched almond in the center of each biscuit. Use an ungreased cookie sheet and sprinkle lightly with salt. Bake about 7 or 8 minutes at 350° F. Makes 6 dozen 1¼-inch biscuits.

**COFFEE
ROASTER**

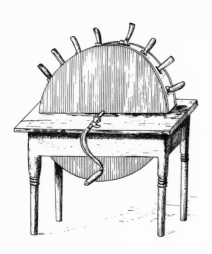

KNIFE-CLEANING MACHINE

CHEESE CUSTARD

½ pound natural cheddar
  cheese
1 egg yolk

1 egg
½ pint heavy cream (1 cup)
Boiling water

Grate the cheese. Beat together the yolk, the egg, and the cream; combine with the cheese. Spoon mixture into 4 to 6 greased custard cups or a soufflé dish. Set in a pan, pour in enough boiling water to come to ½ inch from the top of the custard cups. Bake in a 350° F. oven 20 to 25 minutes or until the custards are set. Makes 4 to 6 servings.

"SAVE-ALL" PUDDING

1 quart milk
½ pound stale bread (half of a
  1-pound loaf)
¼ cup brown sugar
3 eggs, beaten

¼ cup seedless raisins
¼ teaspoon nutmeg
½ teaspoon cinnamon
¼ cup each wine and brandy
Butter or beef suet

Pour the milk over bread crumbs in a bowl; let stand to soften. Press the soft bread and milk through a sieve or food mill. Combine the milk mixture with the brown sugar, eggs, raisins, nutmeg, cinnamon, and combined wines. Pour into a buttered 2-quart casserole. Dot the top with 2 teaspoons butter. Bake in a 375° F. oven about 60 minutes or until a silver knife inserted in the center comes out clean. Makes 6 to 8 servings.

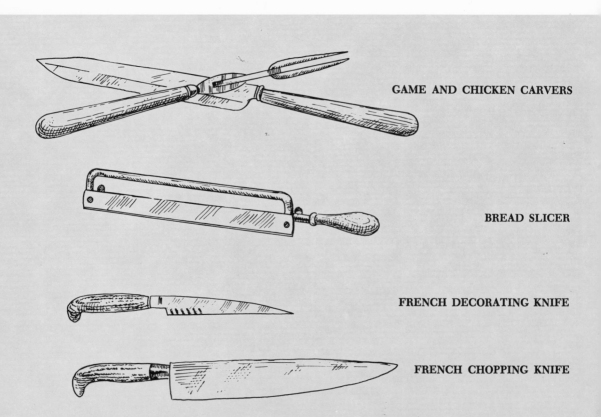

GAME AND CHICKEN CARVERS

BREAD SLICER

FRENCH DECORATING KNIFE

FRENCH CHOPPING KNIFE

BONING KNIFE

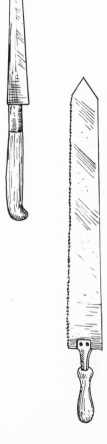

CARAMEL CREAM PRALINES

½ cup granulated sugar
¾ cup boiling water
1 cup light brown sugar
2 cups granulated sugar
1 cup evaporated milk or
   heavy cream
½ teaspoon salt

¼ teaspoon cream of tartar
3 tablespoons butter or
   margarine
1 teaspoon vanilla extract
2½ cups pecan halves and
   pieces

Place ½ cup sugar in a heavy skillet. Over low heat stir the sugar till it melts and turns golden. Remove from the heat. Using long-handled wooden spoon, quickly stir in the boiling water (it will bubble and steam). Return to the heat and cook and stir about 5 minutes more or until cooked down to ½ cup. Pour this caramel sauce into a Dutch oven or other deep, heavy pot. Add the remaining sugars, cream, salt, and cream of tartar. Cook over very low heat till dissolved. When a candy thermometer reads 230° F. or a few drops from the spoon form a soft ball in cold water, remove from the heat; add the butter and cool about 5 minutes or to about 170° F. on a candy thermometer. Beat the candy until creamy (this may take 10 or 15 minutes). Stir in the vanilla and nuts. Quickly drop from a tablespoon onto waxed paper. They will spread to about 3″ in diameter. Let stand till firm. Makes 2½ to 3 dozen.

FRENCH SAW KNIFE

FLUMMERY

2 envelopes unflavored
  gelatin
½ cup cold water
⅔ cup milk, scalded
⅔ cup confectioners' sugar

2 teaspoons vanilla extract or
  rose water
1 pint heavy cream, whipped
  Pears (baked, stewed, fresh
  or canned)

Soak the gelatin in the cold water; dissolve in the scalded milk. Add the sugar and vanilla and stir to dissolve. Set the gelatin mixture in a refrigerator until slightly thickened. (Should the gelatin become too thick, melt over hot water and set to chill again.) Whip the gelatin until fluffy, then fold into the whipped cream a third at a time. Spoon into a mold of 6-cup capacity. Refrigerate until set. Unmold and surround with the pears. Makes 8 to 10 servings.

PEACH OR QUINCE MARMALADE

2 lemons
1 orange
1 cup water
2 pounds ripe peaches or
  quinces

3 pounds granulated sugar
  (7 cups)
½ bottle liquid fruit pectin

Squeeze enough juice from the lemons to make 2 tablespoons; measure into a saucepan. Cut up the orange and lemons, and the skins; remove the seeds. Grind, chop fine, or slice wafer-thin; add to the saucepan. Add the water and simmer covered for 20 minutes. Meanwhile peel and pit the peaches. Chop very fine or grind. Combine the peaches and the cooked citrus fruit, measure 5 cups into a very large saucepan. Add the sugar. Mix well. Place over a high heat, bring to a full rolling boil, and boil hard 1 minute, stirring constantly. Remove from the heat; at once stir in the pectin. Skim off the foam with a metal spoon. Then stir and skim for 7 minutes until slightly cooled to prevent floating fruit. Ladle into glasses. Cover at once with ⅛ inch of hot paraffin. Makes about 11 medium jelly glasses.

Cabbage in Sour Cream, page 109
Mexican Beef, page 102
Sourdough Bread, page 113

Kitchen, Cragfont
Gallatin, Tennessee

Kitchen, Vann Tavern
Calhoun, Georgia

Recipes of the Westward Empire

"G IVE ME YOUR TIRED, your poor, your huddled masses yearning to be free . . ." So goes the legend on the Statue of Liberty, and the world took the appeal quite literally. Of course the movement westward long preceded the erection of the statue. Fortunately, there was enough acreage to accommodate them all as westward moved the nation. The diversity of custom that had already made Americans a new kind of people was compounded as the caravans crossed the continent's midriff. Furs, minerals, the glint of adventurous living, and ultimately the hope of a homestead, drained the Eastern seaboard of brawn, but Europe remained a seemingly inexhaustible supply of manpower. Between 1820 and 1890 almost one third of the population increase was digging canals, building turnpikes, laying rails, manning the mills.

In a background of such epic magnitude, the changing pattern in America's kitchen seems relatively trivial. Yet all these millions who were to bring the Industrial Revolution to its American climax had to eat. (What is more, they were to provide a considerable portion of what the rest of the world would eat.) The cuisine of the United States, adapted and evolved by its migrant population, was in turn to pervade the world as the cultural tide reversed in the next century.

IRON TEAKETTLE

The migrants who were called settlers in the 17th and 18th centuries brought with them the eating and cooking habits of their forebears, accepting maize in place of wheat, catfish in place of whatever swam their native streams, bear and buffalo steak to supplement more

91

familiar livestock. As the settlers moved westward by wagon or by train, their "receipts" were part of the baggage.

Notwithstanding a certain monotony, new dishes and novel ways of preparing them were beginning to enrich the cuisine. For the more sophisticated in all periods, French cookery had a special appeal. Americans with aristocratic leanings valued French cookery and imported chefs, although in the era of Jacksonian democracy this might be impolitic. Yet Eliza Leslie, probably the most popular of the culinary compilers, was able to issue, in the year of Jackson's first election, *Domestic French Cookery.*

A more significant infiltration of French influence came via the territories purchased by Mr. Jefferson. The dishes of New Orleans, which antedated the Americanization of the city (and survived this event), graced the tables of the Deep South. Spanish and Negro as well as French, they might be more accurately characterized as one of the more distinguished facets of American cookery. In the same category is the rich inheritance from Spanish America, a veritably aboriginal cuisine in Spanish guise.

The acquisition of the Floridas, Louisiana, Texas, and California, and later in the century of Alaska and Hawaii, undoubtedly enriched the cuisine that could be claimed—and acclaimed—as American. But the real treasures of a national cuisine were being carried mostly in steerage across the seas. Before the century ended, spaghetti and dumplings, as well as chili and tamales, had become as commonplace as pancakes and doughnuts. Gourmets would relish Mandarin Soup and Hawaiian Chicken. And meanwhile, in the Far North, the prospector continued to pack his sourdough starter, symbol of a vanishing American West.

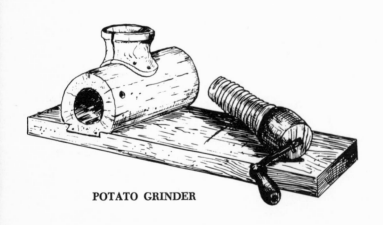

POTATO GRINDER

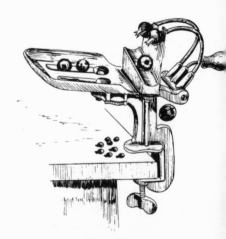

CHERRY STONER

BURGOO

2 pounds shin of beef or veal, cut into 2 or 3 pieces	1 cup carrots
	1 cup corn
	1 cup peas
3 quarts water	1 cup cabbage
1 tablespoon salt	½ cup flour, browned
1 1-pound can tomatoes, or 4 fresh ones	½ cup wine
	1 tablespoon Worcestershire sauce
1 cup potatoes	

Put the shin bone and water in a 5-quart kettle. Add the salt; cover, and simmer 4 hours. Skim often. Remove the bones and any grease that has formed on the top. Add the vegetables and cook until all are tender. Add the browned flour to a cup of the broth, return to the kettle and stir in. Add wine and Worcestershire sauce. Correct the seasonings. Bring to a boil and serve in a tureen. Makes 8 to 10 servings.

LENTIL SOUP

2 cups dried lentils	¼ cup olive oil
3 quarts water	1 teaspoon salt
1 onion, minced	¼ teaspoon pepper
2 cloves garlic, mashed	3 slices bacon, cut in cubes
1 8-ounce can tomato sauce	

Wash the lentils, then put in a heavy soup pot with tight-fitting lid. Add the water and rest of the ingredients. Simmer 2 hours, stir occasionally to keep from sticking. Correct seasonings. Makes 2½ quarts or about 10 servings.

SHINBONE SOUP WITH BUTTER KLÖSSE

3 pounds veal knuckles cut into 3 pieces	1 celery stalk with tops
1 tablespoon salt	1 cup sliced celery
2 quarts water	1 cup sliced carrots
1 quart chicken stock	1 cup diced potatoes
1 large onion stuck with 2 cloves	1 pound hot sausage made into 1-inch balls and browned
2 cloves garlic, minced	½ cup flour, browned
1 bay leaf	Butter Klösse

Put the veal knuckle into a 5- to 6-quart pot. Sprinkle with salt and let stand 20 minutes. Add the water, stock, onion, garlic, bay leaf, and celery stalk. Cover and cook 2½ hours. Skim to remove any grease that has formed on top. Lift out the meat and bones and strain. Return the broth to the pot, adding the meat and discarding bones. Add the sliced celery, carrots, and potatoes. Cook 15 minutes more. Meanwhile, brown the sausage balls. When the vegetables are tender remove 1 cup of the broth and stir into the browned flour. Add the flour to the pot and correct the seasonings. Add the sausages. Drop in Butter Klösse by teaspoonfuls, cover and simmer 8 to 10 minutes. Serve immediately. Makes 8 to 10 servings.

BUTTER KLÖSSE

2 tablespoons softened butter	2 eggs, unbeaten
1 cup flour	½ cup finely chopped parsley
½ teaspoon salt	

With pastry blender or 2 knives cut in the butter, flour, and salt. Add the eggs and parsley. Drop by teaspoonfuls into simmering stock. Cook 8 to 10 minutes without removing the lid.

WARMING PAN

MANDARIN SOUP

1 cup raw lean pork, cut in strips
1 cup mushrooms
1 cup chopped celery
1 cup diced carrots
6 cups chicken or beef consommé
½ cup chopped spinach, fresh or frozen
1 teaspoon monosodium glutamate
1 slightly beaten egg
2 tablespoons cornstarch
2 tablespoons cold water
Salt
Pepper

Sauté the pork strips slightly. Add the mushrooms, celery, and carrots; cook until the vegetables are almost tender. Add the consommé, spinach, and monosodium glutamate. Bring to a boil, add the egg and stir gently. Add the cornstarch dissolved in cold water. Stir and cook five minutes. Season with salt and pepper to taste. Serve hot. Makes 6 servings.

CASTILIAN SOUP

1 large onion sliced in rings
2 tablespoons olive oil
1 teaspoon paprika
3 cups chicken stock
2 tablespoons bread crumbs
Salt and pepper to taste
2 eggs

Sauté in a frying pan the onion and paprika until limp but not brown. Add the stock and simmer 10 minutes. Thicken with bread crumbs. Correct the seasoning. Drop in the eggs and poach in the soup about 2 or 3 minutes. Serve a portion of soup and one egg in individual bowl. This may also be baked in earthenware soup dishes in a 375° F. oven for 3 to 5 minutes. Makes 2 servings.

MINESTRONE SOUP

1 1-pound 4-ounce can garbanzo beans (chickpeas)
¼ cup diced carrots
½ cup diced celery
1 8¼-ounce can diced or sliced beets
1 8-ounce can tomato sauce
1 clove garlic, minced
½ cup cubed potatoes
½ cup shredded cabbage
2 cups chopped spinach
2 cups sliced zucchini
¼ pound diced salt pork
½ cup minced onion
1 tablespoon salt
½ teaspoon pepper
3 quarts water
1 ham bone, cut up
¼ cup rice
1 tablespoon minced parsley
1 cup grated Parmesan cheese

In a large soup pot combine the beans and all the ingredients except the parsley and cheese. Simmer 30 minutes. Remove the bone. Sprinkle on the parsley. Correct the seasonings. Serve with Parmesan cheese. Makes 4 quarts.

SHAKER PEASE PORRIDGE

2 cups split peas
1½ quarts chicken bouillon
2 onions, diced
2 carrots, diced
2 stalks celery, diced

1 turnip, diced
1 teaspoon salt
¼ teaspoon pepper
Buttered rye bread croutons

In a large heavy soup pot simmer the peas, covered, in stock for 2 hours; stir occasionally. Add the onions, carrots, celery, turnip, salt, and pepper; cook 30 minutes longer. Put through a sieve or food mill; reheat. Serve with croutons. Makes 2 quarts of very thick soup.

PAELLA

¼ cup olive oil or peanut oil
1 frying chicken, cut in serving pieces
3 cups chicken stock or canned broth
1 pound shrimps, shelled and deveined
1 teaspoon saffron, crumbled
1½ cups uncooked rice

½ teaspoon salt
¼ teaspoon pepper
2 garlic cloves, chopped
1 cup cooked ham, cubed
½ pound fresh peas or 1 (10-ounce) package frozen
½ pound scallops
3 pimientos cut in strips
2 lemons, cut in wedges

In a Dutch oven heat the oil and brown the chicken all over, a few pieces at a time, removing as it browns. Add the stock and let it come to a boil. Drop in the shrimp and cook only until they turn red. Remove the shrimp, moisten the saffron in a little hot stock and add to the pan. Mix in the rice, salt, pepper, and garlic. Put in the chicken and ham. Cover and cook 20 minutes or until the chicken is tender. Meanwhile, cook the peas and keep warm. Add the scallops and shrimp and cook 10 minutes more. Correct the seasonings. Add the peas and pimiento strips. Serve on a large platter with lemon wedges.

BORSCHT

6 medium beets, cooked, peeled, and grated
1 quart soup stock or canned chicken broth
1½ tablespoons lemon juice

Simmer all together for 30 minutes. Serve with sour cream.

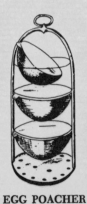

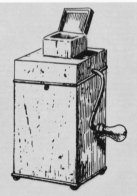

EGG POACHER   **FRENCH JULIENNE MILL**   **WATER FILTER**

PERCH IN SOUR CREAM

6 small perch
1¼ teaspoons salt
¼ teaspoon pepper
3 tablespoons flour for
    dredging
3 tablespoons butter for frying

1 tablespoon flour
1 tablespoon butter
⅔ cup sour milk
½ cup meat stock
Parsley

Clean the fish; cut in portions. Add the salt and pepper, roll in the flour; fry in butter on both sides. When cooked take out of the pan and put on an oven-proof platter. Prepare the sauce in same pan. Mix 1 tablespoon flour with butter, place in the pan and add sour milk and fish or meat stock. Simmer several minutes and let the sauce thicken. Pour the sauce over the fish and place in a hot oven for 10 minutes. Serve in the same dish. Makes 4 to 6 servings.

BAKED HALIBUT PORTUGUESE

1 to 2 teaspoons butter
¼ cup minced onion
1 clove garlic, mashed
1½ to 2 pounds halibut
½ teaspoon salt
⅛ teaspoon pepper

1 1-pound can stewed
    tomatoes
¼ cup sherry
1 teaspoon chopped parsley
4 slices bacon (optional)

Spread the butter generously over a baking dish. Sprinkle the onions and garlic over the bottom of the dish. Place the fish on this; sprinkle with salt and pepper. Combine the tomatoes, sherry, and parsley; pour over the fish. Place the bacon on top. Bake in a 350° F. oven 1 hour or until the bacon is crisp and the fish easily flakes with a fork. Makes 4 servings.

MEXICAN STEWED CHICKEN

3 to 4 pounds of cut-up chicken	1 medium-size chopped onion
Flour	1 chopped tomato
Salt	1 cup raisins
Pepper	½ cup sliced stuffed olives
¼ cup shortening	1½ cups water
	1 stick cinnamon

Dip the chicken in flour, salt, and pepper. Brown in the shortening. Add the onion and tomato and cook 5 minutes, then add the raisins, olives, and sufficient water, about 1½ cups, to allow for simmering of the chicken until it is thoroughly cooked in a covered pan. Simmer for 1½ hours after browning. Add the cinnamon last. Stir for about 5 minutes. Cinnamon may then be removed if desired. Remove the chicken bones before serving. Makes 6 servings.

HAWAIIAN CHICKEN

Young chicken, 3 or 4 pounds	Pepper
2 cups chopped spinach	Salt
Cream of 1 coconut	½ pint milk

Cut up a chicken as if for fricassee, put it in a Dutch oven and cover with water; Simmer until tender. Add the spinach and cook 5 minutes more. Stir in the cream from the coconut. Just bring to a boil and remove from the fire; add pepper and salt to taste. Serve with rice. Makes about 4 to 6 servings.

To make the cream of coconut, break a coconut into pieces, cut off the brown skin, and grate the meat. Put in a saucepan with the ½ pint of milk, and heat slowly. When about to boil, drain off the cream and put the meat in a cheesecloth bag. Squeeze and extract the juice. The pulp is thrown away.

LONE STAR CHICKEN

1 3-pound chicken	2 tablespoons olive oil
1 carrot	1 1-pound can tomatoes
1 stalk celery	1 teaspoon Worcestershire sauce
1 onion	½ teaspoon salt
1 sprig parsley	¼ teaspoon pepper
1 teaspoon salt	½ teaspoon oregano
½ teaspoon pepper	½ cup shredded mozzarella
1 cup minced onions	6 slices American cheese, cut up
2 cups chopped green pepper	
1 clove garlic, mashed	

Simmer the chicken in 2 or 3 cups of water with the carrot, celery, onion, parsley, salt, and pepper for about 1 hour or until

REVOLVING GRATER   CHAFING DISH   MEAT CHOPPER

tender. Meanwhile, in a skillet brown the onions, green pepper, and garlic in oil; add tomatoes and seasonings and cook about 30 minutes, adding water if necessary (about ½ cup). Sauce should be thick. Remove the skin and bones from the chicken. In a 2-quart casserole layer half of the chicken, sauce, and cheeses; repeat. Bake in 350° F. oven about 40 minutes or till bubbling hot. Makes 4 servings.

CHINESE PURPLE-PLUM DUCK

1 4-pound duckling (drawn weight)
½ cup soy sauce
½ cup peanut oil
½ cup canned purple plums, pitted, skinned, and mashed
½ cup syrup drained from canned purple plums
6 slices fresh ginger
⅓ cup green onion tops
1 clove mashed garlic
2 tablespoons Chinese sweet sauce (optional)
¼ teaspoon salt
1 or 2 tablespoons cornstarch
2 tablespoons plum juice

Clean and disjoint the duck. Dip the duck into soy sauce. Cover the bottom of a heavy skillet with peanut oil, about ½ inch deep. When the oil is sizzling, add pieces of duck and brown evenly on both sides. Drain on paper towels. Mix the remainder of the soy sauce with the mashed canned plums, syrup, ginger, chopped green onion tops, garlic, sweet sauce, and salt. Pour the mixture over the duck in the pan, cover and let cook over slow heat for 30 minutes or until the duck is tender. Remove the duck and thicken the sauce in the pan by gradually stirring in, over the low heat, the cornstarch mixed to a smooth paste with the 2 tablespoons plum juice. Cook until smooth and clear. Pour the sauce over the duck. Makes 4 servings.

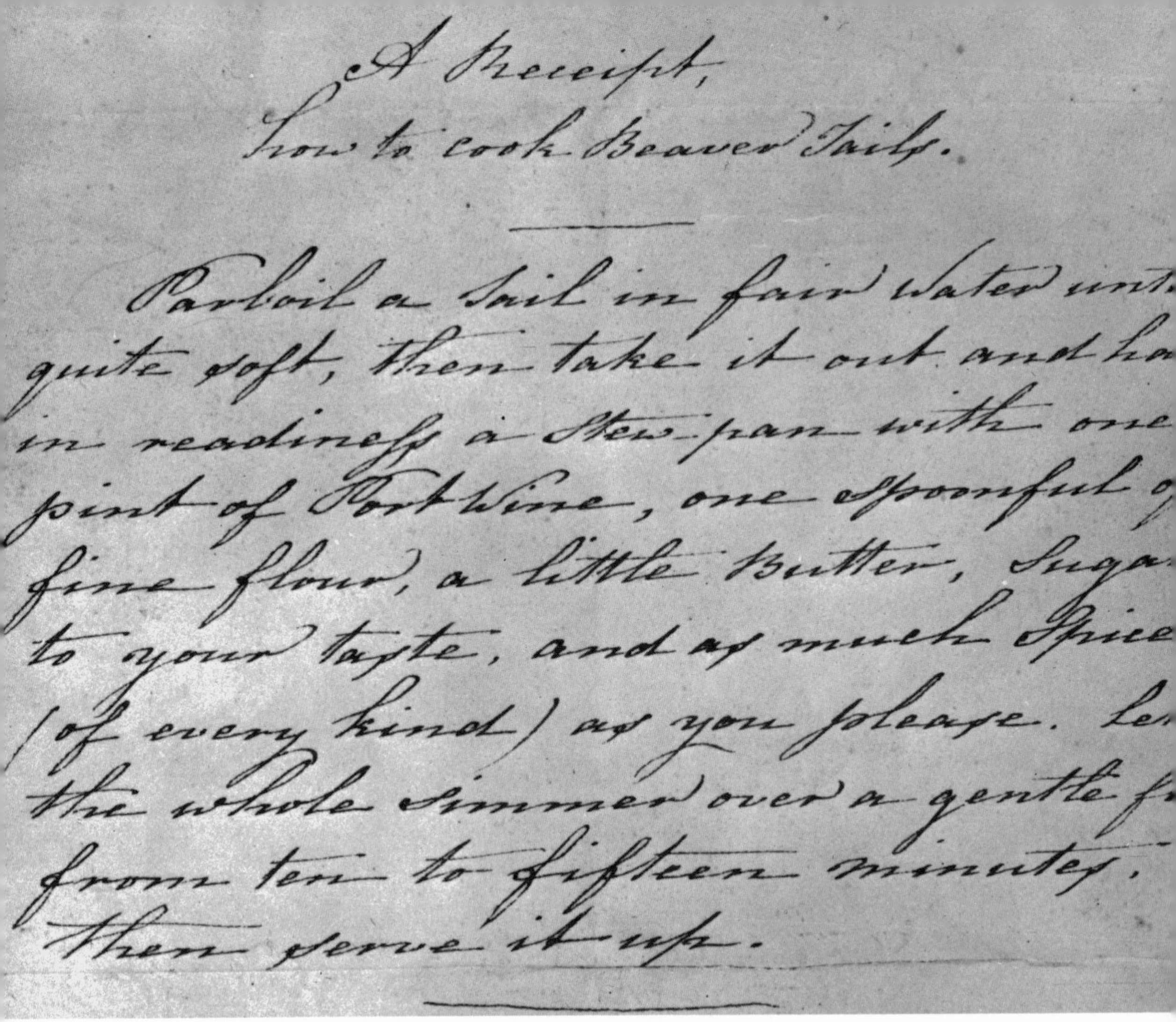

A Receipt,

How to cook Beaver Tails.

———

Parboil a Tail in fair Water until quite soft, then take it out and have in readiness a Stew-pan with one pint of Port Wine, one spoonful of fine flour, a little Butter, Sugar to your taste, and as much Spice (of every kind) as you please. Let the whole simmer over a gentle fire from ten to fifteen minutes, then serve it up.

———

Facsimile of an old "receipt" for cooking a beaver's tail, courtesy of the Detroit Historical Museum

BAKED STUFFED MEAT LOAF

2 tablespoons minced onions
2 tablespoons olive oil
2 peeled tomatoes, chopped
1 cup diced, cooked carrots
1 cup cooked peas
½ cup cooked string beans, cut small
2 eggs
2 teaspoons salt
2 slices bread, cut in pieces
½ cup milk
½ teaspoon pepper
2 pounds ground beef
2 tablespoons olive oil
½ cup beef bouillon

Fry the onion in oil until just tender but not browned. Add the tomatoes, cook for a few minutes, then add the rest of the vegetables; cool. Add 1 egg, beaten, and ½ teaspoon salt. Set aside.

Soak the bread in milk; add 1 egg, slightly beaten, 1½ teaspoons salt, pepper, and the meat. Mix well. On waxed paper or aluminum foil pat out the meat mixture into a long rectangle 9 inches wide and ½ inch thick. Spread on the stuffing. Roll like a jelly roll. Place in 9- x 5- x 3-inch rectangular pan. Bake at 375° F. for 20 minutes then add the bouillon; cover and bake at 350° F. for 1 hour. Makes 8 servings.

SWISS STEAK

1 2-pound round beef steak
½ teaspoon granulated sugar
½ lemon
¼ to ½ cup flour
1 teaspoon salt
¼ teaspoon pepper
3 tablespoons bacon fat

2 onions, chopped
1 green pepper, chopped
3 stalks celery, chopped
1 1-pound can stewed
   tomatoes
½ cup catsup

Rub both sides of the steak with sugar and lemon. Mix the flour with salt and pepper and pound into the meat with the side of a saucer. Heat the fat in large heavy skillet. Sear the steak on both sides; remove to a casserole. In the remaining fat in the skillet sauté the onion, pepper, and celery until just tender. Add the tomatoes and catsup; cook 5 minutes longer. Spoon sauce over the meat; cover casserole. Bake in 275° F. oven for 1½ to 2 hours. Makes 4 servings.

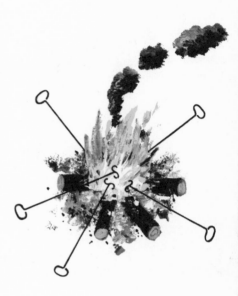

CHILI PIE

1 pound ground beef
1 onion, chopped
1 tablespoon oil
1 cup cooked red beans
½ teaspoon chili powder
½ teaspoon salt

1 tablespoon Worcestershire
   sauce
   Tabasco sauce (a dash)
8 ounces tomato sauce
1 8- or 10-ounce package
   cornbread mix

Brown the ground beef and the chopped onion in the oil. Add the red beans, chili powder, salt, Worcestershire, a dash of Tabasco, and the tomato sauce. Simmer for 15 minutes and then pour into an oiled 9-inch pie pan. Make up the cornbread mix as the label directs. Pour on top. Bake in 450° F. oven for 20 minutes or till the cornbread is done. Invert on a platter. Makes 6 servings.

CHEESE TOASTER

GAS IRON

STONEWARE CHURN

MORTAR AND PESTLE

MEXICAN BEEF

3 pounds round steak cut in
   thin strips
¼ cup flour
1 teaspoon salt
¼ teaspoon pepper
6 tablespoons butter
1 tablespoon olive oil
½ teaspoon powdered thyme
1 bay leaf
2 scallions
1 peeled medium-size onion

6 whole cloves
2 slices diced salt pork or
   bacon
2 cups beef bouillon
20 small mushroom caps (about
   ¾ pound)
1 tablespoon lemon juice
1 cup pitted, drained ripe
   olives
1 cup dry sherry

Dredge the steak pieces in combined flour, salt, and pepper.
Heat 4 tablespoons of the butter and the oil in a large skillet
with a tight-fitting cover. Brown the beef in the hot fat, turning
to brown well on all sides. Add the thyme and bay leaf. Slice
the scallions, tops and all; stud the onion with cloves. Add the
scallions and onion to the beef mixture along with the salt pork
and bouillon. Cover and simmer 1½ hours adding water occasionally if needed to prevent scorching. Sauté the mushrooms
in the remaining butter. When tender (about 5 minutes) add
the lemon juice. Add the mushrooms to the beef and, just before
serving, add the olives and sherry. Adjust salt if needed. Remove
the bay leaf and onion. Heat. Makes 6 servings.

ROAST HAUNCH OF BUFFALO

4- to 6-pound buffalo haunch
or top round of beef
1 cup red wine (claret,
Burgundy, zinfandel)
2 bay leaves
½ cup finely minced onion
½ cup minced celery

¼ cup chopped parsley
2 tablespoons oregano
¼ cup flour
½ teaspoon salt
⅛ teaspoon pepper
3 tablespoons bacon drippings
1 8-ounce can tomato sauce

Marinate the meat overnight in wine combined with bay leaves, onion, celery, parsley, and oregano. Take the meat from the marinade; reserve. Dredge the meat in flour seasoned with salt and pepper. Heat fat in a Dutch oven. Brown meat on all sides in hot fat; add the marinade and tomato sauce. Cover and bake in 325° F. oven about 3 hours or until the meat is tender, turning the roast occasionally. Makes 8 to 10 servings.

STUFFED TORTILLAS

1 pound ground round steak
1 tablespoon cooking oil
2 1-pound cans tomatoes
1 can tomato paste
2 cloves garlic, minced
2 teaspoons oregano
1 teaspon salt
⅛ teaspoon freshly ground
pepper

12 tortillas
12 slices of mozzarella cheese
(2 8-ounce packages)
1 pint of ricotta or cottage
cheese
¼ cup melted butter

Brown the meat in oil. Add the tomatoes, paste, garlic, oregano, salt, and pepper. Simmer gently for ½ hour. Meanwhile, place a slice of mozzarella cheese and a spoonful of ricotta on each tortilla. Roll the tortilla and place seam side down in a shallow baking dish. Pour the sauce down the center. Brush uncovered ends with melted butter. Bake for 15 to 20 minutes in a 350° F. oven. Makes 10 to 12 servings.

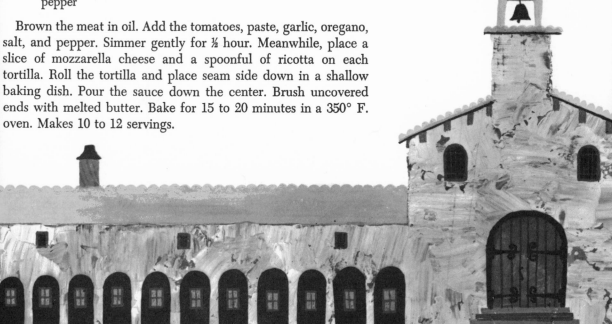

QUICHE LORRAINE

10-inch unbaked pie shell	2 cups light cream
½ pound grated Swiss cheese (3 cups)	1 tablespoon flour
½ pound bacon, fried	½ teaspoon cognac
4 eggs, well beaten	½ teaspoon salt
	Dash nutmeg

Bake the pie shell 6 to 8 minutes in 375° F. oven. Add the cheese and crumbled bacon, and pour on a mixture of the eggs beaten with cream, flour, cognac, and salt; sprinkle on the nutmeg. Continue to bake at 375° F. for 50 to 60 minutes or until the custard is set and golden. Makes 8 to 10 main dish servings.

CHILI CON CARNE

¼ cup corn oil	1 15-ounce can Italian tomatoes
1½ pounds lean round steak or chuck, ground	1 large or 2 small fresh tomatoes, peeled
1 1-pound can black or red kidney beans	1 clove garlic, crushed
2 to 4 tablespoons canned, peeled chili peppers	1 6-ounce can tomato paste

In a Dutch oven in 2 tablespoons hot oil cook the meat, stirring for 30 minutes or until very well done. Meanwhile, put the beans and chili peppers through food grinder. In 2 tablespoons hot oil cook the bean and pepper purée dry. Add the canned and fresh tomatoes, garlic, and tomato paste; cook 30 minutes longer; stir occasionally. Add this mixture to the cooked meat and continue cooking and stirring for another 30 minutes. The mixture will be thick. Serve hot over tortillas. Makes 1 quart.

GREEK RICE

1 cup raw regular rice	⅛ teaspoon pepper
¼ pound butter or margarine (½ cup)	½ pound ground sausage formed into tiny balls
1 cup white wine	1 pound sliced mushrooms
1¼ cups chicken bouillon	10 Greek or black olives, pitted and sliced
4 whole cloves	Parsley
1 small onion	
½ teaspoon salt	

Sauté the rice in butter till golden, stirring carefully to avoid burning butter or rice. Add the wine and bouillon. Stud the onion with cloves and add to the rice with salt and pepper. Bake, covered, 25 minutes in a 350° F. oven. Meanwhile brown the sausage balls on all sides and cook about 10 minutes or till done. Add the mushrooms to the sausage and sauté 2 minutes; drain off the fat. Add the sausage, mushrooms, and olives to cooked rice. Garnish with parsley. Makes 6 to 8 servings.

POTATOES SCALLOPED WITH HAM

1 pound sliced ham
2 thinly sliced onions,
    separated into rings
6 medium, thinly sliced
    potatoes
    Flour

Butter
Salt and pepper
1½ cups milk, or enough to
    cover
1 teaspoon minced parsley
    Bread crumbs

Butter a 2-quart baking dish, cover the bottom with small pieces of the ham. Add a layer of onions, and then potatoes. Sprinkle with flour, dot with butter, season with salt and pepper. Pour in milk to cover. Add more layers of ham, onions, and floured, seasoned potatoes, until the dish is three-quarters full. Pour in more milk to just cover the top layer of potatoes. Sprinkle parsley and a dusting of bread crumbs over the top. Dot with butter. Place the baking dish in a large pan with a little water in the bottom, to catch any over flow of milk as the potatoes cook. Bake in a 350° F. oven for 1¼ hours, or until the potatoes are tender. Makes 6 servings.

SPANISH WHEAT

3 strips bacon
3½ tablespoons chopped onion
1½ cups tomatoes

2 cups cooked cracked wheat
½ teaspoon salt

Cut the bacon into small pieces and fry until crisp. Remove the bacon; add the onion to the pan, and brown slightly. Mix the bacon fat, onion, pieces of bacon, and tomatoes with the cooked wheat, and season. Turn into a 1½-quart baking dish. Bake the mixture in a 350° F. oven 30 minutes. Serves 4 to 6.

SPANISH BEANS

6 slices bacon, diced
1 large peeled and minced
    onion
4 No. 303 cans red kidney
    beans
1 cup syrup drained from
    some canned fruit
¼ cup cider vinegar

1 bay leaf, crumbled
¼ teaspoon powdered thyme
1 pinch rosemary
1 teaspoon dry mustard
1 teaspoon salt
¼ teaspoon pepper
¼ cup strong coffee brew

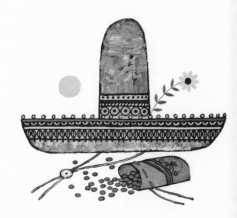

Combine bacon and onion in a Dutch oven or heavy kettle with a tight-fitting cover. Cook over low heat, stirring frequently, until the bacon is beginning to crisp and the onion is transparent. Add the remaining ingredients. Bring to a boil; cover and simmer for about 45 to 60 minutes, stirring occasionally with a fork, being careful not to break up beans. Add a little water from time to time if necessary to keep beans from sticking. Makes 6 servings.

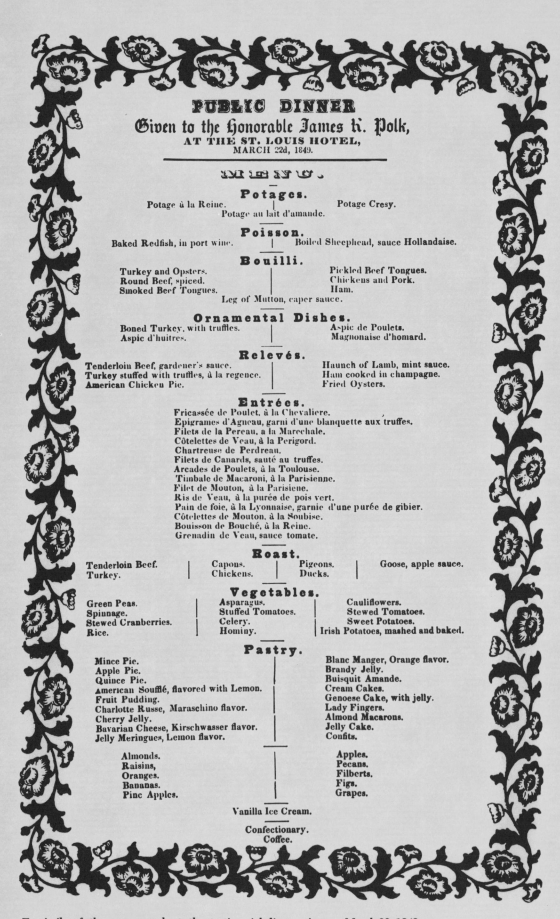

PUBLIC DINNER
Given to the Honorable James K. Polk,
AT THE ST. LOUIS HOTEL,
MARCH 22d, 1849.

MENU.

Potages.

Potage à la Reine. | Potage Cresy.

Potage au lait d'amande.

Poisson.

Baked Redfish, in port wine. | Boiled Sheephead, sauce Hollandaise.

Bouilli.

Turkey and Opsters.   Pickled Beef Tongues.
Round Beef, spiced.   Chickens and Pork.
Smoked Beef Tongues.   Ham.

Leg of Mutton, caper sauce.

Ornamental Dishes.

Boned Turkey, with truffles.   Aspic de Poulets.
Aspic d'huitres.   Magnonaise d'homard.

Relevés.

Tenderloin Beef, gardener's sauce.   Haunch of Lamb, mint sauce.
Turkey stuffed with truffles, à la regence.   Ham cooked in champagne.
American Chicken Pie.   Fried Oysters.

Entrées.

Fricassée de Poulet, à la Chevaliere.
Epigrames d'Agneau, garni d'une blanquette aux truffes.
Filets de la Pereau, a la Marechale.
Côtelettes de Veau, à la Perigord.
Chartreuse de Perdreau.
Filets de Canards, sauté au truffes.
Arcades de Poulets, à la Toulouse.
Timbale de Macaroni, à la Parisienne.
Filet de Mouton, à la Parisiene.
Ris de Veau, à la purée de pois vert.
Pain de foie, à la Lyonnaise, garnie d'une purée de gibier.
Côtelettes de Mouton, à la Soubise.
Bouisson de Bouché, à la Reine.
Grenadin de Veau, sauce tomate.

Roast.

Tenderloin Beef. | Capons. | Pigeons. | Goose, apple sauce.
Turkey. | Chickens. | Ducks. |

Vegetables.

Green Peas. | Asparagus. | Cauliflowers.
Spinnage. | Stuffed Tomatoes. | Stewed Tomatoes.
Stewed Cranberries. | Celery. | Sweet Potatoes.
Rice. | Hominy. | Irish Potatoes, mashed and baked.

Pastry.

Mince Pie.   Blanc Manger, Orange flavor.
Apple Pie.   Brandy Jelly.
Quince Pie.   Buisquit Amande.
American Soufflé, flavored with Lemon.   Cream Cakes.
Fruit Pudding.   Genoese Cake, with jelly.
Charlotte Russe, Maraschino flavor.   Lady Fingers.
Cherry Jelly.   Almond Macarons.
Bavarian Cheese, Kirschwasser flavor.   Jelly Cake.
Jelly Meringues, Lemon flavor.   Confits.

Almonds.   Apples.
Raisins,   Pecans.
Oranges.   Filberts.
Bananas.   Figs.
Pine Apples.   Grapes.

Vanilla Ice Cream.

Confectionary.
Coffee.

Facsimile of the menu used at the testimonial dinner given on March 22, 1849, in honor of James K. Polk at the St. Louis Hotel.

Kitchen, Oakley House
St. Francisville, Louisiana

Kitchen, Salem Tavern
Winston-Salem, North Carolina

The Tea Party (detail)
By Henry Sargent

The Christmas Turkey (detail)
By Francis William Edmonds

WESTERN OMELET

4 tablespoons butter or
  margarine
1½ cups onion sliced in rings
1 cup chopped green pepper
1 1-pound can tomatoes
½ teaspoon salt
¼ teaspoon cayenne pepper
1 cup cooked peas
6 eggs
Dash of salt and pepper

Sauté the onion rings and green pepper in 2 tablespoons of the butter until tender but not browned. Add the tomatoes and seasoning; cook for 10 minutes. Add the peas and cook for 3 minutes more. Remove from heat and keep the mixture warm. Beat the eggs with a dash of salt and pepper until fluffy. Heat the remaining 2 tablespoons of butter in a frying pan and, when sizzling, pour in the eggs and cook over low heat. As soon as all the mixture is set, place ½ cup of the sauce on top and fold over half of the eggs. Remove to a hot platter and surround with the remaining sauce. Makes 4 to 6 servings.

CORN FRITTERS

1⅓ cups sifted all-purpose flour
1 teaspoon salt
1½ teaspoons baking powder
⅔ cup milk
1 egg, beaten
2 cups cooked fresh or frozen
  corn
Shortening

Sift together the flour, salt, and baking powder. Combine the milk and egg and add to the dry ingredients. Mix just until moistened. Stir in the corn. Drop the batter from a tablespoon into hot fat in a deep fryer heated to 375° F. Fry until golden. Makes 12 to 15.

CABBAGE IN SOUR CREAM

1 small head cabbage, finely
  chopped (about 4 to 5
  cups)
1 egg, lightly beaten
¼ cup cider vinegar
1 tablespoon melted butter
1 teaspoon sugar
1 teaspoon salt
¼ teaspoon pepper
½ cup commercial sour cream
1 tablespoon finely chopped
  green pepper
Dash paprika

Cook the cabbage in boiling salted water until tender but still crisp, about 5 minutes. Drain well. In the top of a double boiler over hot water blend together the egg, vinegar, butter, sugar, salt and pepper. Cook, stirring, until thick, about 2 to 3 minutes. Cool slightly. Stir in the sour cream and green pepper. Pour over the drained cabbage in a bowl. Toss to coat well. Serve warm or chilled, sprinkled with paprika. Makes 6 servings.

HEARTS OF LETTUCE WITH GUACAMOLE

1 large ripe avocado	½ teaspoon salt
½ peeled and finely chopped ripe tomato	¼ teaspoon black pepper
	½ teaspoon olive oil
½ seeded and finely chopped green pepper	1 tablespoon lime juice
	½ cup mayonnaise
2 teaspoons grated onion	Hearts of lettuce
½ teaspoon chili powder	

Mash the avocado with a fork. Blend in the remaining ingredients except the mayonnaise. Spread the mayonnaise over the top of the dip to keep it from darkening. When ready to serve, blend in the mayonnaise. Serve as a dressing, on hearts of lettuce or as a dip.

STUFFED TOMATOES WITH SHRIMPS

6 tomatoes, skinned and chilled	3 tablespoons chili sauce
	1 tablespoon vinegar
1 pound or 2 cups cleaned and cooked shrimp	¼ cup mayonnaise
	Grated onion to taste
½ cup minced celery	Lettuce

Hollow out the tomatoes. Combine the remaining ingredients. Stuff the tomatoes with the mixture and serve on shredded lettuce with French dressing if desired. Makes 6 servings.

ESPAGNOLE SAUCE

1 carrot, chopped
1 large or 2 small onions,
   chopped
¼ cup fat
¼ cup all-purpose flour
1 quart beef bouillon
1 stalk celery

1 sprig parsley
1 small bay leaf
   Pinch thyme
1 clove garlic
2 tablespoons tomato sauce or
   ¼ cup tomato purée

In a heavy saucepan combine the chopped carrot and onions with the fat. Cook until the onions turn golden. Stir in the flour, cook and stir till the flour and onions are golden brown. Stir in 1½ cups of the bouillon; add celery and seasonings. Cook, stirring frequently, until the mixture thickens. Skim off any fat; add 1½ cups more stock and continue to cook over low heat, stirring occasionally, for about 1 hour or until the sauce is reduced to 1½ cups. Now add the tomato; cook a few minutes longer. Strain through a sieve or food mill. Add 1 cup more of bouillon and continue to cook slowly for about 1 hour or until the sauce is reduced to 2 cups. Correct the seasonings. Cool; refrigerate. Makes 2 cups.

CORNISH SPLITS

2 packages active dry yeast
½ cup lukewarm water
1 tablespoon sugar
¼ cup milk, scalded
½ cup butter or margarine

2 tablespoons shortening
½ teaspoon salt
½ cup granulated sugar
   About 4 cups sifted all-
     purpose flour

In small bowl soften the yeast in warm water with 1 tablespoon of sugar. To the milk add the butter, shortening, salt, and remaining sugar; when lukewarm, combine the yeast and milk mixture. Stir in enough flour to form a dough you can knead. Place the dough in a bowl; cover; set in a warm place to rise till doubled in bulk. Punch the dough down; shape into little rolls. Place on greased cookie sheets; let rise in a warm place till doubled in bulk. Bake in 400° F. oven about 20 minutes or till golden. Split and serve hot with butter. Makes about 2 dozen.

HUSH PUPPIES

2 cups cornmeal
2 teaspoons baking powder
1 teaspoon salt
½ cup minced onions

1 egg, beaten
⅔ cup milk
   Bacon fat (preferably left
     from fried fish)

Mix together the cornmeal, baking powder, and salt. Stir in the onions, egg, and milk. Mold into finger shapes and fry in hot bacon fat in which fish has been fried. Makes about 2 dozen.

PANETTONE

¼ cup currants
¼ cup brandy
2 packages active dry yeast
½ cup lukewarm water
2 tablespoons granulated sugar
1 cup all-purpose flour
2 eggs, beaten
1 cup granulated sugar
1 teaspoon salt
½ cup butter or margarine, cooled

½ cup lukewarm water
2 cups all-purpose flour
3 tablespoons sliced citron
1 tablespoon each diced candied orange and lemon peel
2 teaspoons lemon rind
Flour
1 egg yolk, slightly beaten

Put the currants to soak in brandy in a covered jar. Soften the yeast in lukewarm water. Add 2 tablespoons sugar and 1 cup flour; stir. Set the bowl in a warm place to rise. Combine the eggs with the remaining sugar, salt, butter, and water. Add to the sponge and stir, along with about 1 cup of the flour. Knead in the remaining cup of flour. Set the dough in a greased bowl; cover and let rise in a warm place till doubled in bulk. Punch down. Stir in the currants and brandy, candied fruits, and lemon rind. Knead again on a lightly floured board. Shape into a ball of dough about 6 inches in diameter. Place on a baking pan. Make several gashes in the top of the ball of dough. Let rise in a warm place until doubled in bulk; brush with yolk. Bake in 375° F. oven about 30 minutes or till golden. Makes 1 loaf 9 inches in diameter and about 3½ inches high.

ICE CREAM FREEZER

CHALLAH

1 package yeast	2 teaspoons salt
¼ cup lukewarm water	3 tablespoons oil
1 tablespoon sugar	5 to 6 cups flour
3 eggs	Poppy seeds
1 cup water	

Combine the yeast, warm water, and sugar and let stand until foamy. Beat the eggs (setting aside 2 tablespoons for future use). Add water, salt, oil, and yeast mixture. Sift 5 cups of flour into a large bowl, add the liquid and mix. Turn onto a board with the remaining flour and knead until smooth and satiny. Place in an oiled bowl, oil the surface lightly, cover with a wet towel. Let rise 1 hour, punch down, re-cover with the wet towel, and let double in bulk. Cut into equal parts to form a braid on a cookie sheet, or divide into 8 equal rounds for each of two loaf pans. Cover and let rise until double. Brush carefully with the reserved egg and sprinkle with poppy seeds. Bake at 375° F. for ½ hour.

SOURDOUGH STARTER

1 envelope of yeast	2 teaspoons salt
2½ cups warm water	1 tablespoon sugar
2 cups flour	

Sprinkle the yeast into ½ cup warm water and let stand for 5 minutes. Stir in 2 cups of warm water, flour, salt, and sugar. Put in a large crock or bowl (starter will bubble to about 4 times its volume). Cover loosely with a towel. Let stand in a warm place (80° to 90° F.) stirring down daily. In 3 or 4 days it is ready to use. When starter is withdrawn from the container replace it with equal amounts of water and flour.

SOURDOUGH BREAD

1 tablespoon melted butter or	½ teaspoon soda
margarine	1 teaspoon sugar
2 cups starter	2 cups flour

Add the butter to the starter. Add all the other ingredients and stir into the starter, adding enough flour to make a thick dough. Turn out on a board and work in enough additional flour to keep the dough from being sticky. Knead until smooth, put in a greased bowl and allow to rise in a warm place until almost doubled. Form it in a loaf, put in a greased tin and allow to double in width. Bake in a 375° F. oven for 30 minutes or until brown.

APPLE STRUDEL

1 egg, beaten
1 tablespoon salad oil
¾ cup warm water
2 cups all-purpose flour
½ teaspoon salt
1 cup butter or margarine, melted and cooled
3 pounds apples, peeled, cored and sliced thin

1 cup fine dry bread crumbs
1 lemon (sprinkle rind and juice over the apples)
1 cup granulated sugar
1 teaspoon cinnamon
1 cup currants or raisins
1 cup ground walnuts
Confectioners' sugar

To make the strudel dough combine the egg, oil, and water. Place the flour and salt in a large bowl and make a well in the center; pour in the egg mixture; stir well with a fork to form a soft dough. Turn the dough out onto a lightly floured surface. Put a little flour on your hand, start to slap or pull at the dough with palm of hand and fingers. It will be very sticky but the more you pull it up and down the better it will be. Use a knife to scrape your fingers clean and to gather the dough together on the board. Flour your hands again and repeat the pulling. It will take 100 or 200 pulls before the dough will be ready. It should start to form a smooth, blistery ball, pull away from the board and not be as sticky as in the beginning. Grease the ball of dough. Cover with a bowl and set in a warm place while you get filling ingredients ready.

To stretch the strudel dough place a clean tablecloth on a card table or kitchen table. Rub flour into the cloth to cover an area about 36 to 40 inches by 24 inches so the dough won't stick. Place the dough in the center of the cloth; with a floured rolling pin, roll dough into as large a square as possible. Using the palms of your hands start very gently pulling the dough outward. Hands will be between dough and floured cloth—keep working around the table gently pulling and stretching. Try not to poke any holes in the dough. When the dough is stretched so that it hangs well over table and is thin enough to see through, it is ready. Cut away any thick edges that might remain. Brush the entire surface with ¼ to ½ cup of the melted butter. Scatter bread crumbs over the buttered strudel, then apples tossed with lemon rind and juice, sugar mixed with cinnamon, currants, and nuts. With the aid of the cloth fold the short sides of the dough over the filling about 1 inch (so it won't fall out). Now, along the longest side, carefully roll as for jelly roll, using the cloth to help push the strudel. Cut the strudel in half and, with spatula, place in a well-buttered 15- x 10- x 2-inch baking pan. Brush with the remaining ½ to ¾ cup butter. Bake in a 400° F. oven 20 minutes. Brush with butter in the pan. Reduce heat to 350° F. and continue to bake and brush about 35 minutes or till golden. Cool in the pan 15 minutes, then cut into pieces and remove to a platter. Serve warm sprinkled with confectioners' sugar. Makes 16 servings.

TEACAKES

2 cups sugar
¾ cup mixed lard and butter, approximately half and half
3 eggs
½ teaspoon soda

3 tablespoons sour milk or buttermilk
1 cup flour
1 teaspoon baking powder
½ teaspoon nutmeg

Cream the sugar and shortening thoroughly. Add the eggs, well beaten. Dissolve the soda in the sour milk and add. Sift in the flour, baking powder, and nutmeg. Add enough flour to make a stiff dough. Refrigerate for several hours, or overnight. Roll *very* thin, using more flour as necessary, and cut with fluted cutters. Bake on greased cookie sheets for about 5 minutes, or until the edges begin to brown. The dough will keep in the refrigerator a week or more if kept covered. Makes 15 dozen.

JAPANESE TEA WAFERS

1 egg white
1 tablespoon sugar

1 tablespoon flour
½ teaspoon softened butter

Put the egg white in a bowl; add the sugar, stir a moment, and then add the flour and softened butter; beat with a wire whisk until well mixed (it should be about as thick as cream). Pour a teaspoonful of this batter on a cookie sheet, slightly greased, and with the back of the spoon spread in until about 4 inches in diameter and almost as thin as tissue paper. Bake at 350° F. till brown. While still warm roll around the handle of a wooden spoon. Do not double the recipe.

GLAZED ORANGE RING

1 cup butter
1 cup sugar
3 eggs, separated
Grated rind of 1 orange

1¾ cups sitted flour
1 teaspoon baking soda
1 teaspoon baking powder
1 cup dairy sour cream

Cream the butter and sugar. Beat in the egg yolks. Add the orange rind. Sift in the dry ingredients alternately with the sour cream. Beat the egg whites stiff, but not dry; fold into the mixture. Turn into a greased and floured 9-inch tube pan. Bake at 325° F. for 45 minutes. Remove from the oven and cool in the pan for about 10 minutes. Loosen carefully around the edges and turn out onto a large dessert plate with a rim. Pour hot glazed syrup slowly over it and into the center.

ORANGE GLAZE

1 cup sugar
½ cup hot water
1 teaspoon grated orange rind

2 tablespoons concentrated frozen orange juice, thawed

Cook the sugar, water, and grated rind until it is reduced to a thick syrup. Add the orange juice, stir in, and drizzle over warm cake.

OHIO PUDDING

4 eggs, well beaten
¼ cup brown sugar
½ cup each mashed cooked
   sweet potatoes and
   carrots (or squash)
1 teaspoon salt

1 cup fine dry bread crumbs
1 quart milk or light cream
1 teaspoon vanilla extract
   Granulated sugar or Cold
   Pudding Sauce

Combine the beaten eggs with brown sugar, mashed vegetables, salt, crumbs, milk, and vanilla. Pour into a well-greased 2-quart baking dish. Bake in 350° F. oven 1 hour 15 minutes or until a silver knife inserted in the center comes out clean. Eat warm with Cold Pudding Sauce, or when partially cool sprinkle with granulated sugar. Makes about 8 servings.

COLD PUDDING SAUCE

¼ pound of butter or
   margarine (½ cup)
1 to 1½ cups sifted
   confectioners' sugar

½ cup heavy cream
1 tablespoon lemon juice or 1
   teaspoon grated rind

Beat the butter; add the sugar, cream, and lemon and beat. Makes 1 cup.

COFFEE GRINDER

BLUEBERRY PIE

1 cup sugar
⅓ cup flour

½ teaspoon cinnamon
4 cups blueberries

Mix together the sugar, flour, and cinnamon. Mix the berries lightly with the flour mixture; reserve.

TWO-CRUST BUTTER PASTRY

2 cups flour
¾ teaspoon freshly grated
   nutmeg
1 cup butter or margarine

About ¼ cup water
1 tablespoon lemon juice
1½ tablespoons butter

Sift the flour with the nutmeg and cut in the 1 cup butter. Sprinkle with water, a tablespoon at a time, mixing lightly until all the flour is moistened. Press the dough into a ball; chill it for an hour. Roll out half the dough and line a 9-inch pie pan. Fill with the berry mixture, sprinkle with the 1 tablespoon lemon juice, and dot with the 1½ tablespoons butter. Roll out a top crust large enough to extend 1 inch beyond the edge of the pan, fold it in half, and make slits near the center for steam to escape. Moisten the edge of the bottom pastry with water, place the folded pastry on top and unfold. Leave a ½-inch rim of pastry beyond the edge of the pan and fold it under the edge of the lower pastry. Seal by pressing together with your fingers on the edge of the pan. Form a fluted edge if desired. Bake in a 425° F. oven for 35 to 45 minutes, or until bubbly and brown. Serve the pie warm.

MINNEHAHA CAKE

1½ cups sugar	2 cups flour
½ cup butter	1 teaspoon baking soda
3 eggs	½ cup milk
2 teaspoons cream of tartar	

Cream the butter and sugar. Add the slightly beaten eggs and mix well. Add cream of tartar to the flour and stir into the egg mixture. Add baking soda to the milk and lightly beat in. Pour into two 9-inch cake pans that have first been greased, wax-paper lined, and greased again. Bake at 350° F. for ½ hour.

FROSTING

½ cup sugar	2 egg whites
2 tablespoons water	1 teaspoon vanilla
¼ cup light corn syrup	1 cup raisins, chopped fine

Mix in a saucepan the sugar, water, and syrup. Bring to a boil and cook to 242° F. on a candy thermometer or until the syrup spins a 6- to 8-inch thread. Just before the syrup is ready beat the egg whites until stiff enough to hold a point. Pour the hot syrup very slowly in a thin stream into the beaten egg whites. Continue to beat until frosting holds a peak. Blend in the vanilla and raisins. Enough for filling and frosting two 9-inch cakes.

Recipes of Victorian America

ONE OVERPOWERING PERSONALITY so dominated two thirds of the 19th century that it gave name to the period and became a way of life. Queen Victoria's was a vigorous, sententious, unquenchable era.

At the beginning of it, when her name stood for the indomitability of the family, the open hearth was still the favored stage on which the immemorial rites of cookery were performed. At its close house-wives were learning to cook with gas. But the dishes presented in this chapter were prepared, for the most part, on an iron range, a gimcrack patented just before Victoria ascended the throne. And in 1884, when the range had its unmarked jubilee, the *Boston Cook Book* thus described it: "All stoves have a fire-box, with more or less space underneath for ashes; a slide damper under the fire, letting in the air; an outlet for the smoke; and a damper which regulates the supply of hot air, sending it around and underneath the oven, or letting it escape into the chimney." There is an air here of matter-of-factness, an absence of romanticism, that may perhaps just describe Victorianism.

This, along with hints on the care of the icebox and the iron sink (two other vanished phenomena) and notes on the Dover eggbeater and the new can opener, may seem as relevant today as a do-it-yourself manual for blacksmiths. But actually they signified that mechanization had reached the woman's world, that grocers stocked ready-to-eat and possible-to-keep vegetables and meats for the first time, that the tyranny of the seasons had been breached.

The cook books and the cooks were also a new breed. The old

COPPER

MEASURING POT

favorite "housekeepers' friend" and "receipt book" continued to be printed, but experts began to supplement the exhortations of the up-lifters with solid, well-organized information on how to run a house. At the beginning of this period, Mrs. Cornelius announced in the preface to *The Young Housekeeper's Friend:* "My aim has been to furnish to young housekeepers the best aid that a book can give . . . and to prevent very many of the perplexities which most young people suffer during the first years of married life. The receipts . . . are fur-nished from my own experience, or that of my immediate friends." About 40 years later, Mrs. Mary J. Lincoln, who acknowledged her debt to the previous compiler and others (in itself a change from the prevailing larceny), wrote in *The Boston Cook Book:* ". . . popular opinion now decides that no young lady's education is complete with-out a course of training in one or more branches of domestic work. And those who are not so fortunate as to have the best of all training —that of actual work under a wise and competent mother—gladly resort to the cooking-schools for instruction."

The "cooking-schools," like the range and the icebox, proved to be ephemeral. Catharine Beecher and other serious manual writers in the earlier part of the era provided the approach that would lead Juliet Corson to open a training school for women in New York in 1874. The Boston Cooking School (of which Mrs. Lincoln, cited above, was first principal) opened five years later, followed by Mrs. Sara Tyson Rorer's Philadelphia institution. The Boston school (especially under Fanny Farmer) became famous, but the future of academic cookery lay in the state colleges of agriculture. In 1890 a School of Domestic Science was formed at the University of Illinois. (An account of this development, and of almost anything relating to cookery, can be found in *The Everlasting Pleasure,* by Kathleen Ann Smallzried.) A legacy of the Victorian American period was the determination that, if the kitchen is to be woman's laboratory, she should be adequately trained to work therein.

Ironically, it turned out that the most celebrated practitioners of cookery would not be women, but the male chefs. The United States, also, was to have its Escoffier and Brillat-Savarin. The era closed with the publication of *The Table* by Alexander Filippini, longtime chef for the House of Delmonico, and *The Cook Book by "Oscar" of the Waldorf.* Its authors had served the gourmets of 19th-century America with dishes fit for a queen (though scarcely one as abstemious as Victoria), and richly deserved the laurels that crowned them the kings of cookery.

QUEEN VICTORIA'S FAVORITE GREEN PEA SOUP

1 quart fresh or frozen peas	2 cups water
½ cup fresh parsley	2 tablespoons butter or
¼ cup fresh mint	margarine
½ cup chopped green onions	1 teaspoon sugar
1 quart beef bouillon	Croutons

In a soup pot combine the peas, parsley, mint, green onions, and bouillon. Cook until the peas are thoroughly tender. You may need to add a little water. Drain the peas, reserving the liquid. Put the peas through a food mill or a blender. Return purée to the broth; reheat. Just before serving add the butter and sugar. Serve with croutons. Makes 2 cups or 4 servings.

MIKADO

Meat from ½ chicken breast, uncooked	1 to 2 tablespoons curry powder
¼ pound lean veal	¼ cup water
¼ pound lean lamb or mutton	Bouquet of herbs
¼ cup butter or margarine	2 teaspoons salt
2 quarts chicken broth	½ teaspoon pepper
½ cup minced onion	3 tablespoons raw, regular rice
½ cup minced green pepper	

Dice the chicken, veal, and lamb. Place the meat in hot butter in a soup pot; cook stirring for 5 minutes. Add the broth, then the onion and pepper. Moisten the curry with ¼ cup water and add to the broth with a bouquet of herbs, salt, and pepper. Cook 30 minutes. Add the rice and cook 30 minutes longer. Remove the bouquet, skim off any fat. Makes 6 to 8 servings.

ONION SOUP

5 tablespoons butter or margarine	2 quarts beef broth
2 large Bermuda onions, sliced	Salt
1 medium turnip or parsnip, peeled, sliced	Pepper
1 medium bunch of celery (leaves and stalks), chopped	1 tablespoon all-purpose flour

In a large saucepan, over medium heat, melt 4 tablespoons butter and sauté the onions until golden. Add the turnip, celery, and beef broth. Simmer for 1 hour. Taste, adding salt and pepper as needed. Pour the soup with vegetables through a strainer, rub the vegetables through; or put the soup through a blender. In the same large saucepan, blend the remaining butter and the flour over low heat until bubbly. Gradually stir in the puréed soup. Bring the soup to boil for 1 minute while stirring. Serve hot. Makes about 1½ quarts or 6 to 8 servings.

LOBSTER BISQUE

1 2-pound lobster	Salt
3 tablespoons butter	White pepper
3 tablespoons flour	Cayenne pepper
1 quart milk	

Plunge the live lobster into about 3 quarts of boiling, salted water in a large kettle. Cover and cook over low heat for 25 minutes. Drain; cool until easy to handle. Remove the meat and coral. Put the shells and spiny tissue into 2 cups of cold water

in a saucepan and boil for 20 minutes. Put the coral in a small pan and dry it out in a slow oven (about 5 minutes). Melt the butter in a saucepan. Stir in the flour. Gradually add the milk, stirring constantly, and cook over medium heat until the sauce is smooth and bubbling hot. Reduce the water on the shells if necessary to about ½ cup; strain. Add to the milk sauce. Rub the coral through a sieve and add. Season to taste with salt, pepper, and cayenne. Add the lobster meat and heat until just steaming hot. Do not boil. Makes 6 servings. If a thicker soup is preferred, use 4 tablespoons flour.

BONNE FEMME SOUP

2 medium heads lettuce, chopped fine
1 medium cucumber, chopped fine
½ cup chopped chervil leaves or ¼ cup snipped parsley
2 tablespoons butter or margarine
1 teaspoon ground nutmeg
2 teaspoons salt
¼ teaspoon pepper
Water
2 tablespoons all-purpose flour
1½ quarts veal stock or chicken broth
4 egg yolks
1 cup heavy cream
2 teaspoons granulated sugar

In a large saucepan, combine the lettuce, cucumber, chervil, butter, nutmeg, salt, pepper, and 1 cup water. Cover tightly and cook over medium heat for 10 minutes. Blend the flour with 2 tablespoons water and stir into the lettuce mixture. Add the veal stock or chicken broth, bring to a boil; reduce the heat, cover, and simmer for 30 minutes. Beat the egg yolks with the cream and sugar. Gradually stir into the hot soup. Serve with croutons. Makes 3 quarts or about 12 (1-cup) servings.

PROVOCATIVE · DELECTABLE · EXQUISITE · SCRUMPTIOUS · AMBROSIAL

FISHBALLS À LA MRS. BENJAMIN HARRISON

1½ pounds salt cod
3 medium-size potatoes
½ cup water
1 tablespoon butter, melted
⅛ teaspoon white pepper

About 3 tablespoons flour
¼ cup butter for frying
6 slices toast
6 poached eggs
6 slices crisp-cooked bacon

Cover the fish with cold water. Let stand for 12 hours. Drain.
Arrange the fish in a heavy saucepan or Dutch oven. Cover again
with cold water. Bring to a boil and drain. Return fish to the
pan. Peel the potatoes and slice them very thin; add to the fish.
Pour in the ½ cup of water. Cover and cook over low heat for
about 30 minutes, or until cod and potatoes are tender, adding
more water if necessary to keep from scorching. Remove from
the heat. Cool until the mixture can be handled easily. Remove
any bones from the fish and drain mixture well. Mash fish and
potatoes and blend in the melted butter and pepper. Form into
cakes about 3-inches in diameter and 1-inch thick. Dip well in
flour. Heat butter in a large skillet and fry cakes, turning to
brown both sides lightly. Serve cakes on slices of toast and top
each with a poached egg, then a strip of bacon. Makes 6 servings.

Salmi of Duck with Olives, page 129

Kitchen, Tower Grove House
St. Louis, Missouri

Kitchen, Kansas Farmhouse
Topeka, Kansas

CRAB RAVIGOTE

4 medium-sized hard-shell crabs or 2 6-ounce packages frozen crabmeat or 2 cans (6½ or 7½-ounces each) crabmeat
¼ teaspoon salt

Dash white pepper
¼ cup Remoulade Sauce
¼ cup mayonnaise
4 anchovy fillets
4 pickle slices

Cook fresh crabs in boiling, salted water to cover for 15 minutes or until the shells are a bright red. Cool and remove meat. Or cook frozen crab as the package directs. Flake meat well. (There will be about 2 cups flaked crab). Chill. Blend in the salt, pepper, Remoulade Sauce, and half the mayonnaise. Serve in shells if available. Top with remaining mayonnaise, anchovy fillets, and pickle slices. Makes 3 to 4 servings.

REMOULADE SAUCE

2 hard-cooked egg yolks
1 medium onion, grated
1 teaspoon powdered mustard
2 tablespoons olive oil

1 tablespoon vinegar
⅛ teaspoon salt
Dash cayenne pepper

Sieve the egg yolks. Blend in the onion, mustard, oil, vinegar, salt, and cayenne. Makes about ¾ cup sauce.

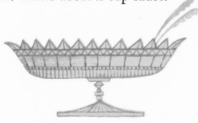

LITTLE PIGS IN BLANKETS

12 large oysters, well drained
Salt
Pepper

6 slices bacon, cut in half
3 slices toast, cut in quarters
Parsley

Dry the oysters thoroughly on paper towels. Sprinkle them with salt and pepper. Wrap each in bacon, fastening securely with toothpicks. Heat a heavy skillet. Fry "pigs" in the skillet until the bacon is crisp, turning to brown all sides. Serve on toast points and garnish with parsley. Makes 12.

BAKED SALMON WITH CREAM SAUCE

2 pounds center-cut salmon (in one piece)	½ teaspoon salt
	¼ teaspoon pepper
4 tablespoons butter	1½ cups light cream
3 tablespoons boiling water.	2 tablespoons chopped parsley
2 tablespoons cornstarch or 4 tablespoons flour	Capers (optional)

Butter a sheet of parchment paper (or heavy brown wrapping paper). Place the salmon in the center of the paper and wrap it up securely. Arrange the fish with folded ends of paper down in a shallow baking pan. Blend together 2 tablespoons of butter and the boiling water. Pour over the fish in its paper jacket. Cover and bake in 350° F. oven for about 40 minutes or until fish flakes easily but is still firm. Melt the remaining 2 tablespoons of butter in a small saucepan. Stir in the cornstarch, salt, pepper, and about ½ cup of the cream. Blend well. Add the remaining cream and cook over low heat, stirring constantly, until the sauce is smooth and thickened. Stir in the parsley. Remove paper from around salmon and arrange it on a serving platter. Pour about ½ cup of the sauce over and sprinkle if desired with capers. Serve the remaining sauce in a sauceboat. Makes 4 to 5 servings.

And after a hearty meal... the master slept

BROILED POMPANO

1 3-pound pompano or striped bass	¼ teaspoon pepper
	1 tablespoon melted butter
½ teaspoon salt	Cucumber sauce

Have the fish scaled, drawn and, if desired, head removed. Wash in cold water and dry it well on paper towels. Make 1-inch long slits to the bone along both sides of the fish, about 2-inches apart. Sprinkle with salt and pepper. Arrange the fish between bars of a wire grill and broil 5 minutes on both sides or until fish is easily flaked, or broil in broiler on rack, turning to brown both sides. Drizzle with melted butter and arrange on hot serving platter. Serve with Cucumber Sauce. Makes 6 to 8 servings.

CUCUMBER SAUCE

⅔ cup finely grated, peeled cucumber	¼ teaspoon salt
	Dash white pepper
¼ cup mayonnaise	

Crush the cucumber with a wooden spoon to extract the juice. Strain. Blend the juice into the mayonnaise and season to taste with salt and pepper. Makes about 1 to 1¼ cups sauce.

SALMI OF DUCK WITH OLIVES

2 ducks	½ onion
Salt	Salt and pepper
2 cups chicken bouillon	½ cup Madeira
1 carrot, peeled	½ cup Espagnole sauce
1 stalk celery	1 cup cut-up olives
1 sprig parsley	1½ cups duck broth
1 clove garlic	Croutons

Cut off wings, legs, and breast from the ducks. Place the remaining carcass in a soup pot and sprinkle with salt. Add the bouillon, carrot, celery, parsley, garlic, and onion to soup pot. Cook, covered, 15 minutes. Then drain off the broth and set aside. Meanwhile place the duck parts in a pan; sprinkle with salt and pepper. Roast in a 450° F. oven about 1 hour, turning the pieces once or twice, until they are tender and golden. Drain off all the fat from the ducks. Pour on the Madeira, Espagnole sauce, and olives. Skim any fat from the duck broth and pour the broth over all; return to the oven 15 minutes longer. Serve decorated with croutons. Makes 3 to 6 servings.

CHICKEN QUENELLES

½ cup stale bread crumbs	½ teaspoon salt
1 cup milk	⅛ teaspoon pepper
1 3-pound uncooked chicken, boned and skinned	¼ cup heavy cream
	3 eggs
1 tablespoon finely chopped salt pork	4 to 6 tablespoons butter or margarine
1 teaspoon grated onion	2 cups chicken broth
1 teaspoon lemon juice	

Cook together the bread crumbs and milk for about 10 minutes or until smooth. Chop or grind the chicken as fine as possible. Combine the chicken, salt pork, milk mixture, onion, lemon juice, salt, pepper, and cream. Separate the eggs and stir the yolks, one at a time, into the chicken mixture. Beat the whites until stiff; fold into the chicken mixture. With the aid of a tablespoon, slipped in boiling water each time, drop spoonfuls of chicken mixture into hot butter in a frying pan. When all of the quenelles are fried, pour on the broth; cover; cook gently 20 minutes. They may be served on mashed potatoes or fried bread with either Béchamel, mushroom, or olive sauce spooned over each, or if you prefer spoon over the broth in which they were cooked. Makes 8 to 10 servings.

ROYAL SWEETBREAD CROQUETTES

1 pair sweetbreads	1 cup light cream
1 double chicken breast, cooked	1 teaspoon salt
1 teaspoon onion juice	¼ teaspoon pepper
1 tablespoon chopped parsley	2 teaspoons lemon juice
½ teaspoon mace	2 eggs, lightly beaten
2 tablespoons butter	⅝ to ¾ cup fine cracker crumbs
3 tablespoons flour	Fat for frying

Cook the sweetbreads in boiling salted water to cover, simmering for 15 minutes or until tender. Drain. Let cool until the meat can be easily handled. Remove membrane from the sweetbreads and chop fine. Skin the chicken and discard bones. Chop or grind (there will be about 2½ cups chopped chicken). In a bowl blend together the sweetbreads, chicken, onion juice, parsley, and mace. Melt the butter in a saucepan. Stir in the flour, cream, salt, and pepper. Cook, stirring, over low heat until the sauce begins to boil and is smooth and very thick. Remove from the heat. Slowly stir in the lemon juice. Stir the sauce into the sweetbread mixture, blending well. Chill mixture until very firm, at least ½ hour. Form into 12 balls about the size of golf balls. Roll them in the beaten egg, then crumbs. Dip again in the egg, then again roll in crumbs. Fry in hot fat. Makes 6 servings.

SAUTÉD SWEETBREADS IN CHAMPAGNE

2 pairs of sweetbreads (1 to 1¼ pounds)	Ice water
1 teaspoon dried parsley	1 cup chilled, extra-dry champagne
½ teaspoon oregano	1 egg, beaten
3 whole peppercorns	½ cup bread crumbs
½ teaspoon salt	¼ teaspoon pepper
2 teaspoons cider vinegar	½ teaspoon salt
3 to 4 cups boiling water	¼ pound butter (½ cup)

Place the sweetbreads in a deep pot; add the parsley, oregano, peppercorns, salt, and vinegar. Pour boiling water over the sweetbreads; simmer 15 minutes. Lift from the pot or drain off the water. Plunge the sweetbreads into ice water to blanch. Take off membranes and skin and remove any tubelike portions. Put the sweetbreads on a flat plate and place another plate on top as a weight; refrigerate for 1 hour.

Place the sweetbreads in a bowl; pour on the champagne; marinate 30 minutes. Reserve the champagne. Slice the sweetbreads in half laterally. Dip them in the egg, then crumbs seasoned with salt and pepper. Sauté in butter in a heavy skillet until golden brown; remove to a platter. Pour the champagne into the skillet, cook down; pour over the sweetbreads; serve at once. Makes 2 to 3 servings.

Facsimile of a drawing of a table setting and description of a summer lunch for 8 people (ca. 1885)

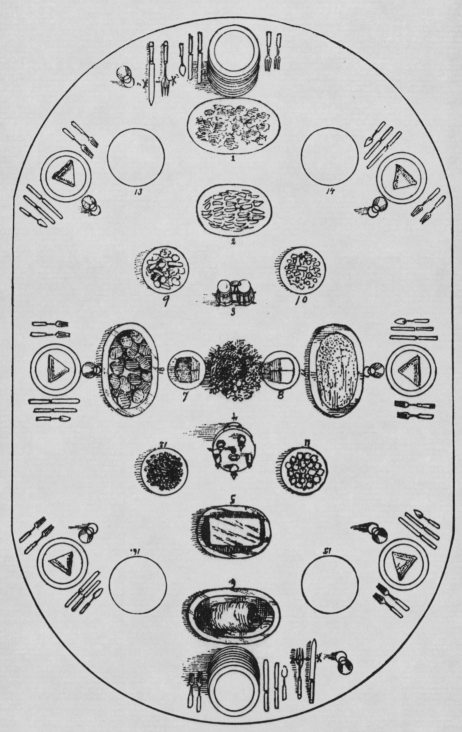

SUMMER LUNCH,
FOR 8 COVERS.

1.	Soft shell crabs.	7.	Brown bread.	13.
2.	Frozen peaches or fruits.	8.	White bread.	14.
3.	Pickles.	9.	Cakes.	15.
4.	Cruet.	10.	Candies.	16.
5.	Ice cream.	11.	Fancy biscuit.	17. Green pease.
6.	Roast lamb.	12.	Chocolate bon bons.	18. Fried Egg plant.

13. ⎫
14. ⎬ Fruit
15. ⎬ you may choose.
16. ⎭
17. Green pease.
18. Fried Egg plant.

In the center—flowers.

ESCALOPS OF VEAL À LA PROVENÇALE

6 veal cutlets (about 1
  pound)
Salt
Pepper
2 tablespoons olive oil
½ cup minced onions
½ cup beef bouillon

1 8-ounce can Spanish-style
  tomato sauce
3 mushrooms, chopped
2 cloves garlic, crushed
1 teaspoon chopped parsley
6 slices buttered toast

Sprinkle the meat with salt and pepper. Brown in hot oil, about 5 minutes for each side. Add the onions and cook until golden. Add the bouillon, sauce, mushrooms, and garlic. Bring the sauce to a boil, then simmer about 10 minutes or until the meat is fork-tender. Sprinkle with parsley. Serve on toast. Makes 6 servings.

BEEF ROULADE

1 cup very finely chopped
  ham
1 egg, lightly beaten
1 teaspoon prepared
  mustard
Pinch cayenne pepper
1 tablespoon water
2 pounds top round beef, cut
  into 6 very thin pieces

Flour
¼ cup bacon fat
1 cup minced onion
1 pint boiling water
2 cloves
½ teaspoon salt
¼ teaspoon pepper

Combine the ham, egg, mustard, cayenne, and water. Use to spread over 6 pieces of beef; roll each up and tie with string. Dredge the meat rolls in flour (about ¼ cup). Brown the meat in fat; remove from the pan. Add the onions to pan and sauté until golden, then add 2 tablespoons flour; stir for 3 minutes. Stir in the boiling water and return the sauce to boiling. Return meat rolls to sauce. Add the cloves, salt, and pepper. Simmer, covered, 3 hours, turning meat rolls once. Serve hot with the sauce strained. Makes 6 servings.

BRAISED BEEF TONGUE

1 4- to 4½-pound smoked beef
  tongue
2 tablespoons butter
3 tablespoons flour
1 quart beef stock or 2 cans
  bouillon with enough
  water to make 1 quart
1 medium-size peeled and
  sliced onion

1 scraped carrot, cut in
  quarters
1 pared, sliced potato
Sprigs parsley
2 small bay leaves
1 tablespoon Worcestershire
  sauce
1 tablespoon mushroom
  catsup

Cover the tongue with boiling water and simmer, covered, for 2 hours. Remove the tongue from the broth. Cool it until it can be easily handled. Cut away the tough portion near the root; skin and remove the bone. Tie the tip of the tongue around the side, fastening it securely. In a baking pan brown the butter; stir in the flour. Gradually stir in the stock. Cook until the sauce is smooth. Add the remaining ingredients and tongue. Cover and bake in a 350° F. oven for 1 hour or until very tender, basting every 15 minutes. Remove the tongue to a warm platter, reduce the sauce to about 1 pint. Strain over the tongue. Makes 8 servings.

CALF'S LIVER MARINÉ

3 pounds calf's liver (in one piece)
Salt
Pepper
4 to 6 slices bacon

2 onions, peeled and sliced
2 thin pieces salt pork, sliced
2 tablespoons vinegar
1 tablespoon olive oil
½ cup claret

Sprinkle the liver with salt and pepper. Cover the liver with strips of bacon; tie up. Place the onions and salt pork in the bottom of a Dutch oven; pour on the vinegar and oil. Refrigerate for 24 hours.

Cook covered over low heat for 1 hour; turning once or twice, then add the claret and cook 20 to 30 minutes longer. Makes 12 servings.

TRIPE À LA BORDELAISE

1½ pounds tripe
1 teaspoon salt
¼ teaspoon pepper
1 onion
1 tablespoon oil
¼ teaspoon each salt and thyme
1 bay leaf
6 whole peppercorns
1 tablespoon lemon juice
1 clove garlic, crushed

¾ to 1 cup flour
2 eggs, well beaten
¾ to 1 cup fine bread crumbs
6 to 8 tablespoons butter or margarine
1 teaspoon finely chopped parsley
1 tablespoon lemon juice
1 teaspoon meat glaze
Nutmeg

Wash the tripe. Cook the tripe in water to cover with 1 teaspoon salt, ¼ teaspoon pepper, and the onion for 2 hours or until tender; drain. Cut the cooked tripe into 12 pieces. Marinate them 1 to 2 hours in the oil mixed with salt, thyme, bay leaf, peppercorns, lemon juice, and garlic. Roll the pieces of drained tripe first in flour, then in egg, and then in bread crumbs. Sauté the pieces in butter till golden brown on each side. Keep warm on a platter. In the same pan melt 1 tablespoon more of butter; add the parsley, lemon juice, meat glaze, and a dash of nutmeg. Pour over the tripe just before serving. Makes 4 to 6 servings.

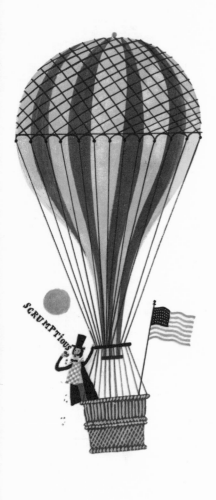

CURRY OF LAMB À L'INDIENNE

3 pounds boned lamb shoulder, cut in 2-inch pieces
2 tablespoons salt
1 teaspoon pepper
6 small onions, peeled
1 sprig parsley
1 stalk celery
1 bay leaf
1 carrot, peeled
¼ cup butter or margarine
¼ cup flour
4 egg yolks, lightly beaten
2 tablespoons lemon juice
2 to 4 tablespoons curry
½ cup water
Hot rice

Wash the meat; drain. Put the meat in a saucepan with 1 quart of water; bring to a boil; drain. Pour 1 quart of boiling water over the meat with salt, pepper, onions, parsley, celery, bay leaf and carrot. Cook covered 40 minutes. Then in another pot melt the butter with the flour to form a smooth paste. Drain liquid from the meat (about 3 cups) into this and cook, stirring, until the mixture thickens. Mix the yolks with lemon juice. Stir a little hot sauce into the yolks, then quickly stir the yolks into the rest of the sauce. Dilute the curry in water; add to the sauce. Pour the hot sauce over lamb. Serve with a border of hot rice. Makes 8 to 10 servings.

LAMB KIDNEYS SAUTÉ

2 teaspoons butter or margarine
2 teaspoons flour
½ cup beef bouillon
1 tablespoon chopped onion
1 teaspoon chopped parsley
1 bay leaf
½ teaspoon salt
⅛ teaspoon pepper
¼ cup Madeira or sherry
6 lamb kidneys, sliced thin
¼ cup chopped mushrooms
1 slice of bacon, cooked
Croutons

Melt the butter in a saucepan; stir in the flour to form a smooth paste, then stir in the broth. Cook, stirring, till smooth and thickened. Add the onion, parsley, bay leaf, salt, pepper, and wine. Cook for a few minutes. Add the kidneys and mushrooms and simmer 5 to 6 minutes. Sprinkle on the crumbled bacon. Garnish with croutons. Makes 2 servings.

STUFFED PORK CHOPS

8 double loin pork chops
    trimmed of fat
2 tablespoons finely chopped
    onions
2 tablespoons finely chopped
    celery
4 tablespoons butter or
    margarine
1½ cups bread crumbs

½ teaspoon powdered sage
4 tablespoons chopped parsley
1 apple, chopped
½ teaspoon salt
⅛ teaspoon pepper
1 egg
Flour
1 cup milk

Cut a pocket in each chop along the edge, or have your butcher do it. Sauté the onion and celery in 1 tablespoon butter until tender. Add the crumbs, sage, parsley, apple, salt, pepper, and egg. Stuff the chops and fasten with a metal skewer. Flour the chops lightly and brown in a frying pan in the remaining butter. Remove to a shallow casserole. Pour in milk, cover with foil and bake in a 325° F. oven for 40 minutes. Turn once. Cook uncovered for 10 minutes more. Makes 8 servings.

LIVER PATÉ

1 can (10½ ounces)
    condensed consommé
10½ ounces tomato juice
1 tablespoon lemon juice
¼ teaspoon tabasco sauce
1½ teaspoons red food coloring

2 envelopes unflavored
    gelatin
½ pound braunschweiger
3 ounces cream cheese
1 tablespoon grated onion

Mix the consommé, tomato juice, lemon, tabasco, coloring, and gelatin. Put the mixture into a 1-quart mold and allow to congeal to a thickness of about ½ inch. Pour or scoop out the unjelled center and reserve it. Combine the braunschweiger, cheese, and onion, and fill the center of the mold with it. Replace the gelatin mixture to the top of the mold, and chill until firm. Unmold and garnish with watercress or parsley.

CHICKEN MOUSSE

1 5-pound chicken
3 stalks celery with tops
1 scraped carrot
1 bay leaf
5 cups water
1 tablespoon salt
3 envelopes gelatin dissolved
   in ½ cup cold water
¼ teaspoon white pepper
1 cup mayonnaise
1½ cups diced celery heart

1 teaspoon Worcestershire
   sauce
2 tablespoons lemon juice
1 cup blanched, toasted,
   slivered almonds
1 cup heavy cream, whipped
2 cups pineapple chunks,
   fresh, or 1 No. 2 can
1 cup white seedless grapes
   Bibb lettuce or watercress

Simmer the chicken with the celery, carrot, and bay leaf in salted water until tender. Cool. Remove the chicken and strain the broth; there should be 4½ cups. Skin, bone, and dice chicken. Add the dissolved gelatin to the broth and put in the refrigerator until it begins to set. Add the chicken, pepper, mayonnaise, celery, Worcestershire, lemon juice, and almonds. Fold in the whipped cream. Oil a 3-quart mold or 2 3-pint molds and fill. Chill for at least 6 hours before turning out on a plate. Garnish with pineapple and grapes and surround with lettuce or watercress if desired. Makes 16 servings.

SCALLOPED EGGPLANT

1 large eggplant, peeled
   Salt
2 cups dry bread cubes
   Water
   Shortening or cooking oil
4 firm tomatoes, peeled and
   sliced, or 2 (1-pound)
   cans peeled tomatoes

½ teaspoon salt
   Dash pepper
   Dash cayenne
1 tablespoon dry bread
   crumbs
1 tablespoon butter or
   margarine

Slice the eggplant ¼ inch thick into a deep bowl; sprinkle salt over the slices and let stand in a cool place for about 1 hour. Soak the bread cubes in cold water. In a skillet, heat the shortening or oil. Drain the eggplant slices, pat dry, then fry on both sides until brown. Drain on paper towels and set aside. In the same skillet, pour off all but 2 tablespoons of oil; fry the tomato slices (or canned tomatoes) until lightly brown, about 5 minutes. Press the water from the soaked bread and add the bread to the tomatoes in the skillet; add ½ teaspoon salt, and the pepper and

Six stove advertisements (1852-1878) from the J. R. Burdick Collection, courtesy of the Metropolitan Museum of Art

cayenne. Stir over low heat to blend well. Preheat the oven to 425° F. In a 1½-quart baking dish, layer the eggplant alternately with the tomato mixture. Sprinkle the top with bread crumbs, dot with butter. Bake for 25 minutes or until the top is browned. Makes 4 to 6 servings.

VOL-AU-VENT OF EGGS

1 beaten egg for glaze	Puff paste

Preheat the oven to 450° F. On a floured pastry cloth, roll out puff paste ¼ inch thick. Cut out 8 rounds with a 2½-inch cutter. Place on an ungreased baking sheet. Brush the surface with cold water and top each circle with another circle. Now with smaller cutter about 1½ inches in diameter, make a cut in center of each top circle, but not through bottom circle. Brush the surfaces with beaten egg. Bake for 5 minutes, then reduce the heat to 375° F. and continue baking for 25 to 30 minutes. Use immediately.

MUSHROOM PURÉE

1 pound mushrooms, stems removed	1 tablespoon butter or margarine
¾ cup milk	1 teaspoon salt
2 cups soft bread cubes	¼ teaspoon pepper

Chop the mushroom caps. In a small saucepan, simmer the mushrooms with milk for 10 minutes. Add the bread cubes and stir over low heat until the mushroom mixture has thickened. Add the butter, salt, and pepper. Press through a sieve or put through a blender. Makes scant 3 cups.

FILLING

6 beaten eggs	½ cup grated Parmesan cheese
¾ cup prepared tomato sauce	

To serve, lightly scramble the eggs in a buttered skillet. Now fill vol-au-vent patty shells on baking sheet—lift off cap and layer alternately mushroom purée, scrambled eggs, and hot tomato sauce. Sprinkle layers with grated cheese and replace top. Makes 6 to 8 servings.

Facsimile of a list of minimum utensils recommended for every kitchen of the 1880's. From Miss Parloa's *New Cook Book* (1884)

Two cast-iron pots, size depending upon range or stove (they come with the stove).
One griddle.
One porcelain-lined preserving kettle.
One fish kettle.
Three porcelain-lined stew-pans, holding from one to six quarts.
One No. 4 deep Scotch frying kettle.
One waffle iron.
Three French polished frying-pans, Nos. 1, 3 and 6.
Four stamped tin or granite ware stew-pans, holding from one pint to four quarts.
One double boiler, holding three quarts.
One Dover egg-beater.
One common wire beater.
One meat rack.
One dish pan.
Two bread pans, holding six and eight quarts respectively.
Two milk pans.
Two Russian-iron baking pans—two sizes.
Four tin shallow baking pans.
One smaller dredger for salt.
One, still smaller, for pepper.
One boning knife.
One French cook's knife.
One butcher's knife.
One large fork.
Two case-knives and forks.
Two vegetable knives.
Four large mixing spoons.
Two table-spoons.
Six teaspoons.
One larding needle.
One trussing needle.
One set of steel skewers.
One wire dish cloth.
One whip churn.
One biscuit cutter.
One hand basin.
One jagging iron.
Three double broilers—one each for toast, fish and meat.
One long-handled dipper.
One large grater.
One apple corer.
One flour scoop.
One sugar scoop.
One lemon squeezer.
Chopping tray and knife.
Small wooden bowl to use in chopping.
Four deep pans for loaves.
Two quart measures.
One deep, round pan of granite-ware, with cover, for braising.
One deep Russian-iron French roll pan.
Two stamped tin muffin pans.
One tea-pot.
One coffee-pot.
One coffee biggin.
One chocolate pot.
One colander.
One squash strainer.
One gravy strainer.
One strainer that will fit on to one of the cast-iron pots.
One frying-basket.
One melon mould.
Two brown bread tins.
One round pudding mould.
Two vegetable cutters.
One tea canister.
One coffee canister.
One cake box.
One spice box.
One dredger for flour.
One for powdered sugar.
Moulding board of good *hard* wood.
Board for cutting bread on.
One for cutting cold meats on.
Thick board, or block, on which to break bones, open lobsters, etc.
A rolling pin.
Wooden buckets for sugar, Graham, Indian and rye meal.
Wooden boxes for rice, tapioca, crackers, barley, soda, cream of tartar, etc.
Covers for flour barrels.
Wire flour sieve—not too large.
A pail for cleaning purposes.
One vegetable masher.
Stone pot for bread, holding ten quarts.
One for butter, holding six quarts.
One for pork, holding three quarts.
One dust pan and brush.
One scrubbing brush.
One broom.
One blacking brush.
Four yellow earthen bowls, holding from six quarts down.
Four white, smooth-bottomed bowls, holding one quart each.
Six cups, holding half a pint each.
One bean pot.
One earthen pudding dish.

STEAMED STUFFED ONIONS

8 large onions, peeled
1 cup sausage meat (about ¼ pound)
1 cup fresh bread crumbs
1 egg, lightly beaten
Salt
Pepper
1 cup beef bouillon

Boil the onions in salted water to cover for 10 minutes; drain. Push or cut out the centers of the onions to make a hole for stuffing. Chop up enough of the centers to make 1 cup. Combine the chopped onions with the sausage, bread crumbs, egg, salt, and pepper to taste. Stuff the onion shells with the sausage mixture. Place the stuffed onions in a 12- x 8- x 2-inch baking dish. Pour bouillon around onions; cover with foil. Bake in a 400° F. oven 30 minutes. Remove the foil; baste onions occasionally, baking 15 to 20 minutes longer or until the stuffing is golden. Makes 8 servings.

COLUMBUS EGGS

4 green peppers
8 eggs
Salt
Pepper
4 to 8 slices of toast
Tomato sauce, heated (canned or your own)

Cut the peppers in half; remove the seeds. Plunge the peppers into boiling water for a few minutes; drain. Place them in a shallow baking pan. Carefully break one egg into each pepper half. Sprinkle the eggs with salt and pepper. Bake in 425° F. oven 15 to 20 minutes or until the eggs are the desired consistency. Serve one or two on toast with tomato sauce spooned over them. Makes 4 to 8 servings.

EGGS, MAÎTRE D'HÔTEL

6 hard-cooked eggs, shelled
4 tablespoons butter
½ teaspoon each chopped tarragon and chervil
1 teaspoon chopped parsley
Salt
Pepper
4 slices toast

Cut the eggs in halves or quarters. Place the eggs in a pan with butter cut into pieces. Sprinkle with the parsley, tarragon, chervil, salt, and pepper. Heat in 350° F. oven about 5 minutes, turning once. Serve on toast. Makes 4 servings.

SUÉDOISE SALAD

1 8-ounce jar fillet of herring, boned
1½ cups cooked, peeled, diced potatoes
1 cup diced, cooked tongue
½ cup diced, cooked beets
½ cup peeled, diced apples
¼ cup diced, cooked carrots
1 tablespoon vinegar
1½ tablespoons olive oil
1 teaspoon prepared mustard
Chopped parsley

Cut the herring in small pieces. Combine the herring with the rest of ingredients except the parsley. Mix well together, then transfer to a serving bowl. Garnish with parsley. Makes 6 servings.

WALDORF SALAD

2 cups peeled, diced apple
½ cup diced celery
2 tablespoons mayonnaise

¼ cup chopped walnuts
(optional)

Combine the apple, celery, mayonnaise, and if desired walnuts. Toss to coat well. Makes 4 servings.

SPINACH SOUFFLÉ WITH GLAZED CARROTS

2 tablespoons butter
3 tablespoons flour
1 cup milk
3 eggs
1 cup chopped, drained, cooked spinach
2 tablespoons grated onion
1 teaspoon salt
⅛ teaspoon pepper

¼ teaspoon nutmeg
2 cups small, baby, cooked carrots or 1-pint can carrots
3 tablespoons butter
2 tablespoons brown sugar
1 tablespoon concentrated orange juice or curaçao

Make a cream sauce with the first three ingredients. When the sauce is thick, cool slightly and mix in the egg yolks. Add the spinach, onion, salt, pepper, and nutmeg. Beat the egg whites and carefully fold in the spinach mixture. Pour into a 5½-cup ring mold. Set the mold in a pan of hot water and bake in a 350° F. oven for about 55 minutes. Let stand 10 minutes before unmolding on a warm platter and fill with glazed carrots.

Sauté the drained carrots in butter and sugar. Add orange juice or liqueur just before removing from the heat. Makes 4 servings.

oh, no never
GIVE a CARROT
TO A
PARROT

PARKER HOUSE ROLLS

2 packages active dry yeast
½ cup warm water
2 cups milk, scalded
¼ cup granulated sugar

Butter or margarine
2 teaspoons salt
About 7 cups all-purpose flour

Dissolve the yeast in warm water. In a large bowl combine the milk, sugar, ¼ cup butter, and salt; cool to lukewarm. Stir in half the flour, then the yeast. Beat thoroughly. Gradually stir in the remaining flour until a soft dough is formed. Turn the dough out on a floured board and knead until smooth and elastic. Place the dough in a greased bowl, brush with melted butter, cover and let rise in a warm place (80° F.) until double in bulk, about 2 hours. Turn out on a floured board, roll dough ½ inch thick. Cut with a floured 2½-inch round cutter. With the back of a knife make a crease across the center of each round. Place a dot of butter in the center, fold over, enclosing the butter. Pinch the sides to seal. Place the rolls 1 inch apart on a greased baking sheet, brush with melted butter. Let the rolls rise until double. Bake at 400° F. for 15 minutes. Makes about 4 dozen rolls.

BRIOCHE

1 package active dry yeast	¼ pound soft butter or mar-
¼ cup warm water	garine (½ cup)
2½ cups sifted all-purpose flour	½ teaspoon salt
2 tablespoons sugar	2 eggs, well beaten
½ cup milk, scalded	1 egg yolk, beaten

Sprinkle the yeast over warm water; let stand a few minutes to dissolve. Add ½ cup of the flour and 1 tablespoon of the sugar to the yeast; cover; let rise in a warm place.

In a large bowl put the rest of the flour. To the milk add the butter, remaining sugar, and salt; cool to lukewarm. Stir the milk mixture and the 2 eggs into the flour. Mix until the dough is smooth. Stir in the yeast mixture. Stir and knead well. Place in a greased bowl, cover, let rise in a warm place 2 to 2½ hours or until doubled in bulk. Punch down. Pinch off a lump of dough. Mold the rest of the dough into a ball large enough to half-fill a brioche mold or bowl-shaped baking pan (1½ quart capacity). Make a crisscross incision in the top of the dough in bowl, gently insert the smaller ball of dough in the crisscross. Cover; set in a warm place to rise. When the dough is double in bulk, brush the surface lightly with egg yolk. Bake in a 425° F. oven until the brioche is brown and shining; about 50 minutes. Makes about 8 servings.

Individual Brioches: The dough may be divided between 8 well-buttered small brioche or custard cups. Bake about 20 to 30 minutes.

MARYLAND BISCUITS

1 cup all-purpose flour	¼ teaspoon salt
2 teaspoons double-acting	½ cup heavy cream
baking powder	

Preheat the oven to 400° F. In a medium bowl, sift the flour with the baking powder and salt; blend in the cream.

Knead to a smooth dough. On a floured board, roll out, fold dough over twice, roll out again, fold over and roll out to a 1-inch thick round. Place on a greased baking sheet and bake for about 15 minutes or until golden. Cool on a rack. Just before serving, split the shortcake, brush inside with melted butter and stack. May be filled with sliced strawberries and whipped cream, or served as is, cut into wedges. Makes about 4 servings.

BAKING POWDER BISCUITS

2 cups all-purpose flour
1 tablespoon double-acting
   baking powder

1 teaspoon salt
¼ cup shortening
¾ cup milk

Sift the flour into a bowl with the baking powder and salt. With a pastry blender or 2 knives scissors-fashion blend in the shortening. Stir in the milk. Knead the dough on a lightly floured board for about ½ minute. Roll ¼- to ½-inch thick; cut with a floured biscuit cutter. Bake on a well-greased cookie sheet in 450° F. oven for 15 minutes or till golden. Makes about 1 dozen.

POPOVERS

Butter or margarine
3 eggs
2 cups milk

2 cups sifted all-purpose flour
1 teaspoon salt

Grease 12 muffin cups generously with butter; place in a 375° F. oven to get hot. Meanwhile, quickly beat the eggs; add the milk. Carefully stir the milk mixture into the flour and salt, being careful not to get lumps. Pour the batter into hot muffin cups. Bake in a 375° F. oven 45 minutes or until popovers are high and golden brown. Loosen each popover. Serve hot. Makes 12 servings.

HAYES CAKE

½ cup butter or margarine,
   softened
1 cup granulated sugar
3 eggs, beaten
1 teaspoon baking soda

½ cup buttermilk or sour milk
2 cups sifted cake flour
1 teaspoon lemon extract
1 teaspoon grated lemon rind

Preheat the oven to 350° F. In a large bowl, beat together the butter, sugar, and eggs, until light and creamy. Stir the soda into the milk and add alternately with the flour to the butter mixture. Beat until smooth; add the lemon extract and rind. Pour the batter into greased 8- x 8- x 2-inch baking pan. Bake for about 50 minutes or until the cake tests done. Cool on a rack. Cut into squares. Makes 9 to 12 servings.

FRENCH PANCAKES

3 eggs, well beaten
½ teaspoon salt
¼ cup confectioners' sugar
1 cup milk

2 tablespoons melted shortening
1 cup sifted all-purpose flour
Confectioners' sugar

In a blender or shaker or mixing bowl, beat together the eggs, salt, sugar, milk, and melted shortening. Shake or beat well. Gradually beat in the flour. In a greased and heated 6-inch skillet, pour in about 1 tablespoon of batter; tilt the pan to spread the batter evenly on the bottom. Bake until dry on top and lightly brown on the bottom; then flip over to lightly brown the other side. Turn out to cool slightly. Fold in quarters and sprinkle with sugar or serve in a liqueur sauce. Makes about 16 crêpes or pancakes.

**Kitchen, Peter Crawford House
Kelso, Washington**

**Kitchen, Old Wade House
Greenbush, Wisconsin**

**Keeping room, Joseph Smith Homestead
Nauvoo, Illinois**

On the Plains—Preparing To Feed (detail)
By J. Goldsborough Bruff

GERMAN PANCAKES

Preheat oven to 425° F. Prepare the batter as for French Pancakes. Heat a heavy 7-inch, well-greased skillet, and pour in 8 ounces of batter (half of the mixture); cook on top of range over medium heat for 2 minutes to lightly brown bottom. Quickly set skillet in the hot oven for about 15 to 25 minutes until the pancake is puffed, dry on top, and lightly browned. Slide out on a heated platter and make a second pancake with the rest of the batter. Sprinkle with powdered sugar, serve with lemon wedges. Cut the pancakes into wedges. Makes 2 7-inch cakes, about 4 to 6 servings.

MINT APPLES

6 small apples (firm cooking apples)
1 package lime gelatin
1 cup boiling water

6 teaspoons crème de menthe liqueur
6 sprigs mint leaves

Peel and core the apples; place them in a small saucepan in which they will fit together, just touching. Dissolve the gelatin in water, spoon over the apples. Cover and simmer gently for 5 minutes. Remove the cover and continue cooking, basting and turning completely with a spoon to color and cook them evenly. Cook about 15 minutes or until done. Do not let them get mushy. Lift them to a small dish. Add the crème de menthe to the liquid in the pan and spoon over the apples. Set aside to cool and glaze, basting occasionally with liquid from the bottom of the dish. Place a sprig of mint in each apple and serve, either in the dish or around a leg of lamb. Makes 6 servings.

CHERRY APPLES FOR PORK OR HAM

Proceed as above, substituting red cherry gelatin and cherry liqueur.

ORANGE APPLES FOR DUCK

Proceed as above, substituting orange gelatin and curaçao or Cointreau.

BROWN BETTY

1 1-pound 9-ounce can
    applesauce (2½ cups)
    (or 2½ cups sweetened
    applesauce)
3 tablespoons melted butter
1½ cups crisp cracker crumbs
    (crushed medium-fine)

3 tablespoons brown sugar
½ teaspoon ground cinnamon
¼ teaspoon salt
Light cream

Heat oven to 375° F. Butter a 1-quart baking dish. Spread about one third of the applesauce over the bottom of the dish. Blend together 2 tablespoons of the melted butter and the crumbs. Sprinkle one third of the crumb mixture over the layer of applesauce. Sprinkle with one third of the sugar, cinnamon, and salt. Repeat until there are 3 layers. Drizzle with the remaining melted butter. Bake in preheated oven 25 minutes or until the crumbs are golden brown. Serve hot with cream. Makes 4 to 6 servings.

BROWNSTONE FRONT CHOCOLATE CAKE

1 cup butter
2 cups sugar
4 eggs, separated
2 ounces melted bitter
    chocolate
1 cup mashed potatoes
1 teaspoon vanilla

1½ cups cake flour
¼ teaspoon cinnamon
2 teaspoons baking powder
⅛ teaspoon salt
½ cup milk
1 cup chopped nuts

Cream the butter and sugar. Add the egg yolks but beat after adding each yolk. Stir in the chocolate, mashed potatoes, and vanilla. Add the sifted dry ingredients alternately with milk. Add the nuts. Fold in stiffly beaten egg whites. Pour into 2 greased and floured 9-inch cake pans. Bake at 350° F. for about 30 minutes or until the cake tests done.

CARAMEL ICING

1 cup granulated sugar
2 cups brown sugar
1 cup dairy sour cream

1 tablespoon butter
1 teaspoon vanilla
⅛ teaspoon salt

Mix the sour cream and sugar. Cook slowly until the sugar is dissolved. Boil gently until it reaches the soft boil stage or about 238° F. on a candy thermometer. Remove from the heat. Add the vanilla and butter. Beat until the mixture is of spreading consistency. Spread between and on top of cake. Sprinkle with chopped nuts if desired.

WHIPPED CREAM PIE

½ cup strawberry or other jam
1 baked 8-inch pastry shell
1 cup heavy cream, whipped

Spread the jam over the bottom of the cooled shell. Spoon the cream over the jam. Cut into 8 servings.

PINEAPPLE AMBROSIA

1 large ripe pineapple, pared
1 cup granulated sugar
4 eggs, separated
¼ teaspoon salt
2 cups milk, scalded
1 teaspoon vanilla extract

Grate the pulp of a pineapple on a coarse grater and mix with ½ cup of the sugar; turn into a serving bowl (about 2-quart capacity) and let stand in the refrigerator. In the top of a double boiler, beat with an egg beater 4 egg yolks and 2 egg whites with ¼ cup sugar and salt. (Reserve the other 2 whites in a deep 1-quart bowl.) Gradually stir in warm (not hot) milk. Place over hot (not boiling) water, stirring constantly, until the custard coats a metal spoon. Cool quickly by setting the pan in cold water; stir in the vanilla. Pour over the pineapple. Beat the remaining egg whites, gradually adding ¼ cup sugar until thick. Spread over the custard. Chill thoroughly. Makes 6 to 8 servings.

MANDARIN ORANGE SOUFFLÉ FROID

1 cup sugar
2 envelopes unflavored
    gelatin
1 cup milk
6 eggs, separated
1 cup orange juice
1 tablespoon grated orange
    rind

¼ teaspoon cream of tartar
¼ cup orange liqueur
1 cup heavy cream, whipped
1 11-ounce can mandarin
    oranges, well drained

Take a 1½-quart soufflé dish. Tear off a piece of waxed paper long enough to wrap around the dish. Fold it to make a long strip about 2½ inches wide. Fasten it around the top of the dish with tape or string, overlapping the paper and dish about 1 inch. Combine ½ cup of the sugar, the gelatin, and milk in a saucepan. Beat the egg yolks and stir into the gelatin mixture. Stir and cook over low heat until the mixture coats a metal spoon and small bubbles begin to form around the edges of the pan. Pour into a mixing bowl; add the juice and rind. Chill until the mixture mounds slightly when dropped from a spoon. Beat egg whites with the cream of tartar until frothy. Beat in the remaining sugar, about 2 tablespoons at a time, continuing to beat well after each addition until the meringue is stiff and glossy. With a wire whisk fold the meringue into the chilled mixture. Fold in the orange liqueur and whipped cream. Turn into the prepared dish, chill until firm, at least 4 hours or overnight. Remove the paper collar. Garnish with mandarin orange sections. Makes 6 to 8 servings.

Recipes of Modern America

WHO COULD HAVE FORESEEN the renascence, in the 20th century, of the kitchen? Strange, indeed, have been the results of the liberation from the Dutch oven, the presses and the molds and the sifters, the graters and mills and mashers, the choppers and grinders, to say nothing of the ice-cream freezer and, for that matter, the ice-box.

Emancipated, the modern housewife can afford to indulge nostalgia and reconstitute that sense of *Gemütlichkeit* or *bonhomie* that is associated with the preparation of good food. The presence of a peppermill with peppercorns, perhaps even a coffee mill (electric), skewers to impersonate the olden spits, a barbecue to echo the hog-roast of yore—such mementoes of bygone eras brighten the gleaming "work areas" and "cooking areas," saving them from being transformed into a mere laboratory for the preparation of vittles.

For the modern kitchen has entered into its present state of grace almost in defiance of its predictable atrophy. The fearsome labor that once signified cookery has long since been taken over by the cannery, the packing plant, the quick-freeze facility. The cuisine in the neighborhood store, needing only a thaw, can surpass many of the dishes possible to the most demanding epicure of the past—for whose chef could have prepared egg roll, tacos, gefillte fish, and crab cakes Maryland and then turn out a pizza or a croissant?

Which only proves that a generation of housewives who *could* cop out prefer not to do so. They appreciate the variety of garlic

ELECTRIC BLENDER

149

grinds, from powder to chunk, the supermarket spice rack that would have made Marco Polo drool, and the dairy and nondairy scrimmage for their trade in spreads. Electronics energizes their ovens. The ovens clean themselves and the refrigerator defrosts itself and little machines specialize in making ice—not necessarily cubes, but spheres or slivers or shavings as milady elects.

This kind of kitchen can be a region of such delight that the planning of its accouterments is one of the decorator arts. Having outgrown its "kitchenette" phase and in the process of putting off its subservience to antiseptic white enamel and stainless steel, the kitchen has commandeered color and freedom of form to challenge the enticements of the "living" room and to become once more a center for family life—as it was perforce in the bad old days, when there was not another warm spot in the house.

As for the art of cookery—this has surely not been taken over by the people who process. Never before have so many cook books been collected, never before have ladies—who might disdain the other "accomplishments" of the earlier Compleat Housewife—been more willing to clip recipes, exchange fascinating techniques of culinary skill, and vie for a reputation as a good cook.

It must not be forgotten that Americans have at last begun to learn the glories of the grape. As a matter of fact, vintners never had it so good. A *carte de vins* may appear in the most unlikely motels. Along with the taste for wine, its availability is improving, and American vineyards are producing for the mass table—when that table is ready to accommodate it—a drink far superior to anything within the reach of most Europeans. Here, as abroad, there will always be devotees of the great and the fine wines, and I count myself among them, but a generation may be coming that will be addicted to neither the cocktail nor the cola. This is a consummation Mary and I devoutly are promoting.

**CORDLESS ELECTRIC
CARVING KNIFE**

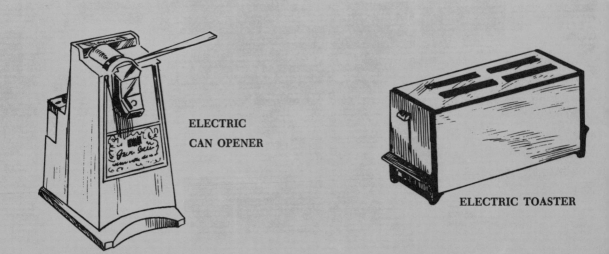

**ELECTRIC
CAN OPENER**

ELECTRIC TOASTER

VICHYSSOISE

4 medium leeks
1 medium onion, chopped
2 tablespoons butter
5 medium potatoes, sliced
1 quart chicken broth

2 teaspoons salt
2 cups milk
2 cups light cream
1 cup heavy cream
Chopped chives

Wash and slice the white part of the leeks. In a large soup pot sauté the leeks and onion in butter until just tender. Add potatoes, chicken broth, and salt; boil until the potatoes are soft. Press through a fine sieve or put in a blender. Scald the milk and light cream. Add the purée and bring to a boil. Chill in the refrigerator. When ready to serve, stir in the heavy cream and top with chopped chives. Makes 8 servings.

QUICK MANHATTAN CLAM CHOWDER

4 slices bacon, in small pieces
½ cup chopped celery
1 cup chopped onion
1 medium green pepper, chopped
1 1-pound can stewed tomatoes

2 cups water
2 medium potatoes, cubed
½ teaspon thyme
2 8-ounce cans minced clams
Salt
Pepper

Fry the bacon until crisp and reserve. In 2 tablespoons of the bacon fat sauté the celery, onion, and green pepper for 5 minutes. Add the tomatoes, water, potatoes, and thyme. Cover and cook until the potatoes are done. Add clams and their juice, and return to a boil. Add salt and pepper to taste. Makes 4 to 6 servings.

COLD SENEGALESE

3½ cups chicken stock
½ teaspoon curry powder
1 cup minced cooked chicken
4 egg yolks

2 cups cream
Salt
Pepper

Heat the chicken stock. Add the curry powder and minced chicken. In a bowl beat 4 egg yolks, stir in some of the hot stock, and blend with cream. Add this egg and cream mixture to the stock. Stir constantly over low heat until just thickened. Add salt and pepper to taste. Let cool and chill in the refrigerator. Makes 6 servings.

CIOPPINO

2½ pounds firm white fish such as striped bass, halibut, and barracuda, cut in pieces (a variety is desirable)
1½ pounds fresh shrimp
2 dozen clams
2 dozen mussels
1 large Dungeness crab or 1½ pounds frozen King crab legs in the shell
1 large onion, chopped
1 large green pepper, chopped
2 stalks celery, chopped
2 large cloves of garlic, minced
¼ cup olive oil
1 1-pound, 13-ounce can tomatoes
2 8-ounce cans tomato sauce
2 cups white or red wine
1 teaspoon salt
Freshly ground pepper
¼ teaspoon dried oregano
¼ teaspoon dried basil
½ cup minced parsley

Wash the fish, shell and clean the shrimp, scrub the clams, wash the mussels and remove the beard, crack and clean the crab. To make the sauce, sauté the onion, green pepper, celery, and garlic in oil until golden. Add tomatoes, tomato sauce, wine, and seasonings. Cover and cook for 15 minutes. Arrange the fish, shrimp, and crab in layers in a large casserole. Pour in the sauce, cover, and bake in a preheated 300° F. oven for 30 minutes. Add the clams and mussels and bake until they open, about 6 to 10 minutes. Sprinkle with parsley and serve at once. Makes 6 to 8 servings.

BROILED HALIBUT MAÎTRE D'HÔTEL

1 3-pound halibut, split in half	Pepper
Melted butter	Parsley
1 cut clove garlic (optional)	Lemon wedges
Salt	

Brush the halibut with melted butter, rub with garlic if desired, and sprinkle with salt and pepper. Place on a greased broiling pan and broil about 15 minutes or until tender. Remove to a hot platter and dot with maître d'hôtel butter. Garnish the platter with parsley and lemon wedges. Makes 6 servings.

MAÎTRE D'HÔTEL BUTTER

1 tablespoon softened butter	¼ teaspoon lemon juice
1 teaspoon finely chopped	½ teaspoon onion juice
parsley	

Mix all the ingredients together with a fork until well blended. Refrigerate until ready to use.

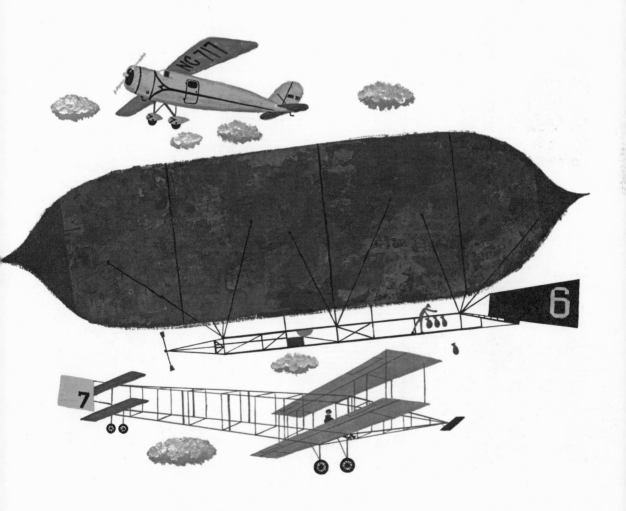

COLD CRAB SOUFFLÉ

2 7¾-ounce cans King crab, flaked
½ cup chopped celery
½ cup chopped green pepper
¼ cup chopped parsley
½ cup chopped pimiento
4 green onions, minced
1 teaspoon salt
⅛ teaspoon white pepper
¼ teaspoon hot pepper sauce
2 envelopes unflavored gelatin
¼ cup cold water
1 tablespoon lemon juice
1 cup mayonnaise
1 pint heavy cream, whipped
Cucumber slices
Watercress

Combine the crab and the next 8 ingredients. Soften the gelatin in the water and lemon juice, and dissolve over hot water. Stir into the mayonnaise. Combine the mayonnaise and the crab mixture. Fold in the whipped cream. Place in an 8-cup mold and chill for several hours. Unmold and serve with a garnish of cucumber slices and watercress. Makes 8 to 10 servings.

CRAB LOUIS

1 pound crabmeat, fresh or canned
1 tablespoon prepared horse-radish
¼ cup chili sauce
2 tablespoons chopped green pepper
2 tablespoons chopped sweet pickle
2 tablespoons chopped green onion
1 tablespoon lemon juice
½ cup mayonnaise
½ teaspoon salt
⅛ teaspoon pepper
1 teaspoon Worcestershire sauce
Lettuce leaves, hollowed-out tomatoes, or avocado halves

Pick over the crabmeat and refrigerate until needed. Make the dressing by mixing together the horseradish, chili sauce, green pepper, pickle, onion, lemon juice, mayonnaise, salt, pepper, and Worcestershire sauce. When ready to serve, mix the crabmeat and dressing. Serve on lettuce leaves or stuffed into tomatoes or avocado halves. Makes 6 servings.

TUNA CASSEROLE

¼ cup butter
¼ cup flour
1 teaspoon salt
⅛ teaspoon pepper
1 cup milk
2 7¾-ounce cans tuna fish, drained and flaked
2½ cups corn kernels
¼ cup pimiento
1 egg, beaten
½ cup fresh bread cubes
Whipped potatoes

Melt the butter in a saucepan and stir in the flour and seasoning. Add the milk and cook until smooth and thickened. Stir in the remaining ingredients except the potatoes. Turn the mixture into a greased casserole and bake in a 375° F. oven for 30 minutes. Garnish with whipped potatoes and return to oven to brown lightly. Makes 6 servings.

CHICKEN MARENGO

2 2-pound broilers, cut in
   quarters
Salt
Pepper
Flour
¼ cup oil
1 cup chicken broth
½ cup white wine or broth
1 garlic clove, crushed

1 stalk celery
1 carrot
1 bay leaf
2 large ripe tomatoes, peeled
   and cut in quarters
½ pound mushroom caps, cut
   in quarters
2 tablespoons chopped parsley

Sprinkle the chicken with salt, pepper, and flour. Heat the oil in a heavy skillet and cook the chicken until lightly browned. Add the remaining ingredients except the mushrooms and parsley. Cover and simmer over low heat for about 30 minutes. Add the mushrooms and cook for 10 minutes more or until chicken is tender. Remove the celery, carrot, and bay leaf. Taste for seasoning and thicken gravy if desired. Sprinkle with the chopped parsley. Makes 6 to 8 servings.

CHICKEN TRIANON

½ cup flour	2 teaspoons cooking oil
¼ teaspoon salt	1 egg
½ cup milk	3 tablespoons milk

To make the crepes, combine the flour and salt in a mixing bowl. Stir in the milk, oil, and egg and mix until smooth. Refrigerate for 30 minutes. Add 3 tablespoons milk to reduce the batter to a thin consistency. Heat a 6-inch skillet and, when very hot, grease lightly. Cover the bottom of the pan with 2 tablespoons of batter and swirl the pan to spread it evenly. Cook until golden on one side, turn, and cook the other side. Stack the crepes separated by pieces of wax paper and keep them warm while making the sauce and filling.

THICK CREAM SAUCE

¼ cup butter	⅛ teaspoon pepper
¼ cup flour	1 cup milk
¼ teaspoon salt	

Melt the butter over low heat and blend in the flour and seasonings. Cook until the mixture is smooth and bubbly. Remove from heat. Stir in the milk. Return to heat and cook, stirring constantly, for 1 minute.

FILLING

1½ cups chopped cooked chicken	¼ teaspoon tarragon
¼ teaspoon salt	Thick cream sauce
	½ cup white wine

Combine the chicken, seasonings, and ¼ cup of the thick cream sauce. Place 2 tablespoons of this mixture on each crepe and roll them. Place them, seam side down, in a shallow, greased baking dish. Cover with foil and bake in a 350° F. oven until heated. Meanwhile, thin the remaining cream sauce with the wine, reheat, and serve over the crepes. Makes 4 servings.

CHICKEN LOAF

4 cups ground or finely minced chicken

2 cups cracker crumbs

¾ cup chicken broth

½ cup light cream or evaporated milk

3 eggs, slightly beaten

2 tablespoons melted butter

3 tablespoons minced green pepper

2 teaspoons minced parsley

2 tablespoons grated onion

1 teaspoon salt

⅛ teaspoon pepper

Egg sauce or pimiento sauce

Mix all the ingredients except the sauce in a bowl. Grease an 8½- x 4½- x 2½-inch loaf pan; line the bottom with a strip of foil that extends 2 inches over the ends of the pan. Pack the chicken mixture into the pan and bake in a preheated 350° F. oven for about 1 hour. Cool in pan for 5 minutes. Turn out onto a heated platter and remove the foil. Serve with an egg sauce or pimiento sauce. Makes 6 servings.

TURKEY CASSEROLE

½ cup butter or margarine

½ cup flour

4 cups turkey broth or chicken broth

1 10-ounce package frozen peas

8 small cooked onions or 1 1-pound can onions, drained

2 cups diced carrots

2 cups diced turkey meat

Salt

Pepper

Melt the butter or margarine in a large saucepan and blend in the flour. Add the broth and cook, stirring constantly, until thickened. Add the remaining ingredients, with salt and pepper to taste. Pour into a 2-quart casserole. Bake in a preheated 400° F. oven until hot and bubbly. Makes 6 servings.

EASY GRANDE MARMITE

5 cups water	2 cloves
1 13¾-ounce can chicken broth	1 bay leaf
1 10½-ounce can beef broth	4 peppercorns
1 pound round steak	2 sprigs parsley
1½ pounds chicken breasts or parts	3 medium carrots, cut in 1-inch slices
1 teaspoon salt	3 small turnips, quartered
2 chopped leeks (white part only) or 6 chopped green onions (no tops)	3 stalks celery, cut in 1-inch pieces
1 medium yellow onion, quartered	½ pound tender green cabbage, shredded
1 teaspoon oil	French bread, sliced and toasted

In a large pot combine the water, broth, steak, chicken, and salt. Bring to a boil and simmer slowly, uncovered, for 30 minutes. Remove scum as it rises. Meanwhile brown the leeks and the onion in the oil. Tie the cloves, bay leaf, peppercorns, and parsley in a piece of cheesecloth. Add this bouquet garni and the browned leeks and onion to the pot and cook for another hour with the pot cover slightly ajar. Add the carrots, turnips, and celery and cook for ½ hour. Add the cabbage and cook another ½ hour. Cut the beef in pieces, remove bones from the chicken, and return the meat and chicken to the soup. Serve toasted French bread on the marmite. Makes 4 to 6 servings.

SAUERBRATEN

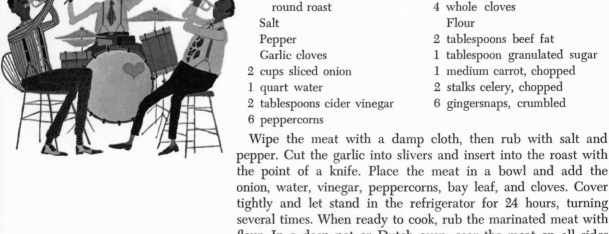

1 5-pound piece of bottom round roast	1 large bay leaf
Salt	4 whole cloves
Pepper	Flour
Garlic cloves	2 tablespoons beef fat
2 cups sliced onion	1 tablespoon granulated sugar
1 quart water	1 medium carrot, chopped
2 tablespoons cider vinegar	2 stalks celery, chopped
6 peppercorns	6 gingersnaps, crumbled

Wipe the meat with a damp cloth, then rub with salt and pepper. Cut the garlic into slivers and insert into the roast with the point of a knife. Place the meat in a bowl and add the onion, water, vinegar, peppercorns, bay leaf, and cloves. Cover tightly and let stand in the refrigerator for 24 hours, turning several times. When ready to cook, rub the marinated meat with flour. In a deep pot or Dutch oven, sear the meat on all sides in beef fat. Add the marinade, sugar, carrots, and celery. Cover and simmer slowly for 3 hours. When meat is tender transfer to a heated platter. Strain the liquid, add the gingersnaps and a little flour, and cook until smooth and thickened. Pour part of the gravy over the meat and serve the rest separately. Makes 6 to 8 servings.

SUKIYAKI

1½ pounds sirloin steak
¼ pound beef suet
2 bunches scallions, washed, trimmed, and cut in 2-inch pieces
3 stalks celery, cut in diagonal pieces
½ pound mushrooms, sliced
2 onions, thinly sliced
1 head Chinese cabbage, shredded
1 pound spinach, stems removed
2 7-ounce cans bamboo shoots, drained and sliced
1 cup meat stock
½ cup soy sauce
3 tablespoons granulated sugar

With a very sharp knife cut the steak across the grain in paper-thin slices. In a large skillet heat the suet and cook the beef quickly until browned. Add the remaining ingredients; cover and cook for 10 minutes over medium heat. Remove cover and cook about 5 minutes more. The vegetables must retain their crispness. Serve with rice. Makes 6 servings.

TEXAS SPARERIBS

5 pounds spareribs
1 clove garlic, cut
Salt
Pepper
½ cup catsup
2 tablespoons honey or brown sugar
1 tablespoon soy sauce
1 tablespoon Worcestershire sauce
1 tablespoon cider vinegar
2 tablespoons onion juice
1 teaspoon chili powder
½ teaspoon dry mustard

Rub the spareribs with garlic and sprinkle with salt and pepper. Combine the remaining ingredients and brush generously on the ribs. Bake in a preheated 350° F. oven for 1½ to 2 hours or until tender. Turn and brush the ribs with sauce several times during the baking. Makes 6 servings.

VEAL PAPRIKA

6 slices bacon, cut in small pieces
4 pounds boneless veal shank, cut in 1-inch pieces
1 cup chopped onion
5 cups chicken broth
1 clove garlic, minced
3 tablespoons paprika
1½ teaspoons salt
3 tablespoons flour
½ cup cold water
1 cup commercial sour cream
Slivered almonds (optional)

Cook the bacon and remove. In the bacon fat brown the veal and onion until golden. Add the bacon, chicken broth, garlic, paprika, and salt. Cover and simmer until veal is tender, about 1 to 1½ hours. Mix the flour, water, and sour cream together. Add this mixture to the veal and cook until thickened, stirring continually. Serve in a casserole, with slivered almonds on top if desired. Makes 8 servings.

SHISH KEBAB

1 5- to 7-pound leg of lamb, boned
1 clove garlic, minced
1 grated onion
½ cup olive oil
1½ teaspoons salt
¼ teaspoon freshly ground pepper
2 tablespoons red wine or wine vinegar

½ teaspoon rosemary
½ teaspoon thyme
4 tomatoes, quartered
4 small Bermuda onions, quartered
2 green peppers, seeded and cut into pieces
16 mushroom caps

Trim any fat off the lamb and cut the meat into 1½- to 2-inch cubes. Mix the next 8 ingredients and cover the lamb with this marinade. Refrigerate for several hours, turning occasionally. When ready to cook, spear the meat and vegetables on skewers. Place mushroom caps on the ends of the skewers and brush on the marinade. Broil, turning and basting, for 10 to 15 minutes or until done, or grill over hot coals. Makes 6 to 8 servings.

LASAGNA NAPOLI

1 cup chopped onion
1 large clove garlic, minced
3 tablespoons olive oil
1 pound ground beef
2 1-pound cans peeled whole tomatoes
2 8-ounce cans tomato sauce
1½ teaspoons salt

¼ teaspoon pepper
1 teaspoon oregano
½ teaspoon sweet basil
½ pound lasagna
1 pound Ricotta cheese
½ pound Mozzarella cheese, thinly sliced
½ cup grated Parmesan cheese

In a skillet sauté the onion and garlic in oil until golden. Add the beef and cook until the meat loses its redness. Add the tomatoes, sauce, and seasonings. Cover and cook 30 minutes, stirring occasionally. Meanwhile cook the lasagna in boiling salted water for about 12 minutes; drain and rinse. Put alternate layers of lasagna, Ricotta, meat sauce, Mozzarella, and Parmesan in a 12- x 8- x 2-inch baking dish. Top with sauce and cheese. Bake in a 375° F. oven for 15 to 20 minutes or until bubbly. Makes 6 servings.

Onion Soup, page 122
Hero, page 163

**Kitchen, Landis Brothers Homestead
Lancaster, Pennsylvania**

**Kitchen, Sunnyside
Tarrytown, New York**

HERO

Loaf of French bread
Mayonnaise
Cheddar or Swiss cheese
   slices
Tomato slices

Green pepper rings
Onion rings
Sliced ham
Liverwurst

Split the loaf of bread lengthwise and spread with mayonnaise. On the bottom half arrange a layer of Cheddar or Swiss cheese slices; a second layer of tomatoes, green pepper, and onion rings; a third layer of ham and liverwurst. Replace the top half of the bread. To serve, cut crosswise into pieces. Makes 4 servings.

CORNED BEEF CHEESEBURGER

1 1-pound can corned beef
⅓ cup chili sauce
1 tablespoon onion juice

⅓ cup chopped dill pickle
8 hamburger buns
8 slices American cheese

Break the corned beef into shreds and mix with the chili sauce, onion juice, and pickle. Split and toast the buns. Spread the bottom halves with meat mixture and place under broiler to heat slightly. Lay on cheese slices and broil until cheese melts. Makes 8 servings.

HAM AND CHEESE SOUFFLÉ SANDWICH

6 slices of bread, crusts
   removed
Butter or margarine
1 4½-ounce can deviled ham
   spread
4 eggs
3 cups milk

½ pound sharp Cheddar cheese,
   grated
⅛ teaspoon Worcestershire
   sauce
4 drops hot pepper sauce
½ teaspoon salt
¼ teaspoon pepper

Spread 3 slices of bread with butter or margarine and 3 slices with deviled ham spread. Put slices together to make sandwiches and cut into fourths. Arrange the fourths in a greased casserole. In a large bowl beat the eggs, add milk, cheese, and seasonings. Pour this custard mixture over the sandwiches and let stand 15 minutes. Set casserole in a pan of hot water and bake in a pre-heated 375° F. oven for about 30 minutes, until puffed. Makes 4 servings.

GENOA PIZZA

1 13¾-ounce package hot roll
   mix
Olive oil
20 ounces prepared spaghetti
   sauce

8 ounces thinly sliced salami,
   cut in julienne strips
½ pound Mozzarella cheese,
   thinly sliced

Prepare the hot roll mix according to package directions and divide the dough in half. Roll each piece out on a floured board and fit into 2 greased 12-inch pizza pans or place on greased cookie sheets. Pinch the dough to form an edge. Brush each pizza with oil. Spread 10 ounces of sauce on each pizza, place salami on the sauce, and top with cheese. Cook in a preheated 425° F. oven for about 20 minutes or until the exposed edges are browned. As a variation, flat anchovies or cooked pepperone may be substituted for the salami. Makes 6 to 8 servings.

EGGPLANT PARMIGIANA

1 large eggplant
2 eggs
1 teaspoon salt
¼ teaspoon pepper

¼ teaspoon oregano
Oil for frying
2 cups tomato sauce
½ cup grated Parmesan cheese
½ pound Mozzarella cheese

Wash the eggplant but do not peel; cut into ¼-inch slices. Beat the eggs lightly and season with salt, pepper, and oregano. In a large skillet heat the oil, which should be ½ inch deep. Dip the eggplant slices in the egg and fry in oil until golden; drain them on a paper towel. Arrange layers of eggplant, Parmesan cheese, and tomato sauce in a 2-quart baking dish. Place Mozzarella cheese on top and bake in a preheated 350° F. oven for about 30 minutes. Place under broiler to brown cheese if desired. Makes 4 to 6 servings.

TOMATOES MONACO

4 large ripe tomatoes
   Garlic salt (optional)

Freshly ground pepper
½ cup grated Cheddar cheese

Cut the tomatoes into slices ½ inch thick. Sprinkle with salt, pepper, and cheese. Place the tomatoes in a shallow greased baking dish. Broil until the cheese becomes bubbly. Makes 4 servings.

COUNTRY CASSEROLE

¼ cup salad oil
½ cup chopped onion
1 cup chopped celery
¼ cup chopped green pepper
1 clove minced garlic
1 pound unpeeled zucchini,
    in ¼-inch slices
2 cups whole kernel corn
½ cup soft bread crumbs
¼ cup chopped pimiento

¾ cup grated Parmesan cheese
½ cup chopped parsley
4 eggs
1½ teaspoons salt
¼ teaspoon freshly ground
    pepper
¼ teaspoon basil
¼ teaspoon thyme
¼ teaspoon marjoram

Heat the oil in a large skillet and sauté the onion, celery, green pepper, and garlic for 5 minutes. Add the zucchini and corn and cook over low heat for 10 minutes more, tossing occasionally. Add the bread crumbs, pimiento, cheese, and parsley. In a large bowl beat the eggs slightly and add the seasonings. Combine the eggs and vegetables and pour into a greased 6-cup casserole. Bake in a 350° F. oven for about 40 minutes or until just set. Makes 8 servings.

NOODLES WITH TOMATO CLAM SAUCE

1 cup chopped onion
1 large clove garlic, minced
3 tablespoons olive oil
1 1-pound can whole peeled
    tomatoes
1 8-ounce can tomato sauce
    with onions
1 teaspoon salt

⅛ teaspoon pepper
½ teaspoon tarragon
¼ teaspoon oregano
1 8-ounce package medium
    noodles
2 8-ounce cans minced clams
    Grated Parmesan cheese

Sauté the onions and garlic in the oil until golden. Add the tomatoes, tomato sauce, and seasonings; simmer for 15 minutes. Meanwhile, cook the noodles according to package directions. Just before serving, add the clams and their juice to the sauce and return to a boil. Arrange the noodles on a warm platter and pour the sauce in the middle. Serve with a bowl of Parmesan cheese. Makes 4 to 6 servings.

MACARONI DANDY

½ 8-ounce package macaroni
1 8-ounce jar pasteurized
    process cheese spread
½ cup hot milk
¼ teaspoon dry mustard
⅛ teaspoon salt

⅛ teaspoon pepper
1 teaspoon Worcestershire
    sauce
2 teaspoons cornstarch
1 tablespoon cold water

Cook the macaroni according to package directions. In a large
pan combine and beat together the cheese spread, hot milk, and
seasonings. Dissolve the cornstarch in water and add to the cheese
mixture. Cook until thickened. Add the macaroni and pour into
a shallow baking dish. Broil until bubbly and golden. Makes 4
servings.

CAESAR SALAD

2 cups bread cubes
½ cup olive oil
1 clove garlic, crushed
2 large heads romaine lettuce
½ teaspoon salt

¼ teaspoon freshly ground
    pepper
¼ teaspoon dry mustard
½ cup grated Parmesan cheese
1 egg
    Juice of 2 lemons

Fry the bread cubes with the crushed garlic in ¼ cup of the
olive oil until golden. Remove and drain. Wash, dry, and chill
the romaine. When ready to serve, tear the lettuce into bite-size
pieces and place in a large salad bowl. Add the remaining ¼ cup
oil and the salt, pepper, mustard, and cheese. Drop the raw egg
on top of the greens and put the lemon juice on the egg. Toss
thoroughly. Just before serving, add the croutons and toss lightly
again. Makes 6 servings.

GREEN GODDESS SALAD

3 heads of assorted lettuce
   (romaine, chicory, Bibb,
   or watercress)
½ cup mayonnaise
¼ cup sour cream

3 tablespoons tarragon vinegar
1 tablespoon lemon juice
1 tablespoon anchovy paste
1 clove garlic, minced
½ cup finely chopped parsley

Wash, dry, and chill the greens. Blend together the remaining ingredients. When ready to serve, tear greens into pieces and toss with the dressing. Makes 6 to 8 servings.

TINY TIM FINGER ROLLS

1 package of 12 refrigerated
   Parkerhouse quick dinner
   rolls
1 beaten egg

Poppy seeds
Sesame seeds
Caraway seeds

Cut the rolls in half. Roll them by hand on a lightly floured board into "pencils" about 4 inches long. Brush with egg and sprinkle some with poppy seeds, some with sesame seeds, and some with caraway seeds. Place on a greased cookie sheet and bake in a preheated 375° F. oven for about 12 to 15 minutes or until lightly browned. Makes 24 rolls.

PRONTO PECAN ROLLS

½ cup melted butter or
  margarine
⅓ cup brown sugar
½ cup chopped pecans

1 8.6-ounce package quick
  refrigerator dinner rolls
  (18 in a package)

Melt the butter or margarine, add brown sugar, and dissolve thoroughly over heat. Stir in the nuts and pour into a 9-inch cake pan. Place the rolls in the pan, flat side down, and brush with butter. Bake in a 375° F. oven for 15 to 20 minutes or until lightly browned. Invert on a serving platter and spoon any remaining mixture on top. Makes 6 to 8 servings.

MOUSSE AU CHOCOLAT

3 ounces semisweet chocolate
  pieces
3 eggs, separated

1 teaspoon vanilla extract
Whipped cream (optional)

Melt the chocolate over hot but not boiling water. Remove from heat, beat in the egg yolks with a whisk, and add vanilla. In a large bowl beat the egg whites until stiff but not dry; fold in chocolate mixture. Spoon into dessert cups or sherbet glasses and refrigerate. Serve with whipped cream if desired. Makes 4 servings.

MOCHA TORTE

1 1-pound package pound
  cake mix
1 cup cold strong coffee
1 4-ounce package instant
  chocolate pudding mix
2 eggs

¼ cup melted butter or
  margarine
1 can (1-pound ¼-ounce)
  chocolate fudge ready-to-
  spread frosting
Whipped cream (optional)

Combine the cake mix and coffee in a mixing bowl and beat with an electric mixer on medium speed for 2 minutes. Add the pudding mix, eggs, and butter and beat again for 1 minute. Pour into a greased 10½- x 15-inch jelly-roll pan that has been lined with oiled wax paper. Bake in a preheated 350° F. oven for about 20 to 30 minutes. Loosen around edges with a knife and turn out onto a clean dish towel. Remove the wax paper and cool. Cut lengthwise into 3 strips. Place 1 strip of cake on a board, frost, and add the next 2 slices with frosting in between. Frost the top. Sides may be covered with whipped cream if desired. Makes 12 servings.

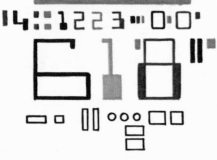

ZABAGLIONE

6 egg yolks
⅔ cup superfine sugar

⅔ cup Marsala wine or sherry

In the top of a double boiler over simmering, not boiling, water beat the egg yolks. Gradually add the sugar and then the wine. Beat constantly until very thick and warm. Use only a very good quality wine. Makes 6 to 8 servings.

STRAWBERRY-GLAZED CHEESECAKE

1 box (6 ounces) Zwieback
½ cup melted butter
¼ teaspoon nutmeg
1¾ cups granulated sugar
2 pounds creamed cottage
   cheese

4 eggs
¼ cup all-purpose flour
½ cup heavy cream
1 tablespoon lemon juice
1 tablespoon vanilla extract

Crush the Zwieback with a rolling pin or in an electric blender. Combine the crumbs with the butter, nutmeg, and ¼ cup of the sugar. Press this firmly onto the bottom of a 9-inch springform pan. Press the cottage cheese through a fine sieve into a bowl and beat in the eggs, one at a time, with an electric mixer. Add the flour and 1 cup of the sugar. Beat in the cream, lemon juice, and vanilla until well blended. Pour the cheese mixture into the crumb-lined pan. Bake in a preheated 350° F. oven for 50 minutes. Turn off the oven heat and leave the cheesecake for 30 minutes longer. Cool and refrigerate overnight. Makes 6 to 8 servings.

STRAWBERRY GLAZE

1 quart strawberries
¾ cup granulated sugar
¼ cup cold water

1½ tablespoons cornstarch
1 tablespoon butter

Hull the strawberries. Reserve the largest berries. Crush enough of the smaller berries to make 1 cup, pressing through a strainer or in a blender. Combine the strawberry purée with the sugar, cold water, and cornstarch in a saucepan. Boil until clear. Stir in the butter and cool. Arrange the large berries on top of cheesecake and spoon on the glaze.

INSTANT ICE CREAM TARTS

2 cups toasted flaked coconut   1 quart vanilla ice cream
¼ cup melted butter   Fruit, sauce, nuts, or jam

Mix together the coconut and butter and line 8 five-ounce custard cups; refrigerate. When ready to serve fill cups with ice cream. Top with any of the following: crushed pineapple, strawberries, chocolate or butterscotch sauce, chopped nuts, apricot or raspberry jam. Makes 8 servings.

BROILED GRAPEFRUIT

2 grapefruit   4 kumquats or maraschino
3 tablespoons honey   cherries
4 teaspoons sweet liqueur

Cut the grapefruit in half and loosen each section from the skin and membrane with a sharp knife. Mix the honey and sweet liqueur and spoon over each half grapefruit. Brown lightly under the broiler. Garnish with a kumquat or maraschino cherry. Makes 4 servings.

CHERRIES JUBILEE

1 1-pound 14-ounce can pitted   ¼ cup kirsch
    Bing cherries   1 quart vanilla ice cream
1 tablespoon cornstarch   (optional)
¼ cup granulated sugar

Drain the cherries and reserve the juice. Mix the cornstarch and sugar in the top pan of a chafing dish. Add the cherry juice and cook until the mixture becomes thick and clear. Add the cherries and heat. Add warmed kirsch and blaze. Serve the flaming cherries alone or over ice cream. Makes 6 servings.

Wine in America

THE HISTORY OF WINE in America is *two* histories. Actually, the wines of California have more in common with those of France than with those of the East. So in recounting the tale of wine in America, we shall have to follow two disparate paths.

America never has lived up to Leif the Lucky's name of Vinland, some 1,000 years ago. The legendary Leif or other explorers who sighted the profusion of wild grapevines twining their tendrils over the land gave them short shrift and went on about their business growing maize and shooting wild turkeys. Later, deciding that the turkey and sweet yams might go well with a glass of wine, they imported French vines and planted them, uprooting the native sons to make room. The new vines all sickened and died, killed by the rigorous winters and fungus diseases to which they had no immunity.

Captain John Smith, in 1606, took time off to report, "We made neere twentie gallons of wine." Whether from native or imported grapes is not known. In 1617 a gaggle of French vintners put in an appearance, amply supplied with European cuttings—which withered away, for the same implacable reasons. However, in the late eighteenth century, with an increase in elegance and pelf in the Colonies, wine got its first leg up, especially in the South. (Rum still took care of New Engand's chill.) But it was not table wine—it was Madeira. Our revered forebears drank Madeira the way their descendants drink cola.

George Washington reputedly drank two bottles a day. Ben Franklin is credited with this aphorism: "Wine is a constant proof that God loves us and loves to see us happy!"

BOTTLE CORKER

171

Even Thomas Jefferson, who must be credited with the first real interest in table wines in this country, started out liking stronger drink. Dessert wines, especially Madeira, were noted in his cellar books. Later, after his fortuitous spell as envoy in France, he discovered the pleasures of table and the drier wines. He made a tour of the Bordeaux vineyards in 1794, met a "Mr. Lur Saluces" of Château d'Yquem (still in the hands of the Lur Saluces family), and discovered such delightful bottles as Château Margaux and Château La Fitte (sic). And it was Jefferson, our only "Renaissance Man," who came finally to the realization that if nature had intended the European grape to grow in the Americas, she would have planted it here. He said, "I think it will be well to push the culture of this grape [the domestic grape] without losing time and efforts in the search of foreign vines, which it will take centuries to adapt to our soil and climate."

The reason European vines failed in the East, where native grapes grew (and still grow) in profusion, is that the grapes are of different families. *Vitis vinifera* is the grape of Europe, and for that matter, the rest of the world. *Vitis labrusca* (and other subspecies) is the grape of Eastern North America. Both groups have infinite offspring, and man has increased these a hundredfold by constant crossbreeding and hybridizing experiments.

The *labrusca* grapes had long been able to endure intense cold and had learned to cope with the deadly plant louse, the *Phylloxera*, by developing an immunity to its root-eating proclivities. Not so *vinifera*. The winters were too rigorous, and the immunity was not there. It remained for California to welcome the *vinifera*.

In passing, it might be well to remark that, while nearly everyone has heard that American rootstocks saved the vineyards of Europe, when the incursion of this pest spread like a scourge in the 1870's and '80's, few seem to realize that it was our vines, experimentally imported into France, that had carried the deadly plague in the first place.

STAVED WOODEN TANKARD

LEATHER BOTTLE

VITICULTURE IN AMERICA

There is probably no state in the Union that has not, at one time or another, grown some grapes and made some wine. In the mid-nineteenth century, Ohio (around Cincinnati) was very prominent—also Missouri, Indiana, Georgia, the Carolinas, and Pennsylvania. Alabama was making as much wine as New York in the 1880's. But these figures concern production by small, independent farmer-producers, who are no more. Today's Eastern production is concentrated in the hands of a few large wineries, not farmers—Taylor's, Widmer's, Great Western, and Gold Seal.

The Eastern wines had special problems to contend with—the grapes, and the kinds of wine made from them. *Labrusca* grapes, and their close relatives, all have what the French would call a *goût sauvage* or wild taste— and aroma too. "Foxy," the wine men call it. It makes for a grapey-tasting wine. Some like the flavor, but to others it lacks subtlety and is foreign to their notion of how wine should taste, based on their acquaintance with the wines of Europe. The Isabella, Delaware, Catawba, Ives, and above all, the ubiquitous Concord are such *labrusca* grapes,

Viticulture in the East

widely used for wine culture. Nicholas Longworth in the early part of the century was making his famous "Sparkling Catawba" out Cincinnati way, with great success. It appeared on most Eastern hotel wine lists, cheek by jowl with Roederer and Clicquot. In more recent years, the Diamond, Elvira, Dutchess, and Iona are grapes that appeal to vintners.

The ascendancy of New York State, today the main Eastern producer, came along much later. An Episcopalian minister, the Reverend Bostwick, planted vines in Hammondsport in 1829, but it was not until the 1860's that the Finger Lakes region became the vineyard of the East. These deep glacial lakes flatten out temperature drops and rises like a well-placed governor on a steam engine; the result is luxuriant hillsides of *labrusca* growing mightily.

The vines are not all *labrusca*. Here and there, under the aegis of dedicated men, such as Frank and Fournier, plantings of hardy *vinifera* grapes were made successfully, and the wines made from them are remarkable good. Other specialists are experimenting with crosses between *vinifera* and *labrusca*, while still others are hybridizing *labrusca* to breed out the less appealing characteristics and to retain the pleasant ones. After all, why must all wine taste one way? There is room for many savors of different wines from different grapes and different climes.

Viticulture in the West

Meanwhile, California had become the center of American viticulture, responsible for 85 per cent of American wine production and 5 per cent of the world's.

Everything started—but very slowly—with Father Junípero Serra, a Franciscan Friar who left Mexico in 1769 and set up a mission in what is now San Diego. This was the first of 21 missions, the first "chain" on the Coast, and at many of them he planted Spanish grapevines, which produced what became known as mission grapes and mission wines. These were the first successful *vinifera* grapes, the grapes of Europe, on American soil. They made wine—of a sort, dessert wine, akin to Angelica. If it depended upon mission wine, California would probably not now hold the exalted position it does. But a Bordelaise émigré, appropriately named Jean Louis Vignes, brought cuttings of his beloved vines of Bordeaux and grew them where the Los Angeles railway station now stands. Then, in 1850, there arrived on the California scene the generally accredited "father" of the grape country—Count Agoston Haraszthy.

As a Hungarian nobleman, Haraszthy knew little of anything other than the grape—noblemen being proscribed from working at anything more mundane. He had earlier appeared at Sauk City, Wisconsin, planting grapes where Holsteins now graze. Failure! His next vineyard was in San Diego. Again failure. San Mateo—ditto. But the good Count (now Colonel) tried again at Buena Vista in Sonoma County. Success at last! Among the vines he planted was that of Zinfandel.

In 1861-62, Haraszthy's success inspired the state to set up a committee to study viticulture in California, and to send the Colonel on a mission to Europe, to bring back cuttings of every vine in sight, not just those of his native Hungary. The legend is that he showed up with 200,000 cuttings! He planted some, gave some, sold many. It was this windfall that really started the wine industry in California. If ever a state owed a debt, it was California to the Hungarian vintner-of-fortune. It is shameful to report that the administration had changed in midstream and Haraszthy was never even paid for his cuttings. He raised grapes, mined gold, minted coins—then set out for Nicaragua, where he distilled rum and ran a sawmill. They say he was eaten by a crocodile in 1859.

Benjamin Wilson produced California's first sparkling wines, harbinger of Korbel, Beaulieu, Kornell, Almadén, Masson, Weibel, and others of today's greats. With increasing affluence, sparkling wines were much in demand. Other vineyards sprang up—in southern California, north of San Francisco in Napa and Sonoma, south and east in Alameda and Santa Clara. Demand was great —6,000,000 south Europeans, wine-drinkers all, had immigrated here.

And then—disaster, in the form of prohibition. After 1918 a little sacramental wine was made, a little medicinal wine, but it was not enough to keep vintners in business. Vineyards were uprooted, especially the better wine grape varieties, which make poor sweet wines and raisins. Experienced European wine makers, grape farmers, workers, and maîtres pulled up stakes. Scofflaws scoffed with liquor, not wine, in the speakeasies of the day. America's slowly developing taste and discrimination went down the drain with bathtub gin. In 1934 the "Noble Experiment" ended, but the damage had been done.

The American wine industry began to come back—especially in California, which since the repeal of prohibition has made the most remarkable progress of any wine area in the world. Techniques developed in California have gone overseas to improve viticulture everywhere. The expertise developed at the University of California at Davis, under Maynard Amerine, has no counterpart. Such vineyards as Krug, Mondavi, Beaulieu, Wente, Martini, Heitz, Mirassou, Buena Vista, Concannon, Cresta Blanca, Beringer, Inglenook, Ray, Christian Brothers, Souverain, Mayacamas, Stony Hill, Llords & Elwood are turning out wines of quality and finesse. But even larger operations such as Almadén, Paul Masson, Brookside, Assumption Abbey, and The Novitiate are doing such a fine job with mass production that the smaller producers are hard put to keep up. Huge operations, such as Gallo, are offering excellent quality at popular prices. All are sure of what they are doing. If the American public's refound taste, perceptiveness, and discrimination continue, the domestic vintners' future is assured.

FRIENDS
EAT
DRINK
LAUGH
LOVE

WHAT IS A GOOD WINE ?

The great George Saintsbury, whose *Notes on a Cellar Book* is holy writ to wine-lovers of the world, declared: "When wines were good they pleased my sense, cheered my spirits, improved my moral and intellectual powers, besides enabling me to confer the same benefits on other people." George Jean Nathan, the essayist and humorist of the 1920's, said more trenchantly: "I like wine because it makes my friends more interesting!" André Simon, the nonogenarian author of over a hundred volumes on wine and food, said with authority: "Wine is a work of art with many facets; it is well worth talking about and learning about for people with inquisitive and cultured minds." Maynard Amerine, American oenologist and wine pundit, put it most simply: "The most important requirement of wine is that it give pleasure."

Wine is, indeed, to give pleasure. It may be defined as a liquid containing five alcohols, dozens of chemicals and minerals. It can be acclaimed along with "a loaf of bread . . . and thou" by the poet. Its virtues can be extolled medically: "Take a little wine for thy stomach's sake." But sooner or later one must return to its primary function—to give pleasure. It should not be held in awe, discussed in hushed tones, pontificated upon by wine bores, apostrophized in learned tomes. Wine is simply a pleasant liquid, of infinite variety, calculated to please most every palate and to make nearly every one the happier for its use.

Wine is not always enjoyed at first encounter—it is often an acquired taste. Chances are your first drink of orangeade resulted in immediate liking—it is such a simple drink. But wines, even the simplest, sweetish, white, low-alcohol, low-tannin types, such as an American Sauternes or a German Liebfraumilch, require a bit of knowing. Such wines as these are relatively uncomplicated and are quickly appreciated. Not so the far more intriguing wines at the other end of the spectrum—such wines as the tannic, somewhat astringent, infinitely complex red wines of Bordeaux. The gamut is in between. And just as friends easily known and quickly intimate do not always wear so well, so the more reticent, more introverted wines tend to become the more interesting and more lastingly preferred. Complexity becomes the arbiter of wine value to the *aficionado* and the goal of the wine producer.

How do we know when wines are good, or when they seem good to us? The answer lies in the senses, about all of which are brought into play. Take color. Wines, to the tyro, are red, white, and pink, but to the expert, they are a vast range of reds, from the blue red of young wines to the brown reds of wines of age; of whites, from nearly water white to greenish whites, chartreuses, yellows; of rosés from just off-red to barely pink. Wine colors are not merely lovely—they often tell a lot about the wine in the bottle. For instance, a white wine that appears unusually dark or brownish can be quickly spotted as a wine that has somewhat oxidized. It is over the top—too old, finished. Except for a few special whites, such as superbly sweet Sauternes or rich German Ausleses and Beerenausleses or heady Tokays, white wines are better drunk young and fresh and gay.

But color is relatively external. Flavor and smell are the great determinants, along with the tactile sense of oiliness or body.

Taste is limited to what the taste buds, all 10,000 of them, can tell us—and they are rather primitive in their reactions. They can only distinguish sweet, sour, bitter, and salt. Hold your nose sometime while eating or drinking, or remember how hard it is to "taste" when you have a heavy cold. It is the combination of taste with the olfactory sensations given by the nose that makes for the total picture. That is the reason the wine expert sniffs first, and why wine glasses should be filled only one-third to one-half full. The space above the wine fills with the aroma and bouquet (if they are there). The taster also sucks in a sip of wine to get it way back under his tongue, where the taste buds are most sensitive. Do not hesitate to do the same. Leave the wine in the mouth for a bit too. Often the taste subtly changes. The aftertaste or "finish" can be important in judging complexity.

At first, wine smells will tend to be all the same to you, but very soon you will begin to recognize the distinctive aromas of certain grapes—the violet overtones of the Cabernet Sauvignon, the flowery spice of the Riesling, the honey sweetness of Sémillon and Sauvignon. And you will also learn to detect the sulfur odor in some white wines; the languorous smell of aged reds; the "stink" of corky or spoiled wine.

Feel, or the tactile sense, is also called into play in drinking wine. It is the body or "bead" that tells if a wine has a watery or an oily quality. Tilt the glass and see the wine "stick." Chew it in your mouth—a wine of high alcoholic content will tend to seem heavier, though sweetness will often cover up viscosity or lack of it. Wine should "feel" vinous, not watery, though the wine that advertises as "so rich you can cut it with a knife" may be overdoing things just a bit.

And finally there is a hard-to-describe additional quality known as "breed." A wine either has it or it has not. You know it when it is there—and when it is not—after drinking enough wine. For you can never learn to distinguish wines without doing homework—drinking them.

How to taste wines

THE TYPES OF WINES

Now it is time to define the subject: What *is* wine?

Basically, wine is simply fermented grape juice. Grapes are crushed to extract juice, the juice is inoculated with yeasts that attack the sugar in the grape juice, converting it to alcohol and releasing carbon dioxide gas in the process. When the sugar (or a portion of it) is thus converted, lo!—you no longer have grape juice, but wine. Interestingly enough, man is not even needed in the process. Wine could have been, and probably was, a "happening." For the bloom on the grape is actually composed of yeast, which cannot help but get into the crush and begin its praiseworthy converting endeavors without a by-your-leave. (In these days of scientific fermentation, these wild yeasts are usually killed by sulfur so that better and more controllable strains may be introduced to the "must" or mash.)

"Natural" or table wines

This process refers to the making of only one type of wine—albeit by far the most important—table wine. As its name implies, table wine is intended to be drunk with food. It is relatively low in alcohol (9 to 14 per cent), and it is "natural," in that no additional ingredient is added to it. Usually, in making table wine, most of the grape sugar is converted—although in some sweet wines, such as Sauternes, unconverted sugar remains. Of course, *something* is done to the wine: It must be fined, and filtered, and racked (names for methods of clarification), then aged, sometimes blended, and bottled.

Champagne and sparkling wines

The second of the four categories of wine is also "natural"—the sparkling wines, of which Champagne is far and away the best known. Champagne, to Americans, is so much a symbol, a thing apart, a mystique, as almost not to be a wine at all. However, Champagne *is* wine, with something special added—a secondary dosage of sugar and yeast, which sets off another fermentation. But since this dosage is added in the bottle, the carbon dioxide cannot escape into the atmosphere. It is captured inside the bottle and results in the lovely bubbles so famous in song and story. That is the true Champagne Process, used for all true Champagnes. Some still wines are simply carbonated by the injection of carbon dioxide gas, in the same manner as a soft drink would be made. There is an appreciable difference in the cost—and in the result. True Champagne is a costly, time-consuming, laborious product to make. Hence its high price, even aside from the unconscionable extra tax bite that Uncle Sam exacts for "bubbles."

Fortified wines

The other two categories of wine are *not* natural. They are made, at least in part, by the hand and skill of man. Both kinds are higher in proof—i.e., alcoholic strength—because man introduces extra spirits into the wine. The first category is the dessert

The Tea Party (detail)
Lithograph by E. B. and E. C. Kellogg
for *Harper's Weekly*

Asking a Blessing (detail)
Chromolithograph by Howet Middleton
from painting by F. O. C. Darley

The William H. Vanderbilt Family (detail)
By Seymour J. Guy

Dining room, The Elms
Newport, Rhode Island

or appetizer wines—sometimes called fortified, because of the added alcohol.

This group includes Sherry, Port, Muscatel, Madeira, and many others that are often drunk before a meal, as an apéritif, or after a meal, or between meals as a pleasant, mild picker-upper. The alcohol in these wines ranges from 19 to 22 per cent. Many of these wines are sweet or sweetish, as the introduction of grape spirits arrests further fermentation, leaving a residue of sugar to sweeten the wine. They are oxidized too, to greater or lesser degree, and some are cooked as well.

The final category represents the flavored wines, of which the Vermouths are by far the best known. These are still wines that have been flavored in one way or another, primarily by infusion with herbs, barks, berries, and the like. One prominent wine producer confided that 60 different ingredients go into his Vermouth, though what they are, and what the proportions, are top secret. Dubonnet is another flavored wine, as are Byrrh, Lillet, Saint-Raphaël—and May Wine. In the United States, of recent years, a new series of flavored wines has emerged, with such swinging titles as Thunderbird and White Satin. The so-called Kosher wines are more comfortably catalogued in this category, as most are cooked and/or flavored and are often sugared.

Flavored wines

WINES BY COLOR

So much for wine by category; now let us consider the division by color. All table wines fall into the reds, the whites, and the pinks (rosés)—but they are, as we observed, not simple red, white, and pink, as in a flag. Wine colors tend to present a palette from dark, almost black, red (like Egri Bikavér from Hungary) to light crimsons of the Bardolino and Beaujolais stamp. The whites run the gamut from browns to water white, through lemons, greens, chartreuses, and the like. Even the pinks show colors from just below a true red to a pink so light as to be hardly discernible at first glance. A common misconception is that the color of the wine follows the color of the grape skin. It may, or it may not.

Red wine

White wine

Pink wine (Rosé)

However, all wine color originates in the skin of the grape, where the pigmentation lies. A red, a white, and a pink wine can all be made from the same grape (a red grape). If the skins are left in the "must" for a week, red wine results; if they are removed immediately after the grapes are crushed, white wine results; if they remain in 24 to 36 hours, the result is pink wine. The best example is Champagne, a yellowish-white wine, usually made of half red and half white grapes. The red skins are simply not permitted to remain in the vat but are removed immediately.

1801. Wine provided at Washington.

D

May 3. a pipe of Brazil Madeira from Col°. Newton . . . 350.

20. [a pipe of Pedro Ximenes, mountain, from Yznardi. 126. gall^s. @ 2^D. 252.
424. bottles of it sent to Monticello. Feb. 1803.

a Quart^r. cask of Tent from d°. 30. gall^s. @ 1.50 45.

a keg of Pacharetti doux. from d°.

doz. of claret from d°.

15. doz. Sauterne from H. Sheaff. @ 8.D . . . . . . 120.

~~140 bottles claret @ 10 D pr doz.~~

~~6 doz. d° @ 12.D.~~

June. 12 2. pipes of Brazil Madeira. from Taylor & Newton . . . 700.

148. bott. claret @ 10.D. pr doz. 123.33
72. d° @ 12.D. 72. . . . 195.33
220

Sep. 28. 2. pipes of Brazil Madeira from Taylor & Newton . . . 700.

Nov. 28. 30. doz. = 360. bottles of Sauterne from Sheaff . . . 240.

1802 Jan. 7. a tierce (60. gall^s.) Malaga from mr Yznardi. Lacryma Christi 106.
the above is 46. years old. viz. vintage of 1755

2. doz. bottles of claret from mr Barnes. @ 8.D. . . . 16.

Feb. 24. 1. pipe dry Pacharetti. from mr Yznardi . . . 202.

[1. pipe Sherry of London quality 10. y. old . . . 188

[½ pipe of Sherry of a different quality . . . 94.
270 bottles of it sent to Monticello. Feb. 1803.

½ pipe of white Sherry . . . 84.

insurance on the wines of Feb. 24. D 22.72

May. 6. duties pd Yznardi on d°. . . 156. 178.72

claret from J. Barnes.

Nov. a half barrel of Syracuse from Capt. McNiel

Dec. 1. 100. bottles Champagne from the Chevalr. Yrujo.} 172.50

1803 Jan. 10. 100. d°. @ .86½ viz. .75 first cost + 11¼ duty . . .

(2. halfpipes of wine of Oeyras. from mr Jarvis at Lisbon. 98. 17
sent to Monticello

Mar. 3. 2 pipes of Brazil Madeira from James Taylor Norfolk. 700.

21. 12. doz. Sauterne from Sheaff. @ 8⅔ D 104.33

1803. Oct. 21. 50. bottles white Hermitage @ 73⅓ cents + 8¾ duty = 82 cents + 9½ freight = 91½ 45.80

23. 150. bottles Rozan Margau @ 82½c + 8¾ duty = 91¼ cents + 8¾ = 1.D. 150.00

150. d°. Sauterne @ 64⅙ + 8¾ duty = 72 9/10 + 8¾ fr^t = 81⅝c 122.57

Dec. 1. 400. d°. Champagne d'Aij (153. broke) | cost .68¾ | duty .07½ | fr^t .19 = .95 }
100. d°. Burgundy of Chambertin | .59½ | .07½ | .19 = .77 .86 } 484.

10. a quarter cask Mountain of crop of 1747. from Kirkpatrick of Malaga fr^t. 10.

Monticello 30. (2. pipes Termo, one the crop of Carrasqueira, the other of Arruda. Jarvis. milreis 170 = 196.35

d°. (1. butt of Pale Sherry from Yznardi 194.85

1804. Mar. 19. a pipe of Brazil Madeira from Taylor 358.07

a box Champagne from d°. 5. doz. @ .62½ cents 37.50

June 20. 138. bottles of wines from Florence [123 Montepulciano] fr^t. & duty 25½c. cost 26c 33.17

July 400. bottles Champagne from N.Y. same as Mar. 19. @ 1.D. [23. broke] 400.

July 20. 98. bottles claret from Sheaff . . . . 82.

Nov. 28. 240. bottles of Hungary wine @ 1.70 }
36. d°. Tokay . . . . . 3.31 } from Bollman 546.43
12 d°. other wines . . . . 4.36 }

Monticello [Dec. 1 pipe dry Pacharetti prime cost 194.85

1. Sherry 15. y. old

[147. bottles Port . .

Montic°. [53. Buccellas. 10. y. old } from Fernandes 152.25

[1. pipe Arrudae wine from Jarvis. Lisbon.

36. bottles Chateau Margaux of 98. @ 7^{tt} }

72. d°. Rozan Margaux of 98. @ 4^{tt}. 10^s } D 778.50 [Lee]

72. d°. Salus Sauterne @ 2^{tt}. 5^s . .

THE WINES OF AMERICA

Today, American wines can hold up their heads with distinction. It is often forgotten that even the wines of the old world are not by any means a vast array of 1st Growth Château Clarets, Domaine de la Romanée Conti Burgundies, or Trockenbeerenauslese Rhine wines. No more than one-tenth of total production of France, and far less of Europe as a whole, ever could be called fine wines. The vast remainder are average wines, and most of these are never even bottled. *Vin ordinaire* in cask, *vin du pays* that seldom leaves its hearthside—these are the staple of the European wine drinker.

In the United States are two major wine-producing areas, East and West. They are entirely different, and their grapes and wines are entirely different.

California has been blessed with some of the finest grape-growing regions in the world, from the point of view of soil, equability of climate, incidence of rainfall, and sunshine. From the Oregon border to the Mexican, here is one vast vineyard growing grapes originally from Europe—*Vitis vinifera*. Of course, not all California vineyards are uniformly productive, nor are the grape varieties used the same. The cool northern counties, blessed with foggy nights and Pacific breezes, are climatically perfect for most of the shy-bearing noble grapes that produce the world's great wines. But hybridization and experimentation have created excellent new varieties of "hot-country" grapes that have taken happily to warmer areas, to produce a splendid harvest of grapes for different wines and wine varieties, both table and dessert.

California wine

A basic difference between the California and European producer is that the latter usually offers only one kind of wine, whereas in California one producer may offer a dozen. The varied topography and acreage in California permit the growing of various kinds of grapes. In France a producer would grow only one, or at most a very few—sometimes by choice, but in the great vineyard areas by law.

Are California wines better or worse or the equals of their European counterparts? It depends on individual taste. However, a wine from Europe and one from California produced from the same grape stock will not taste *exactly* the same because the grape is not the only factor involved. The grapevine in Bordeaux is nourished by the special soil and rainfall, warmed by a local degree and incidence of sunlight. In California, it does the same —but six thousand miles away, with all the attendant variations. Result: two different taste sensations with subtle likenesses.

In the East, primarily in New York State, are the wines of the *Vitis labrusca*. This great family of grapes is descended from wild native vines. The characteristic "foxiness" or grapey taste has been mitigated by some most interesting experiments in

New York wine

Facsimile of Thomas Jefferson's list of wine provided at Washington from 1801 through 1804.

hybridizing, cross-breeding with European varieties, and even the growing of those *vinifera* stocks able to withstand the rigorous Eastern winters. But the "foxiness" of the original Eastern grapes pleases some palates. A true wine buff enjoys the multitude of possible adventures presented by the vast array of wines of the world. Only a snob drinks by the book, by the price tag, or by the certificate of national origin.

Varietal wines

Let us now discuss some of the specifics of the wines to be found. First, the so-called varietal wines take their names from the variety of grapes from which they are made.

For example, the grape that predominates in the most famous red Burgundies of France is the Pinot Noir. The California wine that most closely resembles these Burgundies, and also made from that grape, is labeled Pinot Noir. The grape of the great château wines of Bordeaux is primarily the Cabernet Sauvignon. Wine made from the same grape in California has the label Cabernet Sauvignon. The best of the Beaujolais are from Gamay grapes. Calfornians call the wine Gamay or Gamay Beaujolais. The favored grapes for white wines from France's Burgundy are Chardonnay and Pinot Blanc,´ and these names are used in California for corresponding wines. Chenin Blanc, which lends its name to a varietal wine in California, is used in Vouvray, Pouilly Fumé, and other Loire wines. Rhines and Moselles come from the Riesling and Johannisberg Riesling grapes—hence, California Riesling. Sauternes, Barsac, or Graves come from the grapes known as Sémillon and Sauvignon Blanc. Californians label their comparable wines with the names of these grapes

In the East, such names as Niagara, Elvira, Diamond, and Catawba are varietals, produced from the grapes of these same names.

Generic wines

Below the varietals is another huge category of wines that employ European regional nomenclature, but with their domestic origin clearly indicated—California Burgundy, California Chablis, New York State Claret, etc. These are the generics. They are the handiwork of skilled vintners who blend wines to resemble time honored European wines. But there is no requirement, as in the varietals, to use 51 per cent or more of any one grape variety to legalize the use of the name. A California or New York Claret need not be made from the Cabernet Sauvignon at all, as a true French Claret must be. It is entirely the blender's gambit.

Proprietary brands

A third category of wines offered for sale by American producers are the proprietary or brand-named wines. These are "special" wines, the product of one vintner, who tries to develop wines to which his customers will return, time after time. Hence uniformity is paramount, and that special flavor is to be found only under the one label.

THE WINES OF EUROPE

France is the premier wine-producing country of the world. It produces a far greater percentage of great and superior wines than any other country. It produces more of all wine than any other country (except for Italy in some recent years). It produces a greater variety of wines than any other country.

French wine

The French are not as permissive when it comes to wine or spirits as they are supposed to be about other matters. The *appellations contrôlées,* or delimited geographic designations, are inviolate. They do not guarantee quality, but they do insure point of origin. The label, properly read, will tell you all—as it will in Germany and (to a somewhat lesser extent) in Spain, Portugal, Italy, Austria, Hungary, and elsewhere.

The greatest vineyard area in France, both in extent and in the quality of its greatest products, is unquestionably Bordeaux. A half-billion bottles a year are produced on a quarter-million acres. They are reds (the storied Clarets), whites, and a little pink. The whites range from the sweet Sauternes and Barsacs to flinty dry Graves. The reds are the longest-lived wines in the world, thanks to the preponderance of Cabernet Sauvignon grapes. Ten, twenty, even fifty years of age, will cause no lifted eyebrows in Bordeaux. Many wine *aficionados* confess that, having sampled the gamut of the world's wines, they repair to the Clarets as the ultimate.

The wines of Bordeaux are of two major types—the château wines, which are made from grapes entirely grown, made, and bottled *"au château,"* and the commune or blended wines of a parish or county. For example, Médoc is a large district. In it are such communes as St. Estèphe, Pauillac, St. Julien. Within these are various châteaux. If a vineyard is not attached to a château, the wine made from the grapes may take on the name of the commune. It then is blended with other wines of the same or adjoining communes by one of the large shippers of Bordeaux, and shipped under his house name as a Médoc (after the district) or, if from only one commune, as a St. Julien, a St. Emilion, or St. Estèphe. These wines are often superb values, and most are blended to be drinkable on arrival. No long "laying-down" period is needed for these blended wines.

Bordeaux

The great Château d'Yquem, premier vineyard of Sauternes, and producer of what many consider the prime sweet white wine of the world, makes its wine after the grapes have been attacked by the fungus *Botrytis cinerea,* called *pourriture noble* (patrician rot) by the French. This blessed blight loosens the grape skins and allows moisture to escape. The raisinlike berries yield a nectar for the gods. The same disease produces the great

Beerenauslese and Trockenbeerenauslese wines of Germany, and now even one in the eastern United States.

The official classification of some of the châteaux in 1855 as 1st, 2d, 3d, 4th, 5th is still useful, but should not be followed too religiously. Of course, such great seigneurs as Châteaux Haut-Brion, Lafite, Latour, Margaux, Mouton-Rothschild, Pétrus, Cheval Blanc, and Ausone are among the greatest reds in the world—if not *the* greatest—but there are hundreds of lesser châteaux, unclassified "bourgeois" châteaux, and communal wines well worth searching out, for pleasure as well as for solvency. Look for real bargains in the little-known wines of the Blaye, Bourg, and Entre-Deux-Mers areas.

Burgundy

Bordeaux's only competitor for rank of "greatest" is Burgundy, which produces less than one-third the amount of Bordeaux, and is much smaller in acreage. The heart of Burgundy is called the Côte d'Or (Golden Slope). Attached to it, on the northwest, is Chablis, home of world-famous, steely white wines. South of the Côte d'Or, but still in Burgundy, are the districts of Mâconnais, famous for white Pouilly-Fuissé, and Beaujolais, famous for red Beaujolais (made from the Gamay rather than the Pinot Noir grape of Côte d'Or).

The wines of Côte d'Or are red and white, and include some of the greatest wine names in the world. Among whites are the great Le Montrachet, and its relatives, Chevalier-Montrachet and Bâtard-Montrachet; Meursault; Corton-Charlemagne. Among reds, the most respected include Romanée-Conti and Romanée St. Vivant; Chambertin; Musigny; Bonnes Mares; Richebourg; Grands Echézeaux; and Clos de Vougeot. These are "estate-bottled," similar to the châteaux, cru classé, in Bordeaux.

These are great greats, but very expensive. It is well to seek out good lesser lights and have fun while you save money. Villages or parishes that are renowned for great vineyards also produce wines that are not "estate-bottled" but are demarcated and good—*viz.* Aloxe-Corton, Vosne-Romanée, Chassagne-Montrachet, Puligny-Montrachet, or just plain Beaune or Hospices de Beaune.

Rhône

Loire

There are many other wine areas in France. The southerly Rhône supplies excellent red wines, including the ever popular Châteauneuf-du-Pape. Especially worthy of attention are Hermitage and Côte Roti. The Loire is a great favorite, primarily for white wines. Flinty Pouilly Fumé (not to be confused with Pouilly Fuissé, a Burgundy) is special, as is Sancerre. Vouvray, both still and sparkling, has its devotees.

Alsace

Alsace, a continuation of the Rhineland, has excellent values, as there are not overpriced vineyard names here. As in California, the varietals are named for the grape: Riesling, of course, but also Gewürztraminer and Sylvaner.

There are other wines in the Provence, Midi, and Languedoc,

and one should not overlook Brittany's only "appellation" wine—the light, dry, inexpensive Muscadet.

Italy is a vast reservoir of wines for daily use, with standouts of excellence bobbing up here and there from the Alps to Sicily. And incidentally, the percentage of standouts is increasing at a very rapid rate as the Italian government and voluntary *Consorzi* police to ever greater degree the growing of grapes, the making of wine, the delimitation of districts, and the preparation of labels.

Italian wine

Lombardy and Piedmont in the north are outstanding. The former offers Grignolino, Barbera, Nebbiolo, all red; the latter Valpolicella, Bardolino, and the white Soave and Asti Spumante (the Italian demi-sec Champagne).

Lombardy
Piedmont

Tuscany has a red and white. The best-known Italian wine, recognized by its straw fiasco, is Chianti. (Be advised that only the youngest and least extraordinary Chiantis come in straw-covered *fiaschi*. The noble Chiantis appear in normal Bordeaux-type bottles and bear identifying neck-labels proclaiming their points of origin.) Orvieto, a white wine appearing in a straw flask of different shape, is also from this region.

Tuscany

Around Rome are the wines of Castelli Romani, of moderate virtue. Naples has the lovely-sounding Lachryma Christi, both still and sparkling. Another favorite is the Verdicchio di Jesi from the Marches. All of these are white wines.

Rome
Naples
The Marches
Sicily

Sicily is famous for Marsala, sweet and dry—a red fortified wine, made by adding a cooked concentrate to the wine. It is much prized in cookery, though the dry variant, as an apéritif, deserves greater recognition. Colombo from Sicily is a dry white not to be overlooked.

No mention of Italy is complete without a reminder that Vermouth (the sweet variety primarily) is a product of the area around Turino. The bitters, Campari; the stomachic, Fernet; and the liqueurs, Galliano and Strega, are other widely traveled Italian émigrés.

Turino

Forget the reds (there are few of them); the white wines of Germany are glorious. There is not much of a supply, unfortunately, as the entire grape industry is so far north as to constantly contend with Nature at her worst. It is concentrated along the Rhine and Moselle (German, Mosel) rivers, and their few tributaries. The little towns, surrounded by steep, terraced vineyards, dot the banks for miles.

German wine

As to the Rhines, those of the Rheingau are proverbially best and biggest. Rheinhessen, the Palatinate, and Franconia produce other fine wines.

Rhine

A few to remember are Schloss Vollrads, Schloss Johannisberger, Marcobrunner, Rudesheimer. There are hundreds of others. Usually the town name precedes the vineyard name—for example Hochheimer Kirchenstück, from the town of Hochheim, which gave the British the name of Hock for all Rhine wines. All Rhine wines are demarcated carefully, appearing in traditional flute-shaped, brown-glass bottles. (The so-called Steinweins of Franconia are an exception, coming in squat Bocksbeutels.)

Moselle

The Moselles are more delicate, more flowery, and come in green flutes. Expensive Bernkasteler Doktor is the apogee; Piesporter Goldtröpfchen and Graacher Himmelreich are good bets.

The ubiquitous Liebfraumilch and Moselblümchen are catch-all names for blends of any white wines of Rhine and Moselle. Your guide here must be the shipper's or importer's name on the label, or his special branded names— Blue Nun, etc.

On German labels, *Natur* or *Naturwein* indicates a wine that has not been made from sugared must (in France, sugaring is called chaptalizing). Because Germany is so far north, its grapes often do not have enough of their own sugar for proper fermentation and alcohol production. Therefore artificial sugaring, not of the wine but of the mash during fermentation, is applied to some wines. Those wines that have *not* undergone this process may be identified by the word Naturwein on the label. Other nonsugared wines include those marked Auslese, from specially selected grapes, and Spätlese (from late-picked grapes), both likely to be naturally sweet.

Beerenauslese and Trockenbeerenauslese wines, made only in very favorable years, from most choice grapes, selected with a care beyond that given to the Auslese category, are incredibly sweet when young but mature to something for the gods, the greatest gods, and for the rich ($25 to $50 a bottle)!

Wines of other countries
Switzerland

Switzerland has some pleasant, never great, wines, Neuchâtel being the best-known white and Dôle the best-known red.

Austria

Austria's Loibner Kaiserwein can be delicious and dry; Gumpoldskirchner, delicious and sweet.

Hungary

Hungary's light wines from the banks of Lake Balaton can be splendid—Badacsony and Eger for white; Kadarka and Egri Bikavér (Bull's Blood) the best reds. The most distinctive wines of Hungary, however, are the Tokays. Szamorodni is the drier; Aszu the sweeter. The number of *puttonyos* (baskets) of overripe grapes per cask indicates the relative sweetness of Aszu in increasing scale, and appears on the label.

Yugoslavia

Yugoslavia's wines are primarily thermalized for "keeping," but this does not destroy their pleasant taste, only their maturing qualities. Reds: Merlot, Dingac, Blatina; whites: Zilavka, Rizling, Chipon.

Spain

Spain offers its famed Riojas—red and white. They resemble lesser Bordeaux. But Sherry is the *great* wine of Spain. Sherry is a "strong" wine, 19 to 23% of alcohol. It ranges from pale and bone dry to dark and sweet. Hence, it is an apéritif, a dessert wine, or a between-meal wine. A good Sherry can even be used, to excellent effect, for cooking, but do not buy so-called cooking Sherry.

All Sherry is matured and progressively blended by the *solera* system—whereby great oak butts of wine are kept in a 3-tier arrangement, the newer wines feeding into the butts below. Each year about a third of the wine in the lowest butt is drawn off, blended, and bottled.

There are three basic types of Sherry: the Finos, the Olorosos, and the Pedro Ximénez (a very sweet cousin of the Olorosos). The Finos range from very dry Manzanilla, to pale, dry Fino, to fuller, nutty Amontillado. Olorosos include Amoroso, Oloroso, Cream Sherry, and Brown Sherry, in increasing order of sweetness. The latter have gained newfound popularity, thanks to the American habit of drinking sweet Sherry on-the-rocks.

Portugal

Portugal's Vinho Verde (green wine) is an inexpensive, pleasant, young white. (The greenness refers to age, not color.) But Portuguese pinks are today the darlings of many: Mateus and Lancer's (the crock sparkler).

Portugal's greatest contributions to winedom are the two fortified wines of song and story, Port and Madeira. Port wines are made around the mainland city of Oporto; Madeira is from the islands.

Port is more English than Portuguese. The natives prefer the lighter, natural table wines of the country, but England grew great on fortified Ports. There are two major types of Port, Ruby and Tawny, which are always sweet because of the unconverted sugars. Ruby is a younger wine, rich blue-red in color, fruity and heavy-bodied. It is aged in wood, then bottled and sold. Tawny Port is kept in wood longer, is fined (filtered) at intervals, which removes a certain amount of pigment, leaving a paler, browner liquid. It is always older than Ruby, commands a higher price, is lighter and less heavy of body.

Some Ports are bottled in an exceptional year—Vintage Ports. They throw heavy sediment, must be carefully handled, take 20 years or more to mature, and are seldom seen outside of the Englishman's lair. Crusted Ports are the same, but not all of one year's vintage.

Madeira is a wine of history. It was the tipple of the fathers of our country, who discovered its virtues and the helpfulness of sending barrels of it around the Horn, to swish and to bake under tropic suns. It is still baked.

The types of Madeira are: sweet—Bual and Malmsey; medium—Sercial and Verdelho; drier—Rainwater. They deserve greater popularity and are gaining it.

Greece

Naoussa (red) and Pallini (white) of Greece are very pleasant. Greek resinated wines (Retsina) require a deliberately cultivated taste.

Rumania, Bulgaria, Russia, Israel, the North African countries, South Africa, Australia, New Zealand, Chile, Argentina, Brazil, Peru, and Mexico round out the wine picture. The relative unavailability of these wines makes elaboration unjustified.

HOW TO BUY WINE

How do you buy hats, dresses, shoes? First, it is a matter of taste—*yours*. It is hard to advise out-of-hand. No one can begin to have judgments without *tasting* wines, lots of wines, of all kinds. Set a price level, if you must, select a good, competent wine merchant, tell him your problem and your interest, and throw yourself on his mercy—and judgment. But give him what hints you can. For instance, tell him you like somewhat sweet drinks, that you are planning to serve the wine with a chicken casserole, that there will be eight for dinner. Try two or more selections that fit these requirements and see which you like the best over the weeks. You will begin to eliminate A and C; then try B, your choice, against another entry. And so on. Repeat for meat, fish, egg dishes, desserts, or whatever. Gradually you will become more and more discriminating. You will begin to order wine by cases because by now you will know some wines you like—and case lots come for less money!

Vintage   This much-argued subject will enter into your wine-buying and wine-ordering activities.

People talk about "vintage wine." All wine is "vintage," inasmuch as all wine is made after one year's harvest or another. What they really mean is wine of a good vintage.

It is true that Nature sometimes smiles, sometimes frowns, and sometimes does both in the same year. She sends just the right sunshine or rainfall—or none; she unleashes hailstones and thunderous deluges. She parches the soil, and the grapes. But for all of this, man must take his share of the credit, or blame, for the wine, too. Therefore do not follow vintage years and vintage charts like a horse-player. As the tired old cliché puts it: "Some good wine is made in off years." Moreover, some poor wine *can* be made in good years, if the vintner does not know, or mind, his P's and Q's.

No year in any country is *exactly* like any other in that country, but sometimes the differences are so miniscule as to be meaningless. For instance, the weather in California is remarkably equable—days of sunshine and rain have a nice habit of evening out. Hence, while years certainly do vary some, in both quality and quantity, the vintage date 1962 tells how old the wine is, more important than the qualities of 1962 as a vintage year.

But this is not true for the more northerly vineyards of Europe. Vintage *is* of great concern in Germany, Champagne, Burgundy, Bordeaux, the Loire—not so much in the Rhône, Italy, Spain, Portugal, or other more southerly climes.

Price will often reveal the decisions of the world's wine buyers regarding vintages—or ask your storekeeper for his judgments. Do not be a slave to vintage; but do not be too gullible either. Do not fall for a great-name wine at a bargain—which might turn out to be a bad year even for a château wine. Here are a few of the *good years:*

Germany: 1964, 1959; also 1962, 1961, 1960

France (Bordeaux, Burgundy, Champagne): 1966, 1964, 1962, 1961, 1959, 1955

Other countries and vineyard areas: Not so important.

Good years

The greatest buffs for wine in the world are the doctors. That should prove something.

Wine and health

Wine is, and always has been, known as a drink of natural healthfulness. Even for children (although it is not recommended as a beverage for them) it is far better than teeth-deteriorating sweets and sweet drinks. For the elderly, it is a remarkable builder-upper and soporific. For all of us, it is a great relaxer and reliever of tension—and without tension we do not tend to overeat, oversmoke, overdo.

Another virtue—a 3-oz. serving of average table wine is only 75 to 80 calories. A Martini is about 180; a bottle of beer is 170; a chocolate malt, 210!

SERVING, DRINKING, AND CARING FOR WINES

Now that you have bought your wine, what do you do about it? There is more cant talked about the serving of wine than about any other item that appears on your dining table. If some of it can be dispelled, this chapter will not have been written in vain.

Little glasses, the wedding-present kind, should be used once —to toast the Queen—and then thrown into the fireplace! If one glass is your limit, make it a generous 9-oz. tulip, of clear glass. It will do for white, red, and pink. If you can go for two, get the white 8-oz. and the red 10- or 12-oz. (Big saucer reds are coming in—copying Baccarat's Pavillon glass, invented for the late and great restaurateur, Soulé.)

Wine glasses

The reason for a big glass (aside from not slopping over on your tablecloth) is that you never fill a wine glass to the top. Half-full or less permits the empty top portion to capture the bouquet for your sniffing enjoyment.

Treat yourself to a decent corkscrew, one with a lever or some reversing gadget so that you do not (a) strain yourself; (b) pull through and break the cork. Open red wines an hour or so before serving and let them sit there, corks out. (But not *very* old reds—over 25 years. Open these when you are all gathered 'round. They sometimes collapse a few moments after air strikes them.) Or decant reds. The process of decanting aerates the wine as well as hours of standing. Decanting for sediment is seldom necessary with today's young wines. If you have an older wine, stand it upright for a day, open gently, pour carefully into decanter until the clear liquid appears muddy (a candle behind the stream will help you judge).

Opening the wine bottle

If you like warm whites or cold reds, go to it. Your option.

Temperature of wines

Most wine-drinkers want their whites and pinks nicely chilled (not frozen), their reds at room temperature or a little cooler—say at an Englishman's room temperature in January who has no central heating! Lesser red wines, of modest lineage, may perfectly well be a little chilled—the lower temperature hides many a shortcoming.

Ordering wines in restaurants

Order wines as soon as you have ordered your meal—to give the wine a chance to "breathe" open (if red) and to be chilled properly, if white.

Storing wines

All *table* wines, with corks, should be kept on their sides until the day they are served. This keeps the cork wet, hence swollen, hence tight. (No need to do this with patent-stopper wines.) Air is death to wine. It must not be allowed to enter the bottle until you are ready to broach it.

Keep wines as quiet as possible, and at as constant a temperature as present-day living permits: 55° F. would be ideal. It is a good idea for the city dweller to buy by the case and ask the wine merchant to store the wines (at a nominal annual case charge), letting you draw on them as you need some.

Ages of wines

Wine should not categorically be old, as many people seem to think. White wines are best when young, fresh, and sprightly (except for a few *special* types, such as Sauternes, Ausleses, Tokays). Three or four years of aging is enough, and for little Muscadets, white Beaujolais, Pinot Chardonnays, lesser Graves and Burgundies, even less.

Red wines normally improve with a few years under their corks. Good producers will not release their wines until they are at least bottle-aged to some extent. But one cannot expect a producer of a Claret to hold it 15 years (when it will be about "ready"). Use your own judgment, or ask your wine merchant. As a rule of thumb, Clarets need most age, Burgundies less, Italian and American wines still less—perhaps 4 to 7 years. Shippers' wines are usually quite ready when received. They are blended to be drinkable; however, a year or two of laying down will not hurt them.

What wines with what foods

A question that bothers every wine tenderfoot: what wines with what foods ?

People want hard dicta, inviolable rules. "What goes with what" is a subjective matter. To generalize: Few would willingly select a thin, white wine for beef steak, or a rich, heady Burgundy for brook trout. That is just common sense, as well as common taste. Most people like dry *white* wines with fish, shellfish, poultry, egg dishes. Most people like *red* wines with all red meats, roasts, stews, steaks, game; also duck, goose, veal, cheese dishes. Most people like *pink* wines with ham, pork dishes, rich fish stews and fish such as salmon or snapper, cold cuts, and cook-out meats on a hot summer's day. And most people would select a sweet, white wine (Sauternes, or Barsac, or an Auslese Rhine wine) with dessert.

But there are switches. Coq-au-vin is poultry—yet you cook it in red wine, and drink red with it. Fondue is cheese, yet white wine is preferred.

All the fertility rites of the *sommelier* (wine waiter) with your bottle are not that necessary. But most perform a definite function.

How to serve wine

First, the bottle *should* be shown to the host in a restaurant to insure that it is indeed the bottle he ordered. At home, do a double-take yourself—you may be serving a rare Trocken-beerenauslese when you intended to open an ordinary bottle.

A very little wine should be poured into the host's glass first, for him to sip, to insure that the wine is sound and worthy of the guests. Also, if the corkscrew has deposited any bits of cork in the bottle they will come out with this first pour.

Having confirmed the fact that the wine is drinkable, then pour it in the glasses around the table (about half full only, remember?). There is no need to swaddle the bottle in a napkin. If it is moist, wipe it off. It will not be warmed by your or the waiter's hand. If you do not want your guests to see what you are serving, abstain from serving it. Why not show the label, or even repeat the name of the wine to every guest?

Serving more than one wine

The rule is (to be broken, of course, at your will): Serve the white before the red; the dry before the sweet. If serving one wine, allow a bottle per four guests; serving two wines, figure a bottle of each for six—more to be generous, of course. As André Simon says, "You don't sip wine; you *drink* it!"

If you are serving wine to a dinner party of six or more, where you will need more than one bottle of anything anyway, see if you can get a magnum (two bottles in one large one). It looks handsome and makes a nice splash.

Coda

You cannot learn all about wine by osmosis, or by reading chapters like this. You must do your homework by *tasting*—not such bad homework at that! Vast knowledge will not engulf you overnight, but it *will* come gradually and grow over the years. Wine is a many-splendoured thing. The repertoire goes on through life, its subtlety and enjoyment increasing as your taste for it, and knowledge of it, expands.

André Simon firmly believes that men could find peace in the world if they looked for it over the wine bottle, instead of over water or spirits.

Wine Making in the Home

HOME WINE MAKING USED to be a hit-or-miss proposition, with the results sometimes very disappointing. Today, thanks to the development of equipment and technique, as well as to the increased understanding of the wine-making process, it is an easy task to make good wine at home. Besides, wine making is also a project in which the whole family can participate and in due time enjoy the liquid fruits of its labor.

Just as home cooking has progressed from simple recipes to gourmet delights, so has home wine making improved. Some individuals even claim—and will offer you a glass as good proof—that homemade wines are far more delicious than those available from the best commercial wineries. They will also be quick to tell you how economical such homemade wines can be.

Although the Internal Revenue Service is usually thought of as a stern tax collector, the U.S. Government allows the head of a family to make up to 200 gallons of wine, tax free, per year. Before starting, however, one must obtain a permit from the Federal Alcohol and Tobacco Tax Division of the Internal Revenue Service. Ask for Form No. 1541. The permit is granted free of charge, but it is illegal to begin without it.

You need not grow your own grapes to make a good grade of grape wine. Rather, the grapes can be purchased at a local market. To produce a gallon of wine, you will need between ten and fifteen pounds of grapes, depending on the amount of juice in the type you select. Fewer

FRUIT CRUSHER

Detail of fresco (Story of Noah, 1469–85)
Benozzo Gozzoli in the Campo Santo, Pisa

grapes will be needed if your recipe calls for the addition of water.

The first step in making your own wine is, of course, to select the type of grape you want to use. This may present some difficulty, since only a limited variety of grapes is available in each region of the country. Those who live on the West Coast will probably find the best selection, and those who live in the East will not do badly either. California grapes are considered to be closest to the European varieties, whereas Eastern grapes are thought of as more typically American. In most American cities, at a harvest time in late September and early October, wine-making grapes are available at the wholesale produce markets.

Good varieties are Catawba, Delaware, or Muscat grapes for the white wines; Steuben grapes for the light reds; and Pinot-Noir, Cabernet Savignon, Gamay, or Zinfandel grapes for the red wines. Bear in mind, however, that companies that supply home wine-making equipment also sell grape-juice concentrate, from which excellent wine can be made. Such concentrate can be shipped anywhere. Too, wines can be made from a variety of other fruits, vegetables, and flowers. Recipes are available for making good wines from elderberries, peaches, apricots, pears, celery, carrots, artichokes, roses, and dozens more.

THE CHEMISTRY OF HOME WINE MAKING

The complexity of home wine making varies considerably. Some enthusiasts set aside a special room for the purpose, purchase elaborate equipment, measuring, and testing devices, and experiment with chemical adjustments to help improve the final product. Other wine makers prefer the simple, natural approach. They crush and press their grapes by hand, often use makeshift equipment, and are less quick to make even minor alterations in the fermenting *must*. Rather, they prefer that nature and luck control the final product. The beginning wine maker is probably best advised to start as simply as possible, and this is the approach recommended here.

At the outset, understand that there is no such thing as a "perfect" or an exact recipe for wine. A wine maker may repeat the same procedure a dozen times, and each time achieve a different result. The main reason for this variability is, of course, the variability of the raw materials—the fruit from which the wine is made. The same species of grape varies from month to month, from season to season, and from vineyard to vineyard. In order to allow for these vagaries, one should have at least a minimal understanding of the chemistry of wine making.

Technically, the term wine refers only to the product that results when grape juice is fermented. Wine made by fermenting the juice of other substances must specify in its name the substance from which it was made—elderberry wine, peach wine, or rice wine.

The fermentation process

Must

Yeast

Regardless of what type of wine is being made, the fermenting juice is called the *must*, and the basis of every fermentation process is a single-celled organism called *yeast*. Yeast cells, given the proper conditions, multiply very quickly. These conditions are generally present in the must, as long as the temperature ranges between 60° and 75° F. As the yeast multiplies, it converts oxygen and sugar into water and carbon dioxide. Sugar is naturally present in the must, although often additional sugar is needed. Oxygen, however, is available in the must in only a limited quantity. As this oxygen is used up, the yeast starts to produce alcohol instead of water. Carbon dioxide is still given off. Oxygen is, of course, present in the air above the must, but this is available only to the uppermost level and is quickly used up. This description of the chemistry of wine making covers only the most fundamental aspects—the conversion of sugar into alcohol as the yeast cells multiply during fermentation. Many other processes occur in the fermenting must, but these are very complicated and not necessary for the beginner to study.

EQUIPMENT

Start with simple equipment. You may have old crocks or used five-gallon drinking-water bottles that can be used for the actual fermentation. Wooden barrels are the traditional con-

FRUIT PRESS

tainers, and if you intend to make 30 to 40 gallons of wine, it might be well to obtain used whiskey barrels from a cooperage house or a wine equipment supply dealer. If you intend to make only 5, 10, or 15 gallons of wine, a crock or a few glass carboys are adequate as fermentation equipment. Do not, under any circumstances, use a metal container unless it is stainless steel. Metal tends to have a marked effect on the taste and the bouquet of the wine.

You will also need a glass or plastic funnel and a large wooden or plastic spoon. If you intend to make large quantities of wine, an investment in a press would be wise. For 10 gallons or less, however, pressing can easily be done by hand, and the family can all have fun joining in this ritual. For hand pressing, a straining bag large enough to hold two quarts of liquid can be made from heavy unbleached muslin. A small plastic or porcelain tub is useful for collecting the crushed grapes and the pressed juice. One necessity to eliminate guesswork and insure success in your first wine-making venture is a Brix hydrometer, which measures the sugar content of the juice. The hydrometer can be obtained from any chemical firm.

If you use carboys or jars, a fermentation lock is also a good investment. This device, which is inexpensive, allows gas to escape during fermentation and, at the same time, keeps foreign objects out of the must. During fermentation in barrels, however, a double layer of cheesecloth is equally effective. You will also need a long plastic tube to use as a siphon and jars for storage. If you want to age the wine, you might invest in small wooden casks or barrels, which are available from cooperage houses in 5-, 10-, 25-, and 30-gallon sizes. Be sure to buy a wooden spigot if you use barrels, and corks if you bottle the wine. To insure cleanliness of the wooden barrels (which are recognized as the best storage and aging containers for red wines), purchase a package of sulfur sticks from the drugstore. That's all you need in the way of equipment to make your wine.

FERMENTATION LOCK

THE RAW MATERIALS

Although certain grapes are generally used to make white wines and others to make red wines, both types of wine can be made from the same grape. The juice of all grapes is clear. The color of red wines comes from allowing the skins, which contain color pigment, to ferment with the must. When making white wine, the skins are removed prior to fermentation.

The grapes, or whatever fruit is used to make the wine, should be ripe. Overripe or rotten fruit should be discarded. The grapes should be stemmed before fermentation. Large crushers often are equipped with automatic stemmers, but the home wine maker must perform this task by hand.

By purchasing grape concentrate, the home wine maker simpli-

Selection of grapes

fies his task, since all that need be done to prepare the juice for fermentation is to add water. When grapes are out of season, or if one does not have access to a market selling good-quality grapes, the use of such concentrates is, of course, a huge help.

MAKING A RED WINE

Procedure

Crushing

Now that your equipment is ready, it is a very simple process to make red wines that should be most pleasing to the palate. You will need 10 to 15 pounds of grapes per gallon of wine desired. Buy only ripe grapes. Do not wash them; the fine, whitish dust on the skins is not a spray; it is natural yeast, which will help in the fermentation process. The grapes should be picked from the stems, and be sure to discard the culls—rotten or unripe fruit. Crush the grapes by hand, collecting the juice, pulp, and skins in a plastic tub or other convenient container. Transfer this must into the fermentation container, making sure not to fill more than three-quarters full. Throw in a few handfuls of stems; the stems contain tannic acid, which helps in the development of good body and flavor in the wine during the fermentation cycle.

Test the juice for sugar with your Brix hydrometer. Fill the hydrometer jar about three-quarters full of juice. Place the jar on a level surface, insert the hydrometer, and spin it gently. Do not take the reading until the hydrometer has come to rest and is floating freely in the liquid. If the rating is under 22 percent sugar, you will need to add granulated sugar. Refer to Table I to determine how much. If the sugar level is over 22 percent, you can reduce it by the addition of water. See Table II for these instructions. After taking the reading, wash the hydrometer immediately so that no undesirable residues remain.

HYDROMETER

	Table I		Table II
Per cent of sugar in the must	*Ounces of sugar to be added to each gallon of wine*	*Brix reading of percentage of sugar in wine*	*Ounces of water to be added to each gallon of wine*
10	15	23	5.5
12	13	24	11.5
14	10	26	23
16	8	28	34.9
18	5	30	45
20	3		

Cover the crock or carboy with the fermentation lock, or, if you are using a barrel, cover it with a double fold of cheesecloth. Since grapes are very rich in their own natural yeast cells, fermentation should begin by itself within 24 hours. If, however, the bubbling, boiling process of fermentation does not start within two days, add ¼ ounce of any commercial yeast per gallon of wine. Dissolve the yeast in a cup of lukewarm water and then pour it slowly into the juice. Each day, tamp the crust of skins back into the juice and must. Some vintners turn this crust over completely. Whether you turn it over or simply push it back into the must with a wooden spoon, it is important that it be done daily, for this helps in the complete fermentation process, which should take ten to twelve days.

When the bubbling ceases and the heat of the container is reduced, indicating that fermentation has stopped, pour off the wine and press it. This is done by filling a heavy cloth straining bag with wine and suspending it above a bucket or tub; then, with a hand on each side of the bag, press!

Pressing

A simple hand lever, made of two 3-foot pieces of 2″ x 6″ board will make pressing somewhat easier. Drill two holes through one end of each board, and attach the boards to each other with heavy cord, forming a sort of oversized nutcracker. The straining bag then becomes the "nut" to be cracked—or, in this case, pressed.

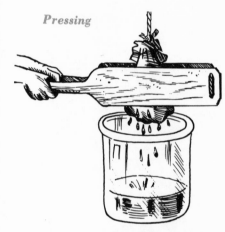

HOME MADE PRESSING OPERATION

If you intend to age the wine, and it is highly recommended that you do so for at least a year, wooden whiskey barrels are preferred. Fill the storage containers to the top and install a water seal or fermentation lock. Any surplus wine that the containers will not hold should be kept in gallon jugs. You will need it later in the racking and fining processes. A process known as refermentation will continue in the storage tank for approximately another ten days. Every time the wine is aired in its early stages, it has a tendency to referment; thus, it is necessary that the water seal be installed. Use melted paraffin to seal the closure of the carboys or barrels.

Racking

After the wine has set for two weeks, it is time for the racking (meaning, "to pour off the clear wine"). Place a clean container at a level below the vessel that is to be racked. Siphon the wine from the higher vessel into the lower one. Be sure that the siphon intake does not settle in the dregs at the bottom. Take care to clean the storage containers thoroughly. If you are using wooden barrels, rinse them and then sterilize them by burning a sulfur stick in each. Strain the wine through a cloth-covered funnel as you replace the wine in the storage containers. Install a permanent cork in the barrels or carboys and cover with melted wax or paraffin to seal completely.

Some vintners rack the wine one or two more times during the first year of aging. This is not absolutely necessary, but it does help clarify the wine. If upon inspection the wine seems cloudy, light a candle and hold it on the opposite side of the glass container; if the flame is clearly outlined, your wine is clear and fine. If, however, the flame is fuzzy and not sharply outlined, the wine needs another racking.

Fining

If the further racking process does not clear the wine, use a fining agent such as powdered gelatin, Sparkolloid, or bentonite. The procedures for fining with these ingredients are as follows:

Powdered gelatin: 6 grams per 10 gallons wine to be fined. Dissolve the gelatin in a cup of water or wine. When it is dissolved, mix it with one quart of wine and beat or shake well. Pour the wine-gelatin solution into the storage container of wine, and stir for 10 minutes.

Sparkolloid (a proprietary fining agent): 3 grams per 10 gallons wine to be fined. Heat one cup of wine to the boiling point; add the Sparkolloid, stir, and pour into the storage container of wine. Be sure to follow the manufacturer's directions in using Sparkolloid, and follow immediately with the bentonite treatment outlined below.

Bentonite: 10 grams per 10 gallons wine to be fined. Dissolve the bentonite in one cup of wine, bring to the boiling point, and pour into the storage container of wine.

Examination of the wine in a few days should reveal a thoroughly fined wine. If residue from the fining appears on top of the container, skim it off and refill to the top with wine or water. Reseal the container with melted wax or paraffin.

Bottling

It is advisable to age your wine in kegs or barrels for at least a year before bottling. For bottling you will need thoroughly clean bottles, corks, and a corking device. Be sure to soak the corks in warm water before use. You may wish to label the wine with dates and ingredients. The bottles should be stored on their sides and kept at a temperature of 60° to 70° F.

**HAND CORKING
MACHINE**

MAKING A WHITE WINE

The procedure for making white wine is a little more tricky than that for red wine. Some of the steps must not be confused with the making of red wine. Care must be taken in handling the grapes for white wine. As suggested earlier, Catawba, Delaware, or Muscat grapes are best. Although these varieties are not always readily available in every part of the country, make an extra effort to find them, for the wine they yield will fully repay you for your trouble. If they are not available, however, any white grapes can be used to make a white wine.

In the manufacture of white wine, the important thing to remember is that the color of any wine is determined by the skins. In making white wine the skins are removed before fermenting, and only the juice is subjected to the process of fermentation.

For your first attempt, it is advisable to make only a small batch, using a glass carboy for the fermenting vat. Stem and crush the grapes and collect in a tub or crock. Now press the grapes to separate the juice from the skins and pulp. Note that, unlike the previous recipe, pressing is done before fermentation. Use any type of homemade press, such as the one already described. The pressing may have to be repeated a number of times until all the juice is extracted. Transfer the juice to the fermentation vessel and cover with cotton cloth.

If fermentation does not begin within a day or two, add yeast (¼ ounce for each gallon of wine), then allow the juice to ferment until all the impurities and solubles have been discharged from the container. Be sure to fill the carboy daily with water or excess juice from the original pressing.

It is necessary to test the must for sugar content with the Brix hydrometer, and adjust as described in the recipe for red wine. Remove wine from the carboy until the level is an inch or so below the bottom of the neck, add the water seal lock, and seal all junctions with melted wax or paraffin.

As in the making of any wine, be sure at this time to clean up the mess. It is imperative that you keep a clean wine-making area; the rigid practice of maintaining sanitary conditions in the manufacture of the wine will insure your success. The most common reason for wine failure is contamination!

In about two weeks the wine will be ready for its first racking. Advance notice is given by the formation of sediment, or lees, in the bottom of the vessel. The lees, the residue of the yeasts, etc., are removed by racking.

Rack as explained in the section on the making of red wine. If bubbling still occurs after racking, it is possible that refermentation has set in. This is not uncommon and may take place when the wine is exposed to the air. Keep a water seal lock in place until the bubbling stops. Rack again in three months. To make the wine crystal clear, you should consider racking again in the spring before the warm weather sets in. If reracking does not clear the wine, fine it as outlined in the section on red wines.

White wine should be aged for at least a year before being bottled. Age your white wine in a keg, making sure that all junctions are sealed with melted wax or paraffin. If you prefer a dry wine, add 2 grams of tannic acid per 10 gallons of wine. Mix the acid powder in a cup of warm wine and pour it into the fermenting vat.

Now you have had the fun and excitement of wine making. Surely you have sneaked in a few tastes along the way! The anxiety of the waiting period is rewarded by the first look, the sniffing of the bouquet, and the taste of your very own wine.

Procedure

Stemming

Crushing

Pressing

Testing

Racking

Fining

Bottling

You recall the suggestion that you try a small batch in your first attempt at making white wine. It *is* tricky, and the weather and the cleanliness of the containers and the area all affect the process—so you *may* end up with a nice batch (small, it is hoped!) of white vinegar. But do not despair. Bottle it, wrap it in gay gift paper, and present it to your wife! Where else could she obtain a bottle of homemade, finely wined vinegar?

But that is the negative side. If you follow the simple instructions given here, your first attempts will provide entertainment, open up a new hobby, and give you, your family, and your friends a great treat—your very own wine.

My own experience in wine making has ranged from utter frustration to complete success—from subdued, solitary vigils to hilarious family involvement. Living near Chicago I have had no trouble in buying wine grapes at harvest time but rather in securing specific types of grapes. Once I nearly drove our produce market friends out of their minds trying to help me locate my choices—all to no avail. I did pick up Muscat, Gamay, Zinfandel, Delaware, and Catawba grapes but not Cabernet Sauvignon nor Pinot Noir. I made several small batches of each and experimented by mixing them. (Record your recipes—you will hit on one variety that you will treasure!)

Procuring the equipment in most large cities is not difficult. I have found used oak barrels for $5 to $8, crocks and carboys for less than $2. Spigots and hydrometers, etc., are all available from many specialty houses. All you really need is a few dollars for the grapes, a small investment in the equipment, a spirit of adventure, and a sincere desire to involve the entire family in one of the oldest and most rewarding activities—making wine!

Come sampling day I may not have a Château Margaux, a Grands Echezeaux, or a Marchesi di Barolo, but I do have a wine that is the most exclusive in the world—my very own!

SULFUR LOCK

WINE BARREL

Wine Glossary

Indicates the quality of agreeable tartness in a wine as contrasted with a sour or spoiled wine. — **Acidity**

As generally used, an apéritif is any alcoholic drink taken before a meal to stimulate the appetite. — **Apéritif**

The legal name of a wine, especially in France, as it must appear on the label. The top tenth of French wines are precisely defined by these label designations (*appellations d'origine contrôlées*), showing not only the origin—by region, district, commune, or estate, in ascending order of presumed excellence—but complying with standards that include the kind of grape used, local customs of viniculture, etc. Thus, Corton-Charlemagne has an estate *appellation* and must be estate-bottled; a Vin de Médoc may be a blend from several communes of that Bordeaux district. Inferior wines have only regional or generic names, such as Vin de Bordeaux or Vin Blanc. In the United States, the European regional names are used generically but must be clearly identified as American: California Chianti, New York Burgundy. The better American wines bear varietal (see *Variety,* below) names. — **Appellation**

A German superior wine made from especially selected bunches of grapes at the harvest (*Lese*), based on the appearance of the beneficent *Botrytis* mold. When individual grapes are so selected, the wine is known as Beerenauslese; when these are left to ripen on the vine before use, the wine is called Trockenbeerenauslese. Each is more esteemed and more expensive than the preceding. — **Auslese**

The major wine region of France, in the southwestern part of the country astride the Gironde River and its tributaries. Its best-known wines are those of Sauternes, Graves, and Médoc, each with innumerable kinds of wine of every grade. The red wines of Bordeaux (called Claret by the English) are mainly from the Cabernet Sauvignon grape; the white wines are from the Sauvignon Blanc and the Sémillon. — **Bordeaux**

The odors derived from a wine as a result of its maturing in the bottle, to be distinguished from aroma, which may appear in a young wine. — **Bouquet**

203

Brandy

An alcoholic beverage distilled from wine made from grapes. A brandy produced from other fruits must be identified by the fruit as: apricot brandy, peach brandy, etc.

Brut

This word is applied to the drier types of Champagne.

Burgundy

An important wine region of France, in the east-central part of the country, southeast of Paris. It provides not only the red and white wines known as Burgundy, but also Chablis and Meursault. All white Burgundies use mainly the Chardonnay grape. Red Burgundies are mainly from the Pinot Noir, except for the Beaujolais group, which uses mainly the Gamay.

Champagne

A region of France east of Paris, the white wine of which, made mainly from the Pinot Noir and Chardonnay grapes, is so processed that a second fermentation occurs in the bottle to produce dissolved carbon dioxide under pressure. On opening the bottle, the gas is released as bubbly effervescence. Outside of the French product, the name may not be used except in the United States, where its use is restricted to wines that employ the French process. Not all "sparkling" wines are Champagne even in a limited sense.

Chateau

In the terminology of the oenologist (wine expert), an estate that includes a vineyard bearing its name. This name may not be used as an *appellation d'origine* unless the wine has been produced according to the standards for which the château has been known. Thus a wine *mis en bouteille au château* is the most guaranteed product of its kind.

Claret

The English name for a Bordeaux red wine (see above).

Crust

The deposit of sediment on the inside of the bottle of old bottle-aged wine.

Decanter

A bottle into which mature red wine is often slowly poured in order to aerate it and to be certain that none of the sediment will reach the glass. As soon as a cloudy appearance indicates the presence of sediment, the pouring from the original bottle ends, and the wine may be served from the decanter.

Dry

In wines, the opposite of sweet. The French word is *sec* for all still wines, but a Champagne that is *sec* is still rather sweet; a truly dry Champagne is *brut*.

A wine—also called, from its use, dessert or apéritif wine—having a relatively high alcoholic content because of the addition of spirits before bottling. The most familiar such wines are Sherry, Port, and Marsala. Vermouth is a fortified wine that is also flavored. | **Fortified Wine**

The English name for Rhine wine. | **Hock**

A general name for Rhine wine, usually one lacking a specific appellation. | **Liebfraumilch**

A wine bottle of 52 fluid ounces. A jeroboam is a double magnum; a rehoboam is a triple magnum. | **Magnum**

A general name for Moselle wine, usually one that lacks a specific appellation. | **Moselblumchen**

A designation given to a German wine to which no sugar has been added before or during the process of fermentation, especially applied to those wines of superior quality that are not otherwise identifiable as unsugared. However, all Auslese, Spätlese, and other outstanding wines (Kabinett) are known to be *Naturweine* without having to be so identified. | **Natur**

The term used to describe the pungent flavor of Sherry. | **Nutty**

A louse that virtually destroyed European vines when American cuttings, which are immune to it, were introduced for experimental purposes into Europe in 1869. The grafting of healthy European vines on American rootstocks proved to be the only means of ending the blight. (See *Vitis labrusca* and *Vitis vinifera* below.) | **Phylloxera**

Describes wine that is ready to drink. | **Ripe**

The wine that has improved in the cask to the point at which it is ready to be bottled. Aging will be completed in the bottle. | **Ripe for Bottling**

A German superior wine made from grapes that have been allowed to ripen beyond the normal harvest, adding to the sweetness and value of the product. | **Spatlese**

Any still, unfortified wine, regardless of color, meant to be served primarily with food. | **Table Wine**

Tawny	Port with a brownish color instead of the usual ruby.
Variety	A term referring primarily to grapes and indirectly to the wines (called "varietal") produced from those grapes. Thus, Chardonnay is a variety of grape, of the species *Vitis vinifera*, and both the Chablis wine of the French district of that name and the California wine named Chardonnay or Pinot Chardonnay are made primarily from that grape. The name of the California wine is varietal, while that of the French wine is regional. Riesling is the name of a variety of grape, and New York, Chilean, and French Riesling are varietal names for wines produced from this grape.
Vermouth	A fortified white wine flavored with spices, herbs, and especially the flower of the wormwood shrub. Regardless of where made, the dry type is known as French and the sweet type as Italian Vermouth.
Vin du Pays	French name for a regional wine that may be excellent when served locally but is not suitable for bottling. It is usually superior to a *vin ordinaire*.
Vin Ordinaire	French name for the bulk of the wine used on a day-to-day basis at table, without bottling or entrance into other than local commerce. It comprises about nine-tenths of the total wine consumption in European wine-drinking countries, but has no market in the United States.
Vintner	A broad term used to designate wine makers, wine blenders, and wholesale wine merchants.
Viticulture	The science of grape-growing.
Vitis labrusca	The most successful native vine of Eastern North America capable of withstanding a rugged climate and immune to *Phylloxera,* but producing wine characterized by a tang that often failed to appeal to devotees of European wines.
Vitis vinifera	The most important species of vine cultivated throughout Europe and transplanted to California. It succumbed to the *Phylloxera* blight, and therefore all existing stocks of this species are grown on roots from resistant American stocks (not *labrusca*). It is believed that the essential characteristics of the *vinifera* were retained, although there is no way to compare contemporary wines with those produced before 1869, when the blight appeared.

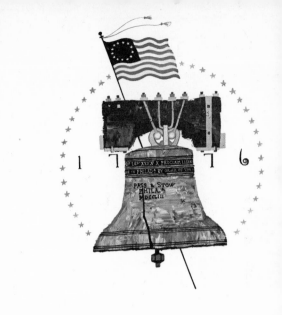